ECONOMIC ISSUES, PROBLEMS AND PERSPECTIVES

CORPORATE INVERSIONS

MOTIVATION AND TAX REFORM ISSUES

ECONOMIC ISSUES, PROBLEMS AND PERSPECTIVES

Additional books in this series can be found on Nova's website
under the Series tab.

Additional e-books in this series can be found on Nova's website
under the e-book tab.

ECONOMIC ISSUES, PROBLEMS AND PERSPECTIVES

CORPORATE INVERSIONS

MOTIVATION AND TAX REFORM ISSUES

FREDRICK WHITE
EDITOR

nova publishers
New York

For permission to use material from this book please contact us:
Telephone 631-231-7269; Fax 631-231-8175
Web Site: http://www.novapublishers.com

Library of Congress Cataloging-in-Publication Data

ISBN: 978-1-63321-966-3

Published by Nova Science Publishers, Inc. † New York

Contents

Preface		**vii**
Chapter 1	Corporate Expatriation, Inversions, and Mergers: Tax Issues *Donald J. Marples and Jane G. Gravelle*	**1**
Chapter 2	Reform of U.S. International Taxation: Alternatives *Jane G. Gravelle*	**19**
Chapter 3	International Corporate Tax Rate Comparisons and Policy Implications *Jane G. Gravelle*	**51**
Chapter 4	Moving to a Territorial Income Tax: Options and Challenges *Jane G. Gravelle*	**91**
Index		**151**

PREFACE

The U.S. corporate income tax is based on worldwide economic activity. If all of a corporation's economic activity is in the United States, then tax administration and compliance is, relatively, straight-forward. Many corporations, however, operate in several jurisdictions, which creates complications for tax administration and compliance. Further, corporations may actively choose where and how to organize to reduce their U.S. and worldwide tax liabilities. Some of these strategies have been referred to as expatriation, inversions, and mergers. This book examines them in light of recent expansion of their use and growing congressional interest. This book also focuses on the global issues relating to tax rate differentials between the United States and other countries. It provides tax rate comparisons; discusses policy implications, including the effect of a corporate rate cut on revenue, output, and national welfare; and discusses the outlook for and consequences of a revenue neutral corporate tax reform.

Chapter 1 – News reports in the late 1990s and early 2000s drew attention to a phenomenon sometimes called corporate "inversions" or "expatriations": instances where U.S. firms reorganize their structure so that the "parent" element of the group is a foreign corporation rather than a corporation chartered in the United States in order to reduce the effect of the U.S. corporate income tax. These corporate inversions apparently involved few, if any, shifts in actual economic activity from the U.S. abroad, at least in the near term. Bermuda and the Cayman Islands—countries with no corporate income tax—were the location of many of the newly created parent corporations, and tax savings were the principal objective.

These types of inversions largely ended with the enactment of the American Jobs Creation Act of 2004 (JOBS Act, P.L. 108-357), which denied the tax benefits of an inversion if the original U.S. stockholders owned 80% or more of the new firm. The Act effectively ended shifts to tax havens where no real business activity took place.

However, two avenues for inverting remained. The Act allowed a firm to invert if it has substantial business operations in the country where the new parent was to be located; the regulations at one point set a 10% level of these business operations. Several inversions using the business activity test resulted in Treasury regulations in 2012 that increased the activity requirement to 25%, effectively closing off this method. Firms could also invert by merging with a foreign company if the original U.S. stockholders owned less than 80% of the new firm.

Two features made a country an attractive destination: a low corporate tax rate and a territorial tax system that did not tax foreign source income. Recently, the UK joined countries such as Ireland, Switzerland, and Canada as targets for inverting when it adopted a territorial tax. At the same time the UK also lowered its rate (from 25% to 20% by 2015).

Recently, several high profile companies have indicated an interest in merging or plans to merge with a non-U.S. headquartered company, including Pfizer and Chiquita. Pfizer, for example, was interested in merging with a smaller British firm, AstraZeneca, and moving headquarters to the UK. For Pfizer, which has accumulated substantial profits in subsidiaries in low tax foreign countries that would be taxed if paid to the U.S. parent, the territorial tax system is likely the most important tax benefit from such a merger. This "second wave" of inversions again raises concerns about an erosion of the U.S. tax base.

Two policy options have been discussed in response: a general reform of the U.S. corporate tax and specific provisions to deal with tax-motivated international mergers. Some have suggested that lowering the corporate tax rate as part of broader tax reform would slow the rate of inversions. Although a lower rate would reduce the incentives to invert, it would be difficult to reduce the rate to the level needed to stop inversions, especially given revenue concerns. Others tax reform proposals suggest that if the United States moved to a territorial tax, the incentive to invert would be eliminated. There are concerns that a territorial tax could worsen the profit-shifting that already exists among multinational firms.

The second option is to directly target the merger inversions. The President's FY2015 budget proposes to treat all mergers as U.S. firms if the U.S. firm's shareholders have 50% or more ownership of the combined firm or maintains management and control in the United States. Similar legislation has also been introduced in the 113th Congress.

Chapter 2 – A striking feature of the modern U.S. economy is its growing openness—its increased integration with the rest of the world. The attention of tax policymakers has recently been focused on the growing participation of U.S. firms in the international economy and the increased pressure that engagement places on the U.S. system for taxing overseas business. Is the current U.S. tax system for taxing U.S. international business the appropriate one for the modern era of globalized business operations, or should its basic structure be reformed?

The current U.S. system for taxing international business is a hybrid. In part the system is based on a residence principle, applying U.S. taxes on a worldwide basis to U.S. firms while granting foreign tax credits to alleviate double taxation. The system, however, also permits U.S. firms to defer foreign-source income indefinitely—a feature that approaches a territorial tax jurisdiction. In keeping with its mixed structure, the system produces a patchwork of economic effects that depend on the location of foreign investment and the circumstances of the firm. Broadly, the system poses a tax incentive to invest in countries with low-tax rates of their own and a disincentive to invest in high-tax countries. In theory, U.S. investment should be skewed toward low-tax countries and away from high-tax locations.

Evaluations of the current tax system vary, and so do prescriptions for reform. According to traditional economic analysis, world economic welfare is maximized by a system that applies the same tax burden to prospective (marginal) foreign and domestic investment so that taxes do not distort investment decisions. Such a system possesses "capital export neutrality," and could be accomplished by worldwide taxation applied to all foreign operations along with an unlimited foreign tax credit. In contrast, a system that maximizes national welfare—a system possessing "national neutrality"—would impose a higher tax burden on foreign investment, thus permitting an overall disincentive for foreign investment. Such a system would impose worldwide taxation, but would permit only a deduction, and not a credit, for foreign taxes.

A tax system based on territorial taxation would exempt overseas business investment from U.S. tax. In recent years, several proponents of territorial taxation have argued that changes in the world economy have rendered traditional prescriptions for international taxation obsolete, and instead prescribe territorial taxation as a means of maximizing both world and national economic welfare. For such a system to be neutral, however, capital would have to be completely immobile across locations. A case might be made that such a system is superior to the current hybrid system, but it is not clear that it is superior to other reforms, including not only a movement toward worldwide taxation by ending deferral, but also providing a minimum tax and restricting deductions for costs associated with deferred income or restricting deferral and foreign tax credits for tax havens.

Chapter 3 – Advocates of cutting corporate tax rates frequently make their argument based on the higher statutory rate in the United States as compared with the rest of the world; they argue that cutting corporate taxes would induce large investment flows into the United States, which would create jobs or expand the taxable income base enough to raise revenue. President Barack Obama has supported a rate cut if the revenue loss can be offset with corporate base broadening. Others have urged on one hand, a revenue raising reform, and, on the other, setting deficit concerns aside.

Is the U.S. tax rate higher than the rest of the world, and what does that difference imply for tax policy? The answer depends, in part, on which tax rates are being compared. Although the U.S. statutory tax rate is higher, the average effective rate is about the same, and the marginal rate on new investment is only slightly higher. The statutory rate differential is relevant for international profit shifting; effective rates are more relevant for firms' investment levels. The 13.7 percentage point differential in statutory rates (a 39.2% rate for the United States compared with 25.5% in other countries), narrows to about 9 percentage points when tax rates in the rest of the world are weighted to reflect the size of countries' economies. (The OECD rates fell by slightly over one-half of a percentage point between 2010 and 2012.)

Regardless of tax differentials, could a U.S. rate cut lead to significant economic gains and revenue feedbacks? Because of the factors that constrain capital flows, estimates for a rate cut from 35% to 25% suggest a modest positive effect on wages and output: an eventual one-time increase of less than two-tenths of 1% of output. Most of this output gain is not an increase in national income because returns to capital imported from abroad belong to foreigners and the returns to U.S. investment abroad that comes back to the United States are already owned by U.S. firms.

The revenue cost of such a rate cut is estimated at between $1.2 trillion and $1.5 trillion over the next 10 years. Revenue feedback effects from increased investment inflows are estimated to reduce those revenue costs by 5%-6%. Reductions in profit shifting could have larger effects, but even if profit shifting disappeared entirely, it would not likely offset revenue losses. It seems unlikely that a rate cut to 25% would significantly reduce profit shifting given these transactions are relatively costless and largely constrained by laws, enforcement, and court decisions.

Both output gains and revenue offsets would be reduced if other countries responded to a U.S. rate cut by reducing their own taxes. Evidence suggests that the U.S. rate cut in the Tax Reform Act of 1986 triggered rate cuts in other countries. It is difficult, although not impossible, to design a reform to lower the corporate tax rate by 10 percentage points that is revenue neutral in the long run. Standard tax expenditures do not appear adequate for this purpose. Eliminating one of the largest provisions, accelerated depreciation, gains much more revenue in the short run than in the long run, and a long-run revenue-neutral change would increase the cost of capital. Other revisions, such as restricting foreign tax credits and interest deductibility or increasing shareholder level taxes, may be required.

This report focuses on the global issues relating to tax rate differentials between the United States and other countries. It provides tax rate comparisons; discusses policy implications, including the effect of a corporate rate cut on revenue, output, and national welfare; and discusses the outlook for and consequences of a revenue neutral corporate tax reform.

Chapter 4 – Among potential tax reforms under discussion by Congress is revising the tax treatment of foreign source income of U.S. multinational corporations. Some business leaders have been urging a movement toward a territorial tax, which would eliminate some U.S. income taxes on active foreign source income.

Under a territorial tax, only the country where the income is earned imposes a tax. Territorial proposals include the Grubert-Mutti proposal (included in President Bush's Advisory Panel on Tax Reform proposal in 2005) and, more recently, a draft Ways and Means Committee proposal and a Senate bill, S. 2091. The Fiscal Commission also proposed a territorial tax. Proposals have, however, also been made to increase the taxation of foreign source income, including S. 727, and proposals by President Obama.

Although the United States has a worldwide system that includes foreign earnings in U.S. taxable income, two provisions cause the current system to resemble a territorial tax in that very little tax is collected. Deferral delays paying taxes until income is repatriated (paid as a dividend by the foreign subsidiary to its U.S. parent). When income is repatriated, credits for foreign taxes paid offset the U.S. tax due. Under cross-crediting, unused foreign tax credits from high tax countries or on highly taxed income can be used to offset U.S. tax on income in low tax countries.

Some proponents of a territorial tax urge such a system on the grounds that the current system discourages repatriations. Economic evidence suggests that effect is small, in part because in normal circumstances a large share of income is retained for permanent reinvestment. Amounts held abroad may have increased, however, as firms lobbied for another repatriation holiday (similar to that adopted in 2004) that allowed firms to exempt most dividends from income on a one-time basis.

Opponents are concerned about encouraging investment abroad. A territorial tax is generally not viewed as efficient because it favors foreign investment, but that increased outflow of investment is likely to have a small effect relative to the U.S. economy. Artificial shifting of profits into tax havens or low tax countries is a current problem that could be worsened under some territorial tax designs, and proposals have included measures to address this problem.

Proposals also address the transitional issue of the treatment of the existing stock of unrepatriated earnings. The Ways and Means proposal would tax this stock of earnings, but at a lower rate, and use the revenues to offset losses from other parts of the plan, which would lead to a long-run revenue loss. S. 2091 has a similar approach. The Grubert-Mutti proposal does not have a specific transitional tax, but would raise revenue largely due to its disallowance of parent overhead expenses aimed at reducing profit shifting. The other two proposals also contain provisions to address profit shifting.

In addition there are complicated issues in the design of a territorial tax, such as how to treat branches and dividends of firms in which the corporation is only partially owned. A number of issues arise from the ending of foreign tax credits, with perhaps the most significant one being the increased tax on royalties, which are currently subject to tax, have low or no foreign taxes, and would lose the shield of excess credits.

The final section of the report briefly discusses some alternative options, including those in S. 727 and in the Administration proposals. It also discusses hybrid approaches that combine territorial and worldwide systems in a more efficient way, including eliminating the disincentive to repatriate.

One such approach is a minimum tax on foreign source income, which is proposed by the President in the context of current rules, but could be combined with a territorial system.

In: Corporate Inversions
Editor: Fredrick White

ISBN: 978-1-63321-966-3

Chapter 1

CORPORATE EXPATRIATION, INVERSIONS, AND MERGERS: TAX ISSUES*

Donald J. Marples and Jane G. Gravelle

SUMMARY

News reports in the late 1990s and early 2000s drew attention to a phenomenon sometimes called corporate "inversions" or "expatriations": instances where U.S. firms reorganize their structure so that the "parent" element of the group is a foreign corporation rather than a corporation chartered in the United States in order to reduce the effect of the U.S. corporate income tax. These corporate inversions apparently involved few, if any, shifts in actual economic activity from the U.S. abroad, at least in the near term. Bermuda and the Cayman Islands—countries with no corporate income tax—were the location of many of the newly created parent corporations, and tax savings were the principal objective.

These types of inversions largely ended with the enactment of the American Jobs Creation Act of 2004 (JOBS Act, P.L. 108-357), which denied the tax benefits of an inversion if the original U.S. stockholders owned 80% or more of the new firm. The Act effectively ended shifts to tax havens where no real business activity took place.

However, two avenues for inverting remained. The Act allowed a firm to invert if it has substantial business operations in the country

* This is an edited, reformatted and augmented version of a Congressional Research Service publication R43568, prepared for Members and Committees of Congress dated May 27, 2014.

where the new parent was to be located; the regulations at one point set a 10% level of these business operations. Several inversions using the business activity test resulted in Treasury regulations in 2012 that increased the activity requirement to 25%, effectively closing off this method. Firms could also invert by merging with a foreign company if the original U.S. stockholders owned less than 80% of the new firm.

Two features made a country an attractive destination: a low corporate tax rate and a territorial tax system that did not tax foreign source income. Recently, the UK joined countries such as Ireland, Switzerland, and Canada as targets for inverting when it adopted a territorial tax. At the same time the UK also lowered its rate (from 25% to 20% by 2015).

Recently, several high profile companies have indicated an interest in merging or plans to merge with a non-U.S. headquartered company, including Pfizer and Chiquita. Pfizer, for example, was interested in merging with a smaller British firm, AstraZeneca, and moving headquarters to the UK. For Pfizer, which has accumulated substantial profits in subsidiaries in low tax foreign countries that would be taxed if paid to the U.S. parent, the territorial tax system is likely the most important tax benefit from such a merger. This "second wave" of inversions again raises concerns about an erosion of the U.S. tax base.

Two policy options have been discussed in response: a general reform of the U.S. corporate tax and specific provisions to deal with tax-motivated international mergers. Some have suggested that lowering the corporate tax rate as part of broader tax reform would slow the rate of inversions. Although a lower rate would reduce the incentives to invert, it would be difficult to reduce the rate to the level needed to stop inversions, especially given revenue concerns. Others tax reform proposals suggest that if the United States moved to a territorial tax, the incentive to invert would be eliminated. There are concerns that a territorial tax could worsen the profit-shifting that already exists among multinational firms.

The second option is to directly target the merger inversions. The President's FY2015 budget proposes to treat all mergers as U.S. firms if the U.S. firm's shareholders have 50% or more ownership of the combined firm or maintains management and control in the United States. Similar legislation has also been introduced in the 113th Congress.

INTRODUCTION

The U.S. corporate income tax is based on worldwide economic activity. If all of a corporation's economic activity is in the United States, then tax administration and compliance is, relatively, straight-forward. Many corporations, however, operate in several jurisdictions, which creates complications for tax administration and compliance. Further, corporations may actively choose where and how to organize to reduce their U.S. and worldwide tax liabilities. Some of these strategies have been referred to as expatriation, inversions, and mergers. This report examines them in light of recent expansion of their use and growing congressional interest.

This report begins with a brief discussion of relevant portions of the U.S. corporate income tax system before examining how inversions were commonly structured. The report then looks at how Congress and Department of the Treasury have reduced the benefits of inversions. The report concludes with an examination of methods that remain to invert and policy options available to prevent or limit these inversions.

Achieving tax savings using an inversion became more difficult with the enactment of the American Jobs Creation Act of 2004 (JOBS Act, P.L. 108-357). The JOBS Act denied or restricted the tax benefits of an inversion if the owners of the new company were not substantially different from the owners of the original company. The Act also allowed a firm to invert only if it had substantial business operations in the country where the new headquarters was to be located.

Although the 2004 legislation largely prevented the types of inversions that drew attention prior to its adoption, several companies have successfully inverted in the past few years by using the substantive business operations mechanism or merging.[1] Treasury regulations have subsequently limited the former mechanism.[2]

Recently, several high-profile companies have indicated an interest in merging or plans to merge with a non-U.S. firm, including Pfizer, Chiquita,[3] and Omnicom (an advertising firm).[4] News reports indicate that a group of Walgreens investors is urging such a move.[5] This "second wave" of inversions again raises concerns about an erosion of the U.S. tax base. While the substantial business avenue appears to have been largely eliminated by new Treasury regulations that increased the required share of activity, the option of merging with a much smaller foreign company remains. U.S. firms may also merge with larger firms, although in this case the tax benefits are less likely to be key factors in the decision to merge.

U.S. INTERNATIONAL TAX SYSTEM

The United States uses a system that taxes both the worldwide income of U.S. corporations and the income of foreign firms earned within U.S. borders. All income earned within U.S. borders is taxed the same—in the year earned and at statutory tax rates up to 35%.

U.S. corporate income earned outside the United States is also subject to U.S. taxation, though not necessarily in the year earned. This occurs because U.S. corporations can defer U.S. tax on active income earned abroad in foreign subsidiaries until it is paid, or repatriated, to the U.S. parent company as a dividend.[6] To mitigate double taxation, tax due on repatriated income is reduced by the amount of foreign taxes already paid.

Income from certain foreign sources earned by subsidiaries—which generally includes passive types of income such as interest, dividends, annuities, rents, and royalties and is referred to as Subpart F income—is generally taxed in the year it is earned. Subpart F applies only to shareholders who may be able to influence location decisions at the corporate level.[7]

ANATOMY OF AN INVERSION

A corporate inversion is a process by which an existing U.S. corporation changes its country of residence. Post-inversion the original U.S. corporation becomes a subsidiary of a foreign parent corporation. Corporate inversions occur through three different paths: the substantial activity test, merger with a larger foreign firm, and merger with a smaller foreign firm.[8] Regardless of the form of the inversion, the typical result is that the new foreign parent company faces a lower home country tax rate and no tax on the company's foreign-source income.[9]

Substantial Business Presence

In this form of inversion, a U.S. corporation with substantial business activity in a foreign company creates a foreign subsidiary. The U.S. corporation and foreign subsidiary exchange stock—resulting in each entity owning some of the other's stock. After the stock exchange, the new entity is a foreign corporation with a U.S. subsidiary, as the exchange is generally in proportion to the respective company valuations. As this form of inversion does not require any change in the effective control of the corporation, it is referred to as a "naked inversion."

U.S. Corporation Acquired by a Larger Foreign Corporation

In this form of inversion, a U.S. corporation would like to bolster its foreign operations and, perhaps, lower its U.S. tax. To do so, the U.S. corporation merges with a larger foreign corporation, with the U.S. shareholders owning a minority share of the new merged company. This results in the effective control of the new company being outside U.S. borders.

While this form of inversion may be driven by business considerations, tax considerations may also be part of the decision. An example of this can be seen in the following statement by the board of directors of a U.S. corporation recommending approval of a merger with a U.K. corporation. The board of directors pursued the merger in part because:

> ... Ensco was headquartered in a jurisdiction that has a favorable tax regime and an extensive network of tax treaties, which can allow the combined company to achieve a global effective tax rate comparable to Pride's competitors.[10]

In this case, a U.S. firm, Pride, merged with a UK firm, Ensco, and the headquarters remained in the UK.

A Smaller Foreign Corporation Acquired by a U.S. Corporation

In this form of inversion, a U.S. corporation would like to bolster its foreign operations and lower its U.S. tax. To do so, the U.S. corporation merges with a smaller foreign corporation, with the U.S. shareholders owning a majority share of the new merged company. This merger results in the effective control of the new company staying with the shareholders of the U.S. corporations.

While this form of inversion may be driven by business considerations, tax considerations may also be part of the decision. An example is the Eaton Cooper merger. The following is an excerpt of a U.S. corporation's (Eaton's) press release announcing the acquisition of an Irish company (Cooper), with the company headquartering in Ireland (with a 12.5% tax rate and a territorial system).

> At the close of the transaction ... Eaton and Cooper will be combined under a new company incorporated in Ireland, where Cooper is incorporated today. The newly created company, which is expected to be called Eaton Global Corporation Plc or a variant thereof ("New Eaton"), will be led by Alexander M. Cutler, Eaton's current chairman and chief executive officer.[11]

At the close of the merger, it was expected that the shareholders of the U.S. company would control 73% of the combined company, with the shareholders of the Irish company controlling the remaining 27%. The press release notes expected tax benefits from the merger at $165 million in 2016, out of $535 million of total cost savings.

In this case, a U.S. corporation used a merger to achieve an inversion while its shareholders retained a significant majority of shares.

Response to Initial Inversions: The American Jobs Creation Act

In the late 1990s and early 2000s, news reports drew the attention of policymakers and the public to a phenomenon sometimes called corporate "inversions" or "expatriations": instances where firms that consist of multiple corporations reorganize their structure so that the "parent" element of the group is a foreign corporation rather than a corporation chartered in the United States. Among the more high-profile inversions were Ingersoll-Rand, Tyco, the PXRE Group, Foster Wheeler, Nabors Industries, and Coopers Industries.[12]

These corporate inversions apparently involved few, if any, shifts in actual economic activity from the United States abroad, at least in the near term. In particular, inverted firms typically continued to maintain headquarters in the United States and did not systematically shift capital or employment abroad post inversion.[13] Further, Bermuda and the Cayman Islands were the location of many of the newly created parent corporations—jurisdictions that have no corporate income tax but that also do have highly developed legal, institutional, and communications infrastructures.

A 2002 study by the U.S. Treasury Department concluded that while inversions were not new— the statutory framework making them possible has long been in existence—there had been a "marked increase" in their frequency, size, and visibility.[14]

Taken together, these facts suggested that tax savings were one goal of the inversion, if not the primary goal. Beyond taxes, firms engaged in the inversions cited a number of reasons for undertaking them, including creating greater "operational flexibility," improved cash management, and an enhanced ability to access international capital markets.[15]

The 2002 Treasury report identified three main concerns about corporate inversions: erosion of the U.S. tax base, a cost advantage for foreign-controlled firms, and a reduction in perceived fairness of the tax system.[16] These concerns, along with a growing awareness of inversion transactions, may have resulted in congressional concern and debate about how to address the issues surrounding inversions, culminating with the enactment of an anti-inversion provision (Section 7874) in the American Jobs Creation Act of 2004 (AJCA; P.L. 108-357).

The AJCA adopted two alternative tax regimes applicable to inversions occurring after March 4, 2003. The AJCA treats the inverted foreign parent company as a domestic corporation if it is owned by at least 80% of the former parent's stockholders. In these cases, the AJCA would deny the firm any tax benefits of the inversion (i.e., it would continue to be taxed on the combined group's worldwide income). The second regime applies when there is at least 60% continuity of ownership but less than 80%. In this case, the new foreign parent is not taxed like a domestic corporation, but any U.S. toll taxes (taxes on gains) that apply to transfers of assets to the new entity are not permitted to be offset by foreign tax credits or net operating losses. The AJCA also exempted corporations with substantial economic activity in the foreign country from the anti-inversion provisions, but it did not define substantial business activity in the statute.[17]

POST-2004 INVERSIONS AND TREASURY REGULATIONS

Although the 2004 Act largely eliminated the generic naked inversions, two alternatives remained that allowed a firm to shift headquarters and retain control of the business: the naked inversion via the business activity exemption, and merger with a smaller company.[18]

Both of these approaches likely preclude direct use of tax havens such as the Cayman Islands. These small tax havens have very little economic activity. Using the business activity route would require significant economic operations in the target country. An inversion by merger would require a large firm that would be at least 25% of the size of the U.S. firm. As discussed below, these types of inversions generally target countries such as Ireland, Switzerland, and, more recently, the UK.

A report in the *Wall Street Journal* in August 2012 highlighted some recent moves abroad.[19] This report claimed 10 companies had inverted, with 6 within the past year or so. This was a small number of companies, but it is useful to look at the methods involved. The *Wall Street Journal* article identified by name 5 of the 10 companies that had moved abroad recently—Aon, Ensco, Rowan, Eaton, and DE Master Blenders 1763—as among the recent ones to move. (The article also referred to Transocean and Weatherford International, but these were firms that had inverted prior to the 2004 legislation: Transocean first to the Cayman Islands, and then Switzerland, and Weatherford first to Bermuda, and then Switzerland).

An article by Bret Wells identified the first three of these firms as using the second form of naked inversion (where the only apparent objective is tax savings), relying on the exception in the anti-inversion rules for firms that had substantial business activities.[20] All three moved to the United Kingdom, where a recent move to a territorial tax, as well as decisions in the European Court of Justice that limited their anti-abuse rules, had made their tax system more attractive.[21] The UK was also in the process of lowering its own corporate rate. Two of the firms are oil drilling firms; drilling in the North Sea might have affected their ability to use this exemption. Aon is an insurance firm.

Wells also mentions another firm, Tim Hortons, which used the second form of naked inversion in 2009 to relocate to Canada. In doing so, the firm was returning to its origins, as it was founded in Canada. It became an American company when Wendy's acquired it in 1995, but it was subsequently spun off in 2006.[22] DE Master Blenders 1763, like Tim Hortons, was returning to its origins as well (a Netherlands firm), as it was spun off from Sara Lee which had acquired it in 1978.[23]

In response, Treasury Regulations (T.D. 9592, June 12, 2012) increased the safe harbor for the substantial business activities test from 10% to 25%, effectively closing off this avenue in the future.[24] This action could be done by regulation because the statute did not specify how the substantial business activity test was to be implemented.

The remaining firm mentioned in the *Wall Street Journal* article is Eaton. Eaton's move abroad was a merger; it merged with Coopers, a firm effectively operating its headquarters in the United States, but one that had inverted prior to the law change.

The post-2004 approaches to inversions no longer involved countries such as Bermuda and the Cayman Islands, but larger countries such as the UK, Canada, and Ireland. The UK, in particular, has become a much more attractive headquarters. Because of freedom of movement rules in the European Union, the UK cannot have anti-inversion laws, which may have played a role in both moving to a territorial tax and lowering the corporate tax rate.

A number of recent mergers have either been effectuated or are in process: Chiquita, Actavis, and Perrigo (the latter two are pharmaceutical firms) moving to Ireland; Valeant Pharmaceuticals and Endo Health Services moving to Canada; and Liberty Global (a cable company) to the UK. Subsequently, the new Irish firm Actavis (itself the result of two prior mergers) merged with Forest Labs.[25] Omnicom (an advertising firm) planned a move to the UK (after proposed merger with a French firm, creating a Netherlands holding company, resident in the UK for tax purposes), but has abandoned its merger.[26]

Most of these firms are not household names or industry giants. Thus, perhaps none has created as much interest as the attempt by pharmacy giant Pfizer to acquire AstraZeneca with a UK headquarters, or the urging of some stockholders of Walgreens to invert to Switzerland. Pfizer represents a significant potential loss of future tax revenue, as much as $1.4 billion per year.[27] According to a recent study by Martin Sullivan, in 2005, when a temporary tax exclusion of 85% of dividends (the repatriation holiday) was in force, Pfizer repatriated $37 billion, the single largest amount of repatriations of any firm.[28] In 2009, Pfizer repatriated $34 billion (and paid U.S. taxes on that amount) to finance the acquisition of Wyeth, but earnings abroad grew from $42 billion in 2009 (after the repatriation) to $73 billion by 2012. These earnings have not been repatriated and taxed in the United States.[29] An inversion by Pfizer would, however, result in current shareholders paying capital gains taxes on any stock appreciation when they are converted into shares of the new company. Shares held in IRAs and 401(k)s would not typically owe this tax, but shares owned directly by individuals and in mutual funds would owe tax even if they did not sell their stock.[30]

Treasury has continued to regulate inversions where regulations are possible. For example, it recently took action to close the Killer B-Helen of

Troy loophole that allowed Liberty Global to shareholders to avoid some capital gains taxes.[31]

POLICY OPTIONS

The AJCA was successful at limiting a form of inversions, at least initially. In particular, the AJCA stopped the practice of basic "naked inversions," in which little activity or presence in the new jurisdiction is required and the new parent is domiciled in a tax haven. Further, through regulation, Treasury has limited the use of the substantial business activity test safe harbor to invert. Recent activity, however, suggests that mergers continue to be used as a vehicle for corporate inversions.

These more recent mergers are increasingly resulting in a UK parent company, due to policy decisions by the UK government. Specifically, the UK lowered its corporate tax rate and adopted a territorial tax system. In addition, anti-abuse provisions for foreign source income were weakened by the European Union courts. The UK has also proposed taxing certain intangible income at a 10% rate (This is referred to as a patent box).

To restrict the occurrence of tax motivated inversions, both a general reform of the U.S. corporate tax and specific provisions to deal with tax-motivated international mergers have been discussed.

U.S. Corporate Tax Reform

Interest in reforming the corporate income tax is longstanding,[32] with recent interest calling for explicit accommodation of international concerns.[33] As noted earlier, two aspects of the U.S. corporate tax system are particularly relevant to corporate location decisions: the corporate tax rate and the taxation of foreign-source earnings. Taken together, these factors can yield a substantial reduction in taxes paid. In the case of the proposed merger of Forest Laboratories Inc. (a U.S. company) and Actavis (an Irish company), the tax reduction is estimated to be roughly $100 million.[34] However, before examining proposals that address these concerns, a discussion of each separately is warranted.

Lower the Corporate Tax Rate

The U.S. corporate statutory tax rate is higher than both the average statutory rates of the other Organisation for Economic Co-operation and Development (OECD) countries and that of the 15 largest economies in the world.[35] This has led many to assert that the U.S. statutory tax rate needs to be lowered to reduce the incentive for inversion transactions.[36] While lowering the corporate tax rate would reduce the incentive to invert, there are reasons to suggest that it would be impractical to reduce the rate to the level needed to stop inversions. Namely, to stop inversions through a reduction in the corporate tax rate would require a U.S. corporate tax rate set equal to the lowest tax rate of a destination company, or zero.

A lower corporate tax rate would reduce the incentive for corporate inversions, primarily by reducing the tax rate applied to repatriated earnings.[37] For a company like Pfizer, with large foreign earnings, a rate reduction could yield significantly lower taxes paid. However, as discussed below, the benefit of a lowered rate is negligible relative to the benefit to corporate taxpayers afforded by territorial tax systems, when income earned in low- or no-tax foreign jurisdictions is never subject to U.S. tax.

Two factors present challenges for lowering the corporate tax rate. First, if revenue neutrality is the goal, there may not be enough base broadening provisions with revenue offsets to provide deep cuts in the corporate tax; and, if such offsets were found, they might have their own consequences for investment. Of course reducing the corporate tax without corresponding base broadening would likely reduce corporate tax revenue, adding to chronic budget deficits.

Adopt a Territorial Tax System

The United States is one of the few countries that has a worldwide tax system and levies a tax on the foreign-source income of domestic corporations. Changing corporate tax residence to a country with a territorial tax system (where foreign earnings would not be taxed at all) is thought to drive inversion decisions. This issue has led to proposals for the United States to adopt a territorial tax system to stop inversion transactions.[38]

One concern about adopting a territorial tax system is the strain it would likely place on the current transfer pricing system.[39] From this perspective, the current worldwide tax system provides a backstop on the amount of profit shifting or base erosion possible, because shifted profits will eventually be repatriated. Under a territorial tax system, this is not the case. Research has found evidence of significant profit shifting, especially related to mobile intellectual property, suggesting a lot of income from foreign sources is really U.S. income in disguise.[40]

Numerous other issues surround the adoption of a U. S. territorial tax. For example, while some support a territorial tax to eliminate the incentive to keep earnings abroad, others oppose it because it likely discourages domestic investment and activity in the United States.[41]

Adopting a territorial tax, as in the case of a rate reduction, would likely reduce corporate tax revenue and add to current budget pressures unless it is offset by other tax increases.

Tax Reform Proposals

Two recent proposals that involve comprehensive reform, the Wyden, Coats, and Begich proposal from the 112th Congress (S. 767) and the proposal by Chairman Camp of the Ways and Means Committee (The Tax Reform Act of 2014),[42] would reduce the corporate rate to 24% and 25%, respectively. The first would move away from a territorial tax by ending deferral. Eliminating deferral would raise a significant amount of revenue that would have been used to reduce the corporate tax rate from 35% to 24%.[43] The second proposal would adopt a territorial tax and offset a reduction in the corporate tax rate. The proposal also contains anti-abuse provisions to tax intangible foreign source income. There has been some agreement that adopting a territorial tax without some significant anti-abuse provisions (which the Camp proposal contains) could be problematic, as it would likely increase profit shifting abroad by U.S. firms.[44] The Senate Finance Committee also issued several tax reform discussion drafts in 2013 that proposed, in the international arena, a current but lower tax on foreign source income (without specifying the type of corporate tax that would be feasible).[45]

Reforming the U.S. corporate tax system may be a desirable objective that can contribute to economic efficiency and growth. However, the types of corporate rate cuts that are feasible given revenue constraints and the concerns about profit shifting for moving to a territorial tax, as reflected in these proposals, suggest that reforming the tax code for the purpose of discouraging tax driven mergers may reduce—but not eliminate—the incentive to invert.

Targeted Approaches

An alternative is to directly restrict the ability of U.S. firms to invert by merger. The President's FY2015 budget proposal contains a provision that would further restrict the use of inversions.[46] The proposal would modify the 80% test enacted in the AJCA to a 50% test and eliminate the 60% test. In effect, this proposal would reduce the percentage of shareholders that are owners of the "old U.S. company" and the "new foreign merged company." The proposal would also require that the new foreign corporation be managed and controlled from outside the United States and prohibit transactions where the new foreign company has substantial business activities in the United States.

Representative Levin, the ranking Member of the House Ways and Means Committee, has introduced a bill, The Corporate Inversion Prevention Act of 2014 (H.R. 4679), which would reflect these changes, retroactive to May 8, 2014. The inversion would not be recognized if the U.S. stockholders have 50% of the shares or if 25% of the business activity is in the United States. A companion bill, which would sunset in two years to provide time for tax reform, has been introduced in the Senate by Senator Levin.[47]

In addition, a number of legislative proposals have been introduced that would limit the tax benefits associated with inversions for certain corporations. For example, H.R. 1554 (Doggett), H.R. 3666 (DeLauro), H.R. 3793 (Maffei), S. 268 (Levin), S. 1533 (Levin), and S. 1844 (Shaheen) would each treat corporations managed and controlled from the United States as domestic corporations regardless of their legal tax home.

Other proposals, H.R. 694 (Schakowsky) and S. 250 (Sanders), would eliminate deferral (taxing foreign source income currently), in addition to limiting the benefits of inversions when management and control continues to reside in the United States. While some support these targeted approaches, others argue that corporate tax reform should be addressed first.

CONCLUDING THOUGHTS

The debate in Congress on inversions is fluid. Some, as noted above, prefer a targeted approach. Others believe that inversions should be addressed only in the context of comprehensive tax reform. While Ways and Means Chairman Camp's Tax Reform Act of 2014 discussion draft does not directly address profit shifting aspects of inversions, it does include elements that may have an impact on such transactions. Profit shifting practices and inversion techniques may be addressed more directly as tax reform proposals unfold. Finance Chairman Ron Wyden has indicated that he would address inversions—his approach is similar to Senator Levin's, as described above—

but in the context of broader tax reform. He has indicated support for making changes relating to inversions retroactive to May 8, 2014.

End Notes

[1] McKinnon, John D. and Scott Thurm, "U.S. Firms Move Abroad to Cut Taxes: Despite '04 Law, Companies Incorporate Overseas, Saving Big Sums on Taxes," Wall Street Journal, August 28, 2012, http://online.wsj.com/news/ articles/SB100008723963904442 30504577615232602107536?mod=WSJ_business_LeadStoryCollection&mg= reno64-sj&url= http%3A%2F%2Fonline.wsj.com%2Farticle%2FSB1000087239639 044423050 4577615232602107536.html%3Fmod %3DWSJ_business_LeadStoryCollection; Bret Wells, "Cant and the Inconvenient Truth about Corporate Inversions." Tax Notes, July 23. 2012, pp. 429-439; Reuven S. Avi-Yonah, "Territoriality: For and Against," Tax Notes International, May 13, 2013, pp. 661-663.

[2] Treasury Decision, T.D. 9592, July 12, 2012.

[3] It is worth noting that a company may invert even if it does not currently expect to pay U.S. tax. See 10K Filing of Chiquita Brands International, Inc. to the Securities and Exchange Commission, March 31, 2009.

[4] Richard Rubin and Zachary R. Mider, "Pfizer Bids for U.K. Address With U.S. Tax Revamp Stalled, Bloomberg," April 29, 2014, http://www.bloomberg.com/news/2014-04-29/pfizer-bids-for-u-k-address-as-u-s-tax-revampstalls.html?utm_content=buffer1c951&utm_ medium=social&utm_source=linkedin.com&utm_campaign=buffer. Omnicom has recently abandoned its proposed merger.

[5] Ameet Sachdev and Peter Frost," Walgreen Pressured To Move Headquarters To Europe," Chicago Tribune, April 14, 2014, http://articles.chicagotribune.com/2014-04-14/business /chi-walgreens-headquarters-to-europe20140414_1_walgreen-co-tax-rate-tax-deals.

[6] CRS Report R40178, Tax Cuts on Repatriation Earnings as Economic Stimulus: An Economic Analysis, by Donald J. Marples and Jane G. Gravelle. Income from branches and passive income earned directly, such as interest and royalties, is taxed currently.

[7] These stockholders are defined as owning at least 10% of a subsidiaries stock and only subsidiaries that are at least 50% owned by 10% U.S. stockholders.

[8] The techniques corporations use to invert—stock-for-stock inversions, asset transfers, or drop-down inversions— apply to all forms of inversions. In drop-down inversions, assets are transferred to the new parent, and some of those assets are transferred to a domestic subsidiary.

[9] William McBride, Corporate Exits Accelerating, Taking Jobs with Them, Tax Foundation, April 25, 2014, http://taxfoundation.org/blog/corporate-exits-accelerating-taking-jobs-them.

[10] Ensco-Pride International Inc. Joint Proxy Statement, "Recommendation of the Pride Board of Directors and Its Reasons for the Merger," April 25, 2011, http://www.sec.gov/ Archives/edgar/data/314808/000095012311039244/ d80026b3e424b3.htm.

[11] Eaton Corporation, "Eaton to Acquire Cooper Industries to Form Premier Global Power," press release, May 21, 2012, http://www.eaton.com/ecm/groups/public/@pub/@ eaton/@corp/ documents/content/pct_361385.pdf.

[12] "While Companies Shift Addresses to Tax Havens, CEO's Stay Put," Bloomberg Visual Data, May 4, 2014, http://www.bloomberg.com/infographics/2014-05-04/companies-shift-addresses-abroad.html.

[13] U.S. Government Accountability Office, Cayman Islands: Business and Tax Advantages Attract U.S. Persons and Enforcement Challenges Exist, GA)-88-778, July 24, 2008.

[14] U.S. Department of the Treasury, Office of Tax Policy, Corporate Inversion Transactions: Tax Policy Implications (Washington: May, 2002), p. 1.

[15] These reasons are cited by Stanley Works in a February 8, 2002, press release. See also the November 2, 2001, proxy statement by Ingersoll-Rand (IR), which cites "a variety of potential business, financial and strategic benefits." The statement is available on the IR website at http://www.shareholder.com/ir/edgar.cfm?Page=2.

[16] U.S. Department of the Treasury, Office of Tax Policy, Corporate Inversion Transactions: Tax Policy Implications, May 2002, p. 21.

[17] Treasury initially defined substantial business activity as being 10% of worldwide activity in regulation.

[18] The third form of inversion, merger with a larger foreign corporation, would result in control moving outside the United States.

[19] McKinnon, John D. and Scott Thurm, "U.S. Firms Move Abroad to Cut Taxes: Despite '04 Law, Companies Incorporate Overseas, Saving Big Sums on Taxes," Wall Street Journal, August 28, 2012.

[20] Bret Wells, "Cant and the Inconvenient Truth about Corporate Inversions." Tax Notes, July 23. 2012, pp. 429-439.

[21] Cadbury-Schweppes, September 12, 2006. The UK rule required that income subject to a tax rate much lower than the UK rates be taxed; this rule was not accepted by the court. See Cleary Gottlieb, "Cadbury Schweppes: UK CFC Rules Too Restrictive," http://www.cgsh.com/files/News/9e29ed20-66c5-4558-93eb-dc8ab51c54c9/Presentation/NewsAttachment/2fcdb202-5144-4e40-8498-dd0d04f99926/cadbury-schweppes.pdf.

[22] Tim Hortons, "The Story of Tim Hortons," http://search.yahoo.com/search;_ylt= A0oG7kHeX4VQXGkAjbVXNyoA?p=tim%20horton's%20inc.&fr2=sb-top&fr=yfp-t-701.

[23] DE Master Blenders 1753, "Our Heritage," 2012 (visited), http://www.demasterblenders1753.com/en/Company/Ourheritage/

[24] Bret Wells, "Cant and the Inconvenient Truth about Corporate Inversions." Tax Notes, July 23. 2012, pp. 429-439; Kristen A. Parillo, "Government Defends Business Activities Test in New Regs." Tax Notes, July 23, 2012, pp. 370- 371.

[25] For news reports, see Zachary R. Mider "Companies Flee U.S. Tax System by Reincorporating Abroad," Bloomberg, January 27, 2014, http://www.bloomberg. com/infographics/2014-01-27/companies-flee-u-s-tax-system-byreincorporating-abroad.html and "Companies Fleeing Taxes Pay CEOs Extra as Law Backfires," Bloomberg, January 27, 2014, http://www.bloomberg.com/news/2014-01-27/companies-fleeing-taxes-pay-ceos-extra-as-law-backfires.html."Actavis, Forest Labs In Biggest Merger In Specialty Pharma," May 5, 2014, Investors Business Daily http://finance.yahoo. com/news/actavis-forest-labs-biggest-merger-223800951.html;_ylt= A0LEV1G3kWdT7jEAEGFXNyoA;_ylu= X3oDMTEyaGV0M2l0BHNlYwNzcgRwb3MDMwRjb2xvA2JmMQR2dGlkA1FJMDQ5XzE-; Tom Fairless, "Publicis, Omnicom Merger Tangled in Tax Red-Tape," Wall Street Journal, April 25, 2014, http://www.marketwatch.com/story/publicis-omnicom-merger-tangled-in-tax-red-tape-2014-04-25.

[26] David Gelles, "At Odds, Omnicom and Publicis End Merger," May 8, 2014, New York Times, http://dealbook.nytimes.com/2014/05/08/ad-agency-giants-said-to-call-off-35-billion-merger/.

[27] Zachary R. Mider, "Tax Break 'Blarney': U.S. Companies Beat the System With Irish Addresses," Bloomberg, May 5, 2014, http://www.bloomberg.com/news/2014-05-04/u-s-firms-with-irish-addresses-criticized-for-the-moves.html.

[28] Martin A. Sullivan, "Economic Analysis: Pfizer's Tax Picture Dominated by U.S. Losses, Repatriation," Tax Notes July 8, 2013, http://www.taxanalysts.com/www/features.nsf/Articles/8A8A34FCBD7C3C3F85257BA200497696? OpenDocument.

[29] For a news article on the proposed Pfizer merger see Kevin Drawbaugh, Pfizer Move to Join Tax-Driven Deal-Making Raises Red Flags in U.S, Reuters, April 14, 2014, http://www.reuters.com/article/2014/04/28/us-usa-tax-pfizeranalysis-idUSBREA3R1FL20140428. For an article on Walgreens see, Ameet Sachdev and Peter Frost, "Walgreen Pressured to Move Headquarters to Europe," Chicago Tribune, April 14, 2014, http://articles.chicagotribune.com/2014- 04-14/business/chi-walgreens-headquarters-to-europe-20140414_1_walgreen-co-tax-rate-tax-deals.

[30] Laura Saunders and Jonathan D, Rockoff, "Pfizer Holders Could Face Tax Hit in a Deal for AstraZeneca," Wall Street Journal, May 8, 2014.

[31] IRS Notice 2014-14. See "IRS Aims at Innovative M&A Inversion Structure," Sidley Austin LLP, at http://m.sidley.com/04-29-2014-Tax-Update/.

[32] CRS Report RL34229, Corporate Tax Reform: Issues for Congress, by Jane G. Gravelle.

[33] CRS Report RL34115, Reform of U.S. International Taxation: Alternatives, by Jane G. Gravelle.

[34] Forest Labs, Acquisition of Forest Laboratories, Inc. by Actavis Plc Call, February 18, 2014, http://www.sec.gov/ Archives/edgar/data/38074/000119312514058927/d679348d425.htm.

[35] CRS Report R41743, International Corporate Tax Rate Comparisons and Policy Implications, by Jane G. Gravelle.

[36] Hank Gutman, Principal, Director of the Tax Governance Institute, KPMG LLP, Changes in the Tax Law: How Are Effects Measured, and Who is Affected?, May 2, 2014.

[37] A corporate rate reduction would also reduce taxes due on U.S. earnings. This is incidental to a corporation's incentive to invert or its competitiveness, because there is no difference of the taxation of U.S. earnings between U.S. and foreign corporations.

[38] McBride (2014).

[39] Gutman (2014).

[40] See CRS Report R40623, Tax Havens: International Tax Avoidance and Evasion, by Jane G. Gravelle for a review of methods and the empirical evidence on profit shifting by U.S, multinational firms.

[41] A territorial tax lowers the tax on returns to investment abroad, increasing after-tax returns and encouraging firms to displace domestic investment with foreign investment.

[42] U.S. Congress, Joint Committee on Taxation, Technical Explanation of the Tax Reform Act of 2014, A Discussion Draft of the Chairman of the House Committee on Ways and Means to Reform the Internal Revenue Code: Title IV— Participation Exemption System for the Taxation of Foreign Income, committee print, 113th Cong., February 26, 2014, JCX-15-14.

[43] Revenue estimates of an earlier version of the bill are available at http://www.wyden.senate.gov/download/?id= 1ba9073f-9ee8-4f8b-a2e3-2b70ebc96d35&download=1.

[44] All of the proposals to move to a territorial tax have been accompanied by provisions that attempt to limit profit shifting, particularly of intangible income. See CRS Report R42624, Moving to a Territorial Income Tax: Options and Challenges, by Jane G. Gravelle, for further discussion.

[45] United States Committee on Finance, Baucus Unveils Proposals for International Tax Reform, http://www.finance.senate.gov/newsroom/chairman/release/?id=f946a9f3-d296-42ad-bae4-bcf451b34b14.

[46] Department of the Treasury, General Explanations of the Administration's Fiscal Year 2015 Revenue Proposals, http://www.treasury.gov/resource-center/tax-policy/Documents/General-Explanations-FY2015.pdf.

[47] See "Senators Announce Bill to Reduce Corporate Inversion 'Loophole'," Tax Notes Today, May 21, 2014.

In: Corporate Inversions
Editor: Fredrick White

ISBN: 978-1-63321-966-3

Chapter 2

REFORM OF U.S. INTERNATIONAL TAXATION: ALTERNATIVES*

Jane G. Gravelle

SUMMARY

A striking feature of the modern U.S. economy is its growing openness—its increased integration with the rest of the world. The attention of tax policymakers has recently been focused on the growing participation of U.S. firms in the international economy and the increased pressure that engagement places on the U.S. system for taxing overseas business. Is the current U.S. tax system for taxing U.S. international business the appropriate one for the modern era of globalized business operations, or should its basic structure be reformed?

The current U.S. system for taxing international business is a hybrid. In part the system is based on a residence principle, applying U.S. taxes on a worldwide basis to U.S. firms while granting foreign tax credits to alleviate double taxation. The system, however, also permits U.S. firms to defer foreign-source income indefinitely—a feature that approaches a territorial tax jurisdiction. In keeping with its mixed structure, the system produces a patchwork of economic effects that depend on the location of foreign investment and the circumstances of the firm. Broadly, the system poses a tax incentive to invest in countries with low-tax rates of their own and a disincentive to invest in high-tax countries. In theory, U.S.

* This is an edited, reformatted and augmented version of a Congressional Research Service publication, No. RL34115, dated December 31, 2013.

investment should be skewed toward low-tax countries and away from high-tax locations.

Evaluations of the current tax system vary, and so do prescriptions for reform. According to traditional economic analysis, world economic welfare is maximized by a system that applies the same tax burden to prospective (marginal) foreign and domestic investment so that taxes do not distort investment decisions. Such a system possesses "capital export neutrality," and could be accomplished by worldwide taxation applied to all foreign operations along with an unlimited foreign tax credit. In contrast, a system that maximizes national welfare—a system possessing "national neutrality"—would impose a higher tax burden on foreign investment, thus permitting an overall disincentive for foreign investment. Such a system would impose worldwide taxation, but would permit only a deduction, and not a credit, for foreign taxes.

A tax system based on territorial taxation would exempt overseas business investment from U.S. tax. In recent years, several proponents of territorial taxation have argued that changes in the world economy have rendered traditional prescriptions for international taxation obsolete, and instead prescribe territorial taxation as a means of maximizing both world and national economic welfare. For such a system to be neutral, however, capital would have to be completely immobile across locations. A case might be made that such a system is superior to the current hybrid system, but it is not clear that it is superior to other reforms, including not only a movement toward worldwide taxation by ending deferral, but also providing a minimum tax and restricting deductions for costs associated with deferred income or restricting deferral and foreign tax credits for tax havens.

INTRODUCTION

The increasingly global scope of U.S. business has a variety of dimensions. In trade, the overall level of exports plus imports has risen steadily and substantially in recent decades, increasing from 16% of U.S. gross domestic product (GDP) in 1976 to 31% of GDP in 2012. Cross-border investment is growing even more dramatically. In 1976, the ratio of U.S. private assets to GDP was 0.20; by year end 2012 the ratio was 1.33.[1]

The bulk of the increase in "outbound" investment has been portfolio investment—investment in financial assets such as stocks and bonds without the active conduct of overseas business operations. But foreign direct investment by U.S. firms—actual foreign production by U.S.-owned companies—has increased too, rising from a ratio of 0.12 to 0.31 of GDP between 1976 and 2012. It is the taxation of U.S. business operations that has been the recent focus of policymakers, and that has raised the question of basic tax reform in the international sector: is the current U.S. tax system for taxing U.S. international business appropriate in this age of globalized business operations, or is reform needed?[2] Moreover, along with the increasing scope of international investment activities, there is an increasing opportunity for tax shelters that take advantage of low-tax foreign jurisdictions. How might revisions in the tax system exacerbate or address these tax shelter issues?

The current U.S. system is a "hybrid" construct, embodying a mix of opposing jurisdictional principles. Not surprisingly, the mixed system—in conjunction with foreign host-country taxes— poses a patchwork of incentive effects for U.S. firms and their global operations, in some cases taxing foreign operations favorably and posing an incentive to invest abroad, and in other cases imposing high-tax burdens and posing a disincentive to overseas investment. In some cases, the system presents a rough tax neutrality toward overseas investment. It is perhaps the hybrid nature of the system that has led to calls for reform. Prescriptions for a "good" tax system vary, and the hybrid system satisfies none of them fully.

This report describes and assesses the principal prescriptions that have been offered for broad reform of the international system. The report begins with an overview of current law and of possible revisions. It then sets the framework for considering economic efficiency as well as tax shelter activities. Finally, it reviews alternative approaches to revision in light of those issues.

THE CURRENT SYSTEM AND POSSIBLE REVISIONS

The System's Structure

There are two alternative, conceptually "pure," principles on which countries base their tax in the international setting: residence and territory. Under a residence system, a country taxes its own residents (or domestically chartered "resident" corporations) on their worldwide income, regardless of its geographic source. Under a territorial or source-based system, a country taxes only income that is earned within its own borders.

In practice, no country uses a pure residence-based tax; historically, virtually all countries tax income foreign investors earn within their borders (although they may grant tax holidays in some cases as an inducement to investment). Some countries, however, do have an exclusively territorial or source-based tax.[3] The United States uses a system that taxes both income of foreign firms earned within its borders as well as the worldwide income of its U.S.-chartered firms.

Despite these nominal "residence" features, however, U.S. taxes do not apply to the foreign income of U.S.-owned corporations chartered abroad. As a result, a U.S. firm can indefinitely defer U.S. tax on its foreign income if it conducts its foreign operations through a foreign-chartered subsidiary corporation; U.S. taxes do not apply as long as the foreign subsidiary's income is reinvested overseas. With some exceptions, U.S. taxes apply only when the income is remitted to the U.S.-resident parent as dividends or other intra-firm payments such as interest and royalties. The deferral feature reduces the effective U.S. tax burden on foreign income and imparts an element of territoriality to the system; it also results in a dichotomous structure for taxing overseas business income: deferral in the case of foreign-subsidiary income and current taxation in the case of branches of U.S. chartered corporations. The bulk of active business investment by U.S. firms is through foreign-chartered subsidiaries.[4]

Along with deferral, another basic feature of the U.S. system is the foreign tax credit. While the United States taxes worldwide income on either a current or deferred basis, it also allows credits for foreign taxes paid on a dollar-for-dollar basis against U.S. taxes otherwise owed.[5] This treatment avoids the double-taxation that would otherwise apply and concedes the first right of taxation to the country of source. In effect, the United States gives the foreign host country the first opportunity to tax the income, and collects only what tax is left (up to its own rate) after the foreign host country collects its share.

When the foreign tax is higher than the U.S. tax, the credit is limited to the U.S. tax that would be due on the foreign income. The purpose of the limit is to protect the U.S. domestic tax base: without it, foreign countries could impose very high taxes without discouraging inbound U.S. investment, because the cost of the higher taxes would be shifted to the U.S. treasury. With the limitation, if foreign taxes exceed the U.S. tax that would be due, the excess foreign taxes cannot be credited. Foreign tax credits that exceed this limitation are termed "excess credits." Currently foreign tax credits are allowed on what is sometimes termed an "overall" basis, so that income and tax credits from all countries are combined. This treatment allows for "cross-crediting," where credits paid in excess of U.S. tax in one country may be used to offset U.S. tax in a country where the foreign tax is lower than the U.S. tax. To prevent abuse, tax credits are divided into "baskets," which separate passive income easily shifted to low-tax countries. Currently, there are two baskets, one for active income and one for passive income. Over half of foreign-source active business income is earned by firms with overall excess credits.[6]

To address tax avoidance by shifting passive income into low-tax jurisdictions, Subpart F restricts the applicability of deferral in some situations. Subpart F provides that U.S. stockholders (e.g., parent firms) of foreign corporations are subject to current U.S. tax on certain types of subsidiary income, whether or not the income is repatriated. Only stockholders owning at least 10% of subsidiary stock and only subsidiaries that are at least 50% owned by 10% U.S. stockholders are subject to Subpart F. Countries that have territorial tax systems generally also have some type of anti-abuse provision to protect their tax base.

Tax deferral results in heightened importance for the system's rules for dividing income between related firms; the more income a firm can assign, for tax purposes, to a foreign subsidiary in a low-tax country, the lower its overall tax burden. The current system generally requires firms to set hypothetical "transfer prices," which are required to approximate the prices two firms would agree on if they conducted their transactions at arm's length. The system is complex and difficult to administer.

The foreign tax credit's limitation also places pressure on the system's rules for determining the source of income ("sourcing" rules). Because firms can only credit foreign taxes against the portion of taxable income attributable to foreign sources, taxpayers must assign both revenue and costs to either domestic or foreign sources. Although the tax code contains rules for making such allocations, they are likewise complex and difficult to administer.

In sum, the United States taxes its resident corporations on their worldwide income, but permits indefinite deferral of active business income earned through foreign subsidiaries. Where U.S. taxes apply, foreign tax credits alleviate double taxation but are limited to offsetting U.S. tax on foreign income. Subpart F is designed to deny deferral to what is generally passive income.

Possible Revisions

Because the current U.S. tax system is a mix of a worldwide system and a territorial system, the fundamental tax reform issue is whether moving toward either "pure" system—a territorial or worldwide residence-based regime—

would be an improvement. Moving toward a territorial system would involve permanently exempting most foreign-source active business income. (Most territorial proposals, however, would continue taxing passive income, as under current law's Subpart F.) Moving toward a worldwide tax would eliminate the deferral benefit and might also entail further restricting cross-crediting by increasing the number of baskets for the foreign tax credit limit. Some revisions that maintain the current system but tighten the rules for deductions include proposals to disallow certain deductions of the parent company (such as interest) that reflect the share of income that is deferred.

The report defers the discussion of the precise changes fundamental reform would entail. First, however, the report explains the tools economists have developed for evaluating the various international tax systems.

NEUTRALITY, EFFICIENCY, AND COMPETITIVENESS

The term competitiveness has often been invoked in the debate about U.S. policy in a global economy, including discussions of U.S. tax policy.[7] In economic analysis, however, it is not *countries* that are competitive, it is *companies* that are. A company generally thinks of itself as competitive if it can produce at the same cost as, or a lower cost than, other firms. But a country's firms cannot be competitive in all areas. Indeed, even if firms in a country are more productive than firms in all other countries in every respect, a country would still tend to produce those goods in which its relative advantage is greatest. The other countries need to produce goods with their resources as well. This notion is called comparative advantage, and it is an important concept in economic theory.[8]

When discussing national policy, including tax policy and its effect on the international allocation of capital, the issues are generally framed around issues of efficiency, neutrality, and optimal policies rather than notions of competitiveness. These terms can mean the same thing, or they can be slightly different. Neutrality generally refers to provisions that do not alter the allocation of investment from that which would occur without taxes. When markets are operating efficiently, a neutral tax policy will also be an efficient policy, since it will maintain the efficient allocation that would occur without taxes. Moreover, even when there are market imperfections, neutrality may still be the policy most likely to be efficient, given the difficulty in identifying and measuring market imperfections.

Optimal policy differs from efficiency in that it usually refers to a particular agent or actor choosing a policy that maximizes his or her own welfare. A country can also choose a policy that leads to the greatest welfare for its own citizens, even if that policy distorts the allocation of capital (is not neutral) and leads to less efficient worldwide production. The optimal policy from the perspective of a country, in other words, may not be the most efficient in terms of the worldwide allocation of capital, and may not be the optimal policy from the perspective of world economic welfare.

Economists have traditionally used three concepts to evaluate tax rules that apply to outbound investment. These concepts are referred to as neutrality concepts, although, as shown below, they are not always neutral in the sense of not distorting the allocation of investment. The concepts are capital export neutrality, capital import neutrality, and national neutrality. To evaluate the consequences of any multinational tax reform, it is crucial to understand these concepts, whether they are valid, and what they imply for policy. The concepts were developed when virtually all foreign investment took place as direct investment of multinational companies; virtually no foreign portfolio investment (ownership of foreign stock by U.S. citizens) existed. The growth in this portfolio investment has led to a new neutrality concept, referred to as capital ownership neutrality. These traditional and new concepts are addressed in turn.

Understanding Capital Export Neutrality, Capital Import Neutrality, and National Neutrality

Capital export neutrality requires a country to apply the same tax rate to its firms' investments, regardless of where they are located, and is embodied in a residence-based tax system. Capital import neutrality requires the same tax on firms with different nationalities that invest in a given location and is embodied in a territorial or source-based tax. National neutrality requires that the nation's total return on investment, including both that nation's taxes and its firms' profits, is equal in each jurisdiction, foreign and domestic. This form of neutrality is obtained by taxing foreign-source income and allowing a deduction for foreign taxes.

Some of these neutrality rules may also be rules for optimization. National neutrality is often described as optimal, but that outcome is only the case with perfectly mobile capital and no retaliation by foreign countries. There is also an optimizing rule for choosing the tax rate on inbound investment, which depends on how responsive that investment inflow is to the return.

Evaluating policy, discussed subsequently, is complicated because while some countries have territorial or source-based taxes, no country imposes a pure residence-based tax. Although worldwide taxation as practiced in the United States and other countries has some attributes of a residence-based tax, it is a mixture of residence- and source-based tax. Tax is imposed on foreign firms operating within the United States, a source-based attribute. On outbound investment, the application of tax to repatriated income creates some resemblance to residence tax, but the foreign tax credit limitations cause it to depart from such a tax, and deferral provisions introduce an element of a source-based tax.

Because these concepts are so frequently misunderstood, it is useful to employ a simple illustrative example to explain them with the pure tax systems that are consistent with capital export neutrality and capital import neutrality. In these simple systems, national neutrality is the same as capital export neutrality, and its nuances will be discussed in the following section where more realistic tax systems are discussed. In this instance, it may be helpful to demonstrate the difference between residence-based and source-based taxes in achieving economic neutrality.

Consider a world beginning with no taxes, and assume that capital is perfectly substitutable across countries, implying that a firm will earn the same after-tax return in each location. The return is 10%. There are three countries: a high-tax country that imposes a 50% tax rate, a low-tax country that imposes a 25% tax rate, and a zero-tax country. All investment is made through the companies' direct operations, hence, there is no substitution of capital across firms and the capital owned by each country is fixed. The high- and low-tax rate countries have capital that can be used to invest in their own country, or in the other two countries. To simplify, the zero-tax country is assumed to have only labor and no capital.

Table 1 shows the return to firms in the absence of any tax and with the two tax systems in place but before investment has shifted (which would alter the pre-tax return). Residence taxation, which produces capital export neutrality, has no effect on the allocation of investment by either country's firms because each firm still earns the same return in each location. Source-based taxation, however, will result in higher returns in the zero- and, to a lesser extent, low-tax countries. As a result, capital will flow out of the high-tax country, raising its return and lowering the wages of the workers in that country and into the zero-tax country, lowering its return and raising the wages of the workers in that country. The effect on the low-tax country depends on the size of that country and its labor force relative to the rest of the world. In addition to the effects on the return to capital and wages, output is produced inefficiently, which reduces world welfare.

Table 1. Illustration of the Effects of Residence- and Source-Based Taxation

	Return by Location of Investment (%)		
Nationality of Firm	High-Tax Country	Low-Tax Country	Zero-Tax Country
No Taxes			
High-Tax Country	10%	10%	10%
Low-Tax Country	10%	10%	10%
Residence Tax			
High-Tax Country	5%	5%	5%
Low-Tax Country	7.5%	7.5%	7.5%
Source-Based (Territorial) Tax			
High-Tax Country	5%	7.5%	10%
Low-Tax Country	5%	7.5%	10%

Source: Compiled by the Congressional Research Service.

Note: The high-tax country has a 50% tax rate, while the low-tax country has a 25% tax rate.

Table 1 can also be used to show that the residence-based system is also consistent with national neutrality, but the source-based system is not. For the high-tax country, in each location it earns 5% in tax revenue and 5% in profits (for a total of 10%). Thus the total return to the nation is equated in each jurisdiction. The same is true of the low-tax country, although the total return is split into 2.5% taxes and 7.5% profits. The source-based system does not meet that standard. Even before investment shifts, the high-tax country, while earning 10% domestically and in the zero tax haven country, is earning only 7.5% in the low-tax country, since that country's government is collecting the tax. The same is true of the low-tax country with respect to investment taxed by the high-tax country.

National neutrality departs from capital export neutrality in the more complex, real world circumstances. It, in fact, requires that foreign-source income be taxed and that any taxes imposed by the country of location be deducted (rather than the current rule of some countries, including the United States, that allow taxes to be credited). If foreign countries impose taxes, national neutrality does not lead to worldwide neutrality, since foreign investment is discouraged in countries that impose taxes.

National neutrality is really about optimal policy, which maximizes the welfare of the country's residents. It is an optimal policy if all capital is perfectly mobile; if not, it is actually optimal for a country to impose even more tax on outbound investment than is suggested by the neutrality standard.

In sum, according to these longstanding measures of neutrality and efficiency, capital export neutrality is appropriate for maximizing world output, national neutrality is appropriate for maximizing a nation's welfare, and capital import "neutrality" is not neutral at all.

Capital Ownership Neutrality

A new concept of neutrality has appeared in recent years. The term capital ownership neutrality (CON) is closely associated with Desai and Hines, professors, respectively, of business at Harvard and economics at the University of Michigan.[9] The term itself, however, appears to have been coined by Michael Devereaux,[10] a British economist. The underlying justification for the new standard's development, the growth of portfolio investment, was also discussed independently about the same time in a paper by Frisch.[11] Essentially, capital ownership neutrality is the same as capital import neutrality in that, under certain very restrictive assumptions, it is achieved by source-based taxation, and some of the earlier discussions viewed it as a resurrection of capital import neutrality.[12]

The issue of ownership neutrality developed because international investment markets changed. At the time the previous notions of neutral international tax systems were first developed— generally, the early 1960s— virtually all U.S. investment abroad was carried out through foreign direct investment by U.S. firms.[13] U.S. portfolio investors held almost no stock in foreign firms.

Until the mid-1980s, the share of foreign stocks in U.S. residents' stock portfolios was less than 1%. Thus, it was reasonable to assume, as in the discussion above, that there was no substitution across the nationality of firms, but rather only across locations—that is, U.S. investors could not substitute investment abroad through foreign firms for investment in U.S. firms with foreign operations. Over time, however, the share of foreign stock owned by U.S. investors increased, and by the end of 2006, it was 22% of corporate equity owned by U.S. investors.[14] This increase did not occur smoothly: it increased in the latter part of the mid-1980s to about 6%, leveled out for a number of years, then again rose around 1993 and 1994 to about 11%, where it stayed until around 2001, and then rose again.

A closer look at the CON concept indicates that, to make the argument that capital ownership neutrality (and therefore source-based taxation) should be the guiding principle for an efficient and neutral tax system, three requirements are needed. First, firms are assumed not to substitute operations in one location for those in another—capital is completely immobile across locations. Second, firms must differ in their productivity—that is, some firms are more efficient than others—and there must be substitution across portfolios that results in firms being shut out of lines-of-business that they could run more efficiently. Third, there must be no mechanisms available to obtain the benefits of productive efficiency—short of owning the productive capital assets. For example, relatively inefficient firms cannot rent efficient technologies or hire efficient managers away from efficient firms.

If only the first requirement is met (immobility across locations), any system of taxing investment abroad would be neutral because the particular distortion—allocation of investment across locations—is simply assumed away. It doesn't matter if overseas operations are taxed higher or lower than domestic investment, because investment has no reason to move. Residence taxation would be efficient as well as source-based taxation, because the national affiliation of firms would not matter to productivity (although residence taxation would not be optimal for the high-tax country that would have no revenues).[15]

If the two remaining assumptions also apply—productivity differs and no mechanisms exist to boost efficiency—it can be shown that residence-based taxation is inefficient while source-based taxation produces efficiency. For example, returning to **Table 1**, suppose some firms in each country are particularly productive and can earn 12% before tax rather than 10%. With residence-based taxation, the after-tax return of the high-tax country's productive firms, which would yield an after-tax return of 6%, would not be enough for these firms to operate and, if the only way to realize the higher return is to own the capital, the higher pre-tax yields of these more efficient firms would not be realized. With source-based taxation, the efficient firms in each country would operate and displace the less efficient ones.

In the more realistic tax systems where countries also tax capital income in their own location, the high-tax country's especially productive firms would still operate in their own country. That is, by taxing income within its borders, a high-tax country that is attempting to practice capital export neutrality with a worldwide tax still faces neutral ground in its home country. Thus, any distortion arising in practice from the current system would involve foreign firms and the solution of exempting foreign-source income from tax is the solution consistent with capital ownership neutrality.

Consider each of the restrictions in turn. The first is the assumption that capital is immobile across locations; as noted above, there is considerable evidence that it is not and, indeed, that it is quite elastic. So at best, it would be a question of picking which type of distortion is worse. As long as capital is mobile across jurisdictions, "capital ownership neutrality" is not neutral. At most, the model shows that there is no way to achieve neutrality and that one is in a second-best world.

The second restriction requires a high, perhaps perfect, degree of substitution in portfolios of different types of stocks that would lead to the exclusion of stock of high-tax countries. There is considerable evidence to suggest that such perfect substitution is not the case. It has long been known that there is a significant home bias in the holding of both portfolio and direct assets. Despite global securities markets, American residents continue to hold 80% of their stock portfolios in stock of U.S. firms. If portfolio investment were perfectly substitutable, the U.S. share would be expected to be closer to the share of total assets. The U.S. accounts for about a third of total fixed investment of the OECD countries.[16]

The fact that the portfolio share has grown does not in itself provide evidence of a significant elasticity; rather, it may reflect a variety of technical and institutional changes that make holding foreign stocks more feasible. Moreover, the portfolio shares are consistent with the notion that the holdings that do exist are not so much due to tax differences but to a general desire to diversify assets across countries to reduce cyclical risk. Two-thirds of investment is in other countries with similar tax rates. At the end of 2005, the two largest shares were for the U.K. (16%) and Japan (15%). While the U.K., with a 30% corporate rate, has a lower statutory rate than the U.S. (39% including state taxes), Japan has a rate of 41%. The next two largest claimants with 7% and 6% have rates of 35% and 35%.[17] There are significant shares in two tax havens, Bermuda (5%) and the Cayman Islands (3%). According to the Department of Treasury, however, the Bermuda investments are largely former U.S. firms that have moved their location to avoid U.S. tax (a phenomenon called inversion, which was subsequently addressed with legislative restrictions), and the Cayman Islands investments are in offshore financial centers (again likely a tax avoidance issue rather than direct production issue).[18]

An imperfect portfolio substitution elasticity also suggests that the phenomenon of eliminating efficient firms is less likely to happen. Firms that are especially productive and efficient will earn higher returns than other firms in similar circumstances of nationality and location, and they would be expected to be retained in both domestic and foreign investors' portfolios. Any firms whose size is contracted by portfolio shifts due to tax rates are more likely to be the marginal firms that have a normal level of productivity.

Finally, this model assumes that there are no other ways to enjoy the additional productivity of more efficient firms. In effect, the model begins with the assumption of productive advantages without defining in formal terms—so that the effects can be modeled—the source of the productivity.

For example, if the greater productivity of the firm is due to the employment of managers with greater skills, then that productivity arises at a cost, and these management skills embodied in the individuals resident in a given country should be free to move to their highest use, and allocated efficiently. Because they add a surplus value, they would not be driven out of the market, and worldwide efficiency requires a capital export neutrality approach to labor resources as well as capital.

If the asset is uniquely tied to the firm—such as a value through a trademark, intangible R&D, or even a management set-up—the model does not allow for the fact that ownership of the productive assets and ownership of the intangible asset can, in most cases, be separated. Trademarks and patents can be franchised and sold. Or, if the intangible cannot be separately sold (for example, if the R&D could be easily copied and thus is not patented but kept secret), there are ways for the firm to operate without ownership of the capital assets, such as factories, machinery, and equipment, that give rise to normal products. These assets could be leased by the firm with the intangible asset. Moreover, if the asset is not closely tied to management, the firm could arrange for contract manufacturing, a technique commonly used to shift profits. These techniques may be less than perfect if there are principal-agent costs,[19] but this effect is of questionable importance.

In light of the many ways in which the efficiency costs of capital ownership non-neutrality are unlikely to be significant compared to location distortions, it seems questionable to use meeting this standard of neutrality to evaluate tax reform changes and questionable to see source-based taxation as an efficient international tax regime.

ASSESSING THE EXISTING TAX SYSTEM

The above examples illustrate the various traditional concepts of neutrality and how they are embodied in basic tax structures. However, as described at the report's outset, the U.S. tax system is a hybrid—neither a pure territorial or residence-based system. Accordingly, it presents a patchwork of incentive effects, sometimes posing an incentive to invest abroad and, in other situations, presenting either a disincentive or tax neutrality. This section looks at the existing system's principal incentive effects.

First, in some cases the U.S. system resembles residence-based taxation—it taxes foreign branch income on a current basis while allowing a foreign tax credit. Even where current taxation applies, however, the U.S. system departs from pure residence taxation by placing a limit on its foreign tax credit. If pure residence-based means taxing income of residents at the same rate, regardless of where it is earned, an unlimited foreign tax credit would be required. Under such a credit, when the foreign tax is lower than the home country tax, the home country would collect a residual, equating the total tax imposed to that on its domestic investment. When the foreign country's tax is higher, the home country would have to refund the excess so that, again, the tax on the foreign investment would be the same as the tax on domestic investment. In practice, however, an unlimited foreign tax credit is not feasible because of its potential threat to the home country tax base (here, that of the United States). Without a limit, countries host to foreign investment could simply raise their taxes on inbound investment without limit and without fear of driving foreign investors away. The foreign investors could simply credit their high foreign taxes against their home-country tax bill. The U.S. thus limits its foreign tax credit to offsetting U.S. taxes on foreign (and not domestic) income.

The incentive effects of a worldwide system with a limited credit depend on exactly how the credit is limited. If the limit applies separately for each country (a "per-country" limit), the system would achieve neutrality on outbound investment with respect to low tax-rate countries, but not high tax-rate countries. If taxes can be averaged across countries—that is, if a firm calculates a single limit aggregated across countries, the neutrality consequences are less clear. In that case, the excess credits from the investment in a high-tax country can be used to offset tax due on investments in the low-tax country (can be "cross credited"). For example, assume profits were $100 in a high-tax location with a 50% rate and $100 in the no-tax location, with the home country tax rate 25%. With no cross crediting, a firm from the 25% tax rate country uses the foreign tax of $50 to wipe out the home country tax of $25, with only the tax of $50 applying, while the firm would pay a home country tax of $25 on the income earned in the zero tax jurisdiction. The total tax is $75. With cross crediting, the total foreign-source income is $200, the total foreign tax paid is $50 (in the high-tax country, on $100 of profit), and the total home-country tax due is also $50 (25% of $200 of income in both countries). All foreign tax is credited and the total tax is $50.

Cross crediting, as allowed in the U.S. tax system, can therefore reduce the disincentive to invest in high-tax countries if the firm already has investment in the zero tax country, because the excess credits have a value. Similarly, it can increase the incentive to invest in the zero tax country if the country already has investment in the high-tax country, since excess credits can effectively remove any residual tax in the zero tax country. In either case, foreign investment is encouraged relative to domestic investment. In practice, the U.S. tax system permits extensive cross crediting; it does not require a per-country limitation, although it does require firms to calculate separate limits for passive and active business income.

Second, the U.S. tax system departs from residence-based taxation in its use of deferral. As described above, U.S. taxes generally do not apply to the foreign business income of foreign-chartered subsidiaries. This feature of the tax system introduces elements of a territorial or source-based taxation into the system, and also introduces a distortion in firms' decisions of whether to return profits to the United States or reinvest them abroad. Moreover the interaction of deferral with cross crediting provides some scope for firms to choose the times and places of repatriation to minimize tax liability. In general, the availability of deferral—like the territorial taxation it at least approaches—poses an incentive for U.S. firms to invest in low-tax countries. Also, once capital has been invested abroad, the provision encourages firms to retain their earnings overseas rather than returning them to the United States.

This mixture of treatments also provides methods for avoiding tax apart from the direct effects on investment allocation. Deferral provides an incentive to artificially shift profits to low-tax jurisdictions. Because firms can choose between branch operations and investment via foreign-chartered subsidiaries, they can use a branch form when operations are starting up and typically lose money to allow losses to be deducted from the U.S. worldwide income tax, and then shift to a subsidiary form when the operation becomes profitable.

In sum, the current system poses a patchwork of incentive effects that is in keeping with its hybrid nature. Where current taxation applies—for example, to branch income—there is a disincentive to invest in high-tax countries, and either an incentive or neutrality toward investment in low-tax countries, depending on whether the investing firm can use cross-crediting of foreign taxes. Where deferral is available, the system poses an incentive to invest in low-tax countries. The system also provides mechanisms for artificially sheltering income from tax.

TERRITORIAL TAXATION: THE DIVIDEND EXEMPTION PROPOSAL

The preceding sections showed why the theoretical argument that territorial taxation is optimal is difficult to defend. Some have argued, however, that while territorial taxation may not be the most efficient system in a perfect world, it is nonetheless superior to the hybrid, patchwork system that is the current U.S. system—a "second best" argument. A territorial tax was recently proposed by the National Commission on Fiscal Responsibility and Reform, although the specific details were not provided.[20] To best understand this argument for territorial taxation, it is helpful to examine the specific version proposed in a 2001 American Enterprise Institute monograph by economists Harry Grubert and John Mutti. A similar plan was set forth in 2005 by President Bush's advisory commission on tax reform.[21] While the Grubert-Mutti proposal had been the focus of attention for many years, more recent proposals, described subsequently, are quite different.

Grubert and Mutti described their proposal as a "dividend exemption" system, thus focusing on the chief modification their plan would make to the current regime: it would exempt from U.S. taxes dividends repatriated to U.S. parents from foreign subsidiary corporations, thus moving from current law's deferral for foreign income to a permanent exemption. More generally, an exemption system can be viewed as a territorial tax system whose application is restricted to active business investment abroad, but that continues to tax portfolio investment of firms (such as interest, royalties, and similar income) on a current basis.

Several additional features of the plan are important to the advantages it might have over the current system. First, the plan would not permit foreign tax credits to be claimed for foreign taxes paid with respect to repatriated earnings. The repatriations, after all, would be exempt from U.S. tax, thus obviating the need for relief from double taxation. Second, deductions allocable to tax-exempt foreign-source income would be disallowed. Here, the reasoning is that the purpose of deductions is to remove items of cost from the tax base; because overseas income would no longer be in the U.S. tax base, removal of associated costs would not be necessary. Importantly, this would mean that a portion of debt incurred by a U.S. parent corporation would not be deductible—the portion assumed to be used in financing tax-exempt foreign subsidiaries.

As described in the preceding sections, the capital import neutrality and capital ownership neutrality standards both recommend adoption of territorial taxation, but traditional economic theory is skeptical of the theoretical justification of the two standards. Grubert and Mutti argue, however, that even if CIN and CON are rejected on theoretical grounds, an exemption system is superior to the current hybrid system in terms of several important factors: efficiency, simplicity, and the raising of tax revenue.

First, efficiency: Grubert and Mutti argue that current law's application of tax to repatriated foreign earnings encourages wasteful and inefficient behavior on the part of corporations in devising methods of repatriating foreign earnings without paying U.S. tax. Under an exemption system, such wasteful planning would be unnecessary. Also, because foreign tax credits would no longer be applicable, cross-crediting of excess foreign tax credits would no longer shield investment in low-tax foreign locations from U.S. tax, and the artificial diversion of technology-exploiting investment to low-tax locations would no longer occur.[22]

Nevertheless, elimination of these sources of inefficiency alone would not be sufficient to make an exemption system less wasteful than current law. If elimination of tax on repatriations were the only feature of an exemption system, the system would likely increase inefficiency by encouraging added investment in low-tax countries. Rather, the crucial element to an exemption system's purported superiority is its elimination of interest deductions for overseas investment. The inclusion of this provision would actually result in an increase in the average tax burden for overseas investment, thus generating an efficiency gain from an improved allocation of investment away from low-tax overseas locations and into the domestic economy.[23]

An exemption system may also increase tax revenue. The Grubert and Mutti analysis concludes that the system would generate $7.7 billion annually in added U.S. revenue.[24] (Their estimate is based on 1994 data, so it would likely be larger in the current economy.) More recently, the Joint Committee on Taxation has estimated the revenue gain at about $6 billion per year.[25] As with the efficiency gains, however, the increase in tax revenues is crucially dependent on denial of deductions for costs allocated to tax-exempt foreign income. Without the new restrictions, an exemption system would likely reduce tax revenue. The Joint Committee on Taxation has estimated that current law's deferral reduces revenues by approximately $6 billion.[26] By the same token, an exemption system would lose tax revenue compared with the current system if the current system were to deny deductions to deferred income.

In the area of simplicity, proponents of an exemption system emphasize its reduction in the need for tax planning. Note, however, that tax complexity—and its accompanying difficulties for tax administration—exist when entities or activities are taxed according to different rules. Under an exemption system, foreign subsidiary corporations would be tax exempt as under current law, and because the exemption would be permanent rather than temporary, its import for firms' tax planners would be magnified. Accordingly, the tax system's transfer pricing rules for allocating income among U.S. parent firms and their foreign subsidiaries would become more important; more pressure would apply to rules that are inherently difficult to enforce. The same would be true for the distinction between active and passive income, because active income would be permanently exempt and passive-investment income would be taxed on a current basis. Firms would have an even greater incentive to move from branch to subsidiary operations for start-up firms.

In a recent article critical of territorial tax proposals, Kleinbard pointed out analyses by Grubert and others that emphasized the growth in the importance of royalties as a share of repatriated earnings for multinationals, suggesting that the exploitation of intangible assets by multinationals in foreign locations is increasing. However, where the Grubert and Mutti analysis sees this as an important reason to adopt an exemption system—cross-crediting of foreign taxes would no longer pose an incentive to low-tax investment under an exemption system—Kleinbard sees it as a liability. The growth of intangibles, argues Kleinbard, would place enormous pressure on the administration of transfer prices.[27]

Proponents of an exemption system concede that it is not perfect, but argue that it is at least superior to the highly imperfect system now in existence. Even this defense, however, has its shortcomings: the most economically attractive aspects of the exemption proposals could, in principle, be adopted piecemeal, and its most distortionary aspects could be left behind. Specifically, more restrictive rules for deducting interest and other costs could be adopted without exempting dividend repatriations from U.S. tax. Such plans could enhance economic efficiency more than would the full-blown exemption systems.

More recent proposals, such as those proposed by the Ways and Means Committee and in a bill by Senator Enzi (S. 2091), differ in substantial ways from the Mutti-Grubert proposal. They do not include the allocation of deductions and propose, or consider, some relief for royalties. These proposals also contain anti-base erosion provisions or options for limiting profit shifting whose adoption and effectiveness is uncertain. Finally, they propose to be revenue neutral in the budget horizon but this neutrality relies on a one-time taxation of existing accumulated earnings and thus would lose revenue in the long run. On the whole, therefore, these proposals would likely encourage more investment abroad. The fleshing out of a detailed territorial tax provision that might be considered legislatively has also served to highlight one of the major concerns about moving to a territorial tax: the possible increase in international profit shifting and tax avoidance.[28]

Even with these criticisms and even when considering the Mutti-Grubert version of the exemption, another question is this: why accept second best? The report next examines what moving toward a residence-based system would look like, in practice.

A Residence-Based System in Practice

The capital export neutrality standard recommends a system that would be based on residence— that is, a system that taxes the income of home-country firms, regardless of where it is earned. The present section looks at the shape a residence-based system would likely take.

Current law's deferral system would be repealed under a residence-based system, and U.S. taxation would apply on a current basis to the income of foreign subsidiaries, whether or not the income is repatriated. If it were not for foreign taxes, deferral's repeal would move the system to the brink of capital export neutrality (except for the portfolio investment concern): the tax burden on foreign investment would roughly equal the tax rate on domestic investment. Foreign taxes, however, complicate matters and make pure capital export neutrality difficult to achieve, in practice. The problem arises when a foreign host country's tax rate exceeds the U.S. domestic tax rate. In such cases, pure capital export neutrality would require an unlimited foreign tax credit. Foreign taxes would offset U.S. taxes on domestic as well as foreign income—only by this mechanism could the high foreign tax burden be brought into line with taxes on domestic investment. Yet, as noted in the preceding section on the existing tax system, an unlimited foreign tax credit is impractical: foreign governments could, in effect, draw on the U.S. Treasury by raising taxes on U.S. investors, *ad infinitum*.

Advocates of a residence-based system have in some cases advocated a more restrictive form of the foreign tax credit limitation that would place more limits on "cross crediting" than does current law's two-part limit. For example, at various times in the past, the United States has required firms to calculate their limitation on a country-by-country basis (a so-called "per-country" limitation), under which taxes paid to one country could not be credited against U.S. tax on income from another country.[29] The Wyden-Gregg Tax Reform Act, S. 3018, introduced in the 111th Congress would, in the context of a general corporate reform that would broaden the base and reduce the rate, eliminate deferral and institute a per country foreign tax credit limit. A similar bill, S. 727 sponsored by Wyden and Coats was introduced in the 112th Congress. An alternative or additional approach to restricting cross crediting was implemented by the Tax Reform Act of 1986 (P.L. 99-514), which, instead of requiring separate limits for each country, specified a variety of different types of income for which separate limits ("baskets") were required. The American Jobs Creation Act of 2004 (AJCA; P.L. 108-357), however, reduced the number of separate limits to current law's two.[30] Note, however, that a more restrictive foreign tax credit limitation would not necessarily move a residence-based system closer to pure capital export neutrality. As noted above, while cross crediting may pose an incentive to invest in low-tax countries, it also mitigates the disincentive to invest in high-tax countries.

Capital export neutrality requires equal tax burdens on foreign and domestic investment. There are several features of the current system that favor domestic over foreign investment, and whose modification would move the current system in the direction of capital export neutrality. The most important of these is the 9% tax deduction for domestic production enacted in 2004 by AJCA. Other tax benefits that are restricted to domestic investment are the Section 179 "expensing" allowance for machines and equipment and the research and experimentation tax credit.

As noted above, Grubert and Altshuler revisited the topic of international tax reform in 2006. In their analysis, they compared the exemption system with what they termed a "burden neutral" worldwide taxation system. In constructing this latter system, they couple elimination of deferral with a reduction in the statutory U.S. tax rate that applies to foreign earnings—thus using the added tax revenue from deferral's repeal to, in effect, "purchase" a cut in the tax rate. The goal of the exchange is to not damage what they term the "competitive position" of U.S. multinationals. As a consequence of the countervailing changes, the burden on investment in a range of low-tax countries would increase; the burden of a range of income that is repatriated under current law would fall, but the overall burden on overseas investment would be unchanged.

Grubert and Altshuler note that the overall advantage of their burden-neutral worldwide proposal over current law depends on outcomes which are, as yet, unknown: how many firms would be in an excess credit position under the plan and what the burden-neutral tax rate would be. They also caution that the plan would have another weakness: foreign countries would have an incentive to raise their tax rates in the face of current U.S. taxation because inbound U.S. investment would be less sensitive to the foreign rates.[31] They further note that their plan's reduction of tax rates at the corporate level would shift more of the overall U.S. tax burden on corporations from the corporate to the shareholder level—a virtue in the modern world where capital is increasingly mobile since shareholder-level taxes are generally imposed on a residence basis and thus achieve allocative efficiency.

A MINIMUM TAX APPROACH: CHAIRMAN BAUCUS AND THE SENATE FINANCE COMMITTEE DISCUSSION DRAFT

Chairman Baucus has released a discussion draft of a proposal that is not entirely residence based or source based, but a plan that taxes some foreign source income in full and provides lower rates on others, while retaining the foreign tax credit.[32] Under the plan, income derived from activities with a U.S. source as well as passive and mobile income (presumably similar to current Subpart F income) would be taxed in full when earned. Other foreign source income would also be taxed when earned, but at a rate lower than the U.S. rate. The discussion draft describes two options, one where this income would be taxed at 80% of the U.S. rate and one where active income would be taxed at 60% of the U.S. rate and other income at 100%. The 80% and 60% are only suggestions at this point. Minimum tax approaches have also been suggested, without specifics, by the President.[33]

A minimum tax on foreign source income might be a compromise between moving to a territorial system and eliminating deferral or imposing stricter rules in the context of the current system. Another form of compromise might be requiring a percentage of income to be paid out. This type of system would eliminate the repatriation tax, because income would be taxed (at some rate) regardless of repatriation.

The discussion draft also includes provisions aimed at limiting profit shifting, including an interest allocation rule (similar to that of Grubert and Mutti) that would disallow deductions associated with exempt income.

PRESIDENT OBAMA'S PROPOSALS TO RESTRICT DEFERRAL AND CROSS-CREDITING

It is also possible to move toward further restrictions on deferral without eliminating it entirely. One such proposal, contained in H.R. 3970, the tax reform proposal introduced by Chairman Rangel of the Ways and Means Committee, would disallow certain deductions of parent company costs (the most important being interest) that reflect the share of income that is deferred. This provision, projected to raise revenue of $106 billion over 10 years, would make investment in low-tax countries much less attractive.[34] The revenue from this provision and other changes were to be used to lower the corporate statutory tax rate.

This proposal also included a foreign tax credit pooling proposal, which would allow a share of foreign tax credits equal to the share of income repatriated. This provision limits the ability of firms to repatriate income from high tax countries and use excess foreign tax credits to shield income from low-tax countries from the foreign tax credit. President Obama proposed these changes, along with others, in his various budget proposals.[35] (The allocation of deductions, however, excluded research and development expenditures). The deferral provision was projected to raise $5.9 billion in FY2014 and $37.2 billion over 10 years and the foreign credit and the foreign tax credit pooling provision was projected to raise $5.5 billion in FY2013 and $60.8 billion over 10 years.

Another provision (contained in the FY2010 proposals, but not in later outlines) would eliminate "check-the-box," a provision that allows firms to elect to treat subsidiaries as separate entities or disregarded entities. These regulations permit firms to avoid current taxation on certain income that would be subject to Subpart F anti-abuse rules (such as interest on loans from a subsidiary in a low-tax country to a related subsidiary in a high-tax country). This provision was originally projected to raise $86 billion over 10 years.[36]

A provision in the FY2013 proposal would treat excess income from intangibles as Subpart F income and assigns them to a separate foreign tax credit basket. This provision is projected to raise $2.7 billion in FY2014, and $23.0 billion over 10 years. It may have been a substitute for "check-the-box" revisions.

The proposals also included a provision that would disallow foreign tax credits when the associated income is not received, as can occur with an arrangement termed a "reverse hybrids." This provision was adopted in 2010 (P.L. 111-226). P.L. 111-226 contained a number of provisions that were directed at perceived abuses of the foreign tax credit. Several other more limited proposals were included in the President's budget proposals.[37] In the FY2013 proposal, these international proposals are projected to raise $16.2 billion in FY2014 and $147.5 billion over 10 years.

The Administration also presented a framework for tax reform that mentioned five elements: the allocation of interest for deferred income (first bullet point above), a tax on excess intangibles (third bullet point), a minimum tax on foreign source income in low-tax countries, disallowing a deduction for the cost of moving abroad, and providing a 20% credit for costs of moving an operation from abroad to the United States.[38]

A minimum tax on foreign source income might be a compromise between moving to a territorial system and eliminating deferral. Another form of compromise might be requiring a percentage of income to be paid out.

TAX HAVENS: ISSUES AND POLICY OPTIONS

The topic of "tax havens" has been a focus of recent international tax policy discussions. (This topic is treated in more detail in another CRS report.)[39]Tax havens do not fit neatly into the traditional CEN/CMN/NN evaluation framework outlined above—perhaps because the tax haven issue involves as much artificial shifting of income and investment as it does questions about how investment is actually allocated. To the extent tax havens abet the shifting of income from its true geographic source to low-tax jurisdictions (the havens themselves), they raise questions about protecting the U.S. Treasury from revenue losses. They also raise questions about tax fairness (not all taxpayers are in position to reduce their U.S. taxes by using tax havens). And to the extent tax havens reduce the tax burden on investment that truly occurs overseas, they also raise the same questions about economic efficiency and neutrality addressed by the traditional framework outlined above.

"Tax haven" is not a precisely defined term, but in most usages it refers to a country—in many cases small ones—where non-residents can save taxes by conducting various investments, transactions, and activities. Attributes that make a country a successful tax haven include low or non-existent tax rates applicable to foreigners; strict bank and financial secrecy laws; and a highly developed communications, financial, and legal infrastructure.

At the heart of the tax haven issue is the discrepancy between real economic activity and what is only apparent. Much of the economic activity that appears to occur in tax havens actually occurs elsewhere, and is only associated with particular tax-haven countries because of sometimes spurious relationships between the person or firm conducting the activity and the tax-haven country. Thus, for example, much (or even most) of the income reported by U.S.-controlled subsidiaries chartered in tax havens may well have its true economic location either in some other foreign country or even in the United States itself. In several small tax-haven locations, incomes of U.S.-controlled foreign subsidiaries are many times larger than GDP. In Bermuda and the Cayman Islands, this income was respectively, over six times and over five times.[40]

In part, U.S. firms may find tax havens useful tax-saving mechanisms because of particular aspects of the U.S. tax structure. Here, no illegal tax evasion or even transfer-price manipulation may be necessary to obtain tax savings. An example is the technique sometimes termed a corporate "inversion" reorganization, under which the overall parent of a corporate group shifts from a U.S.-chartered entity to a foreign corporation organized in an offshore-tax haven. The rearrangement can potentially reduce or eliminate U.S. tax that would otherwise be due when foreign income is repatriated.[41]

U.S. firms can also use tax havens to shift income out of foreign countries where there are corporate income taxes to the zero-tax environment many tax havens offer. Short of outright tax evasion, techniques for shifting income include manipulation of transfer prices affixed to intrafirm sales and other transfers, and the structuring of intrafirm lending and interest charges so as to shift income out of high-tax countries to tax havens (sometimes called "earnings stripping"). Transfer price manipulation can also theoretically be used to shift what is actually U.S.-source income to offshore-tax-haven subsidiary corporations.

Along with income shifting and expatriation by corporations, tax havens in some cases apparently abet the outright evasion of taxes, in some cases by

U.S. citizens. For example, income from illegal activity in the United States can be shielded from U.S. authorities if a tax haven offers sufficient bank secrecy. Or, taxes on legally generated U.S. income are apparently evaded in some cases by depositing the income in secrecy-protected foreign bank accounts.[42] The focus of this report, however, is the activities of multinational firms, so its concern with tax havens is more with legal (albeit what some might term "abusive") income shifting rather than outright tax evasion.

In part, the ability of firms to divert income from other foreign locations to tax havens has implications for the real location of investment: just because a tax haven is not the true source of income does not make the associated tax savings any less real for the underlying investment, wherever it may be located. Interpret the effect of tax havens on actual investment in terms of the efficiency framework outlined in previous sections of the report. First, regarding the allocation of investment between the United States and foreign locations, existing data indicate that the United States is a relatively "high tax" country, even if tax havens are omitted from the calculation.[43] Thus, much of the income shifted to tax havens is likely shifted from countries whose taxes are lower than U.S. taxes to begin with. As a result, it is likely that tax havens on balance magnify the distorting effects of deferral, thus further diverting U.S. investment to foreign locations and, in turn, reducing economic efficiency and U.S. national welfare. This efficiency effect, however, may be mitigated by a reduction in the tax-induced distortion of location decisions across foreign countries.[44]

Along with efficiency effects, tax havens reduce tax revenue collections by capital-exporting countries. In the case of U.S. firms' use of tax havens, the revenue loss can accrue both to the United States (in the case of income shifted from domestic sources) and other countries (in the case of income shifted from other countries with higher taxes). Tax havens likewise have the potential of damaging perceptions of tax fairness when public reports appear of large firms and wealthy individuals using tax havens to avoid or evade substantial taxes.[45] Accordingly, a policy question is how tax evasion, or what might be termed "abusive" tax avoidance through tax havens, can be reduced.

One possible approach to tax havens is multilateral (that is, multi-country) action. The concept here is that tax havens flourish in part because of a lack of coordination in tax-administration between non-haven countries and that efforts to suppress tax-haven activities cannot be successful without solidarity among non-haven countries.[46] One prominent multilateral effort has been the Organization for Economic Cooperation and Development's (OECD's) "harmful tax practices project," initiated in 1996. The focus of the OECD's project has been to identify tax havens and to induce them to increase their "transparency" (presumably reduce secrecy about financial transactions) and to increase the number and scope of exchange of tax information agreements with tax havens.[47]

A unilateral approach was proposed by the Clinton Administration with its FY2001 budget proposal. The basis of the plan was to be a list of jurisdictions identified by the Treasury Department as tax havens. Foreign tax credits and the deferral benefit would be restricted for taxpayers using the identified tax havens.[48] More narrow unilateral approaches proposed in the past have primarily involved increasing information reporting requirements.

Several legislative proposals, including proposals in President Obama's budget, and a number of congressional proposals have been made to address evasion and avoidance. Some provisions were adopted in the Hire Act in 2010 (P.L. 111-147).[49]

General Reforms of the Corporate Tax and Implications for International Tax Treatment

Despite increasing globalization of the U.S. economy, foreign direct investment remains a small share of the U.S.-owned capital stock. For that reason, it would perhaps not be appropriate for international concerns to dominate the formulation of corporate tax policy. Nevertheless, there are specific forms of corporate tax revisions that might have important consequences for international taxation.

Under the current U.S. system, taxes on corporate profits at the individual level (dividends and capital gains) tend to be collected (due to tax treaties) on a residence basis. If taxes at the individual level could be increased and taxes at the corporate level decreased, the tax would shift toward a residence-based system without any other changes and without any additional concerns about portfolio substitution. In 2003, relief for double taxation was provided by reducing the tax rate on corporate dividends from the ordinary tax rate to 15% for those in brackets above the 15% rate, and to 5% for others. The 5% rate is now scheduled to fall to zero.

Using 2004 figures, where data on qualified dividends are available, the 35% corporate tax rate could have been rolled back to a 31% rate, or even less, for the same revenue cost if a corporate rate reduction rather than reductions in the individual level tax had occurred.[50] There are many other potential changes that could raise revenue to permit a further lowering of the corporate rate. At the individual level, these might include higher capital gains tax rates, accrual taxation of gains on corporate stock, and limits or modest taxes on retirement savings (which would benefit from corporate rate reductions). At the corporate level, a number of base broadening provisions might be considered. It could be feasible to lower the corporate tax rate to 25% with relatively modest changes in tax rules.[51]

A lower U.S. corporate tax is desirable if one believes that the most serious distortion in the international tax system is the tendency of capital to flow to low-tax foreign jurisdictions because of deferral. Such a proposition is a reasonable one, as the United States is generally a high-tax country. Lower corporate tax rates are also responsive to concerns that portfolio substitution disfavors U.S. owned firms. Nevertheless, even significant reductions in the U.S. tax rate are unlikely to have significant effects on overall U.S. output because the corporate tax is relatively small compared with GDP. A recent estimate suggests that lowering the rate to 25% without making any other changes would increase U.S. output by only 2/10 of 1% of GDP.[52]

Although international concerns should not necessarily dominate the issues surrounding corporate tax policy,[53] they do suggest the economic desirability of certain types of corporate tax reforms that would improve economic efficiency in the international area.

End Notes

[1] Data on trade, U.S. assets abroad, and foreign assets in the United States are from the website of the U.S. Department of Commerce, Bureau of Economic Analysis, at http://www.bea.gov. The fixed assets data were adjusted to include estimated stocks of inventory and intangible capital.

[2] Interest in international reform comes from a variety of sources. For example, the President's executive order (E.O. 13369) establishing his advisory panel on tax reform cited international competitiveness concerns as one principal reason for considering tax reform; the panel's final report included a fundamental change in the structure of the U.S. international system as part of one of its reform options. See President's Advisory Panel on Federal Tax Reform, *Simple, Fair, and Pro-Growth: Proposals to Fix America's Tax System* (Washington, November 2005). In Congress, in June 2006, the House Ways and Means Committee's Subcommittee on Select Revenue Measures held a hearing on international tax reform. The topic is also receiving attention in the academic and professional world: the *National Tax Journal* published a four-article forum on international tax reform in its December 2001 issue.

[3] President Bush's Advisory Panel on Tax Reform published a list of countries that use a territorial system either by statute or treaty. The territorial countries are: Australia, Austria,

Belgium, Canada, Denmark, Finland, France, Germany, Greece, Hungary, Iceland, Italy, Luxembourg, Netherlands, Norway, Portugal, Slovak Republic, Spain, Sweden, Switzerland, and Turkey. The following countries tax foreign-source income at some point and rely on foreign tax credits to relieve double taxation: Czech Republic, Iceland, Japan, Korea, Mexico, New Zealand, Poland, the United Kingdom, and the United States. President's Advisory Panel on Federal Tax Reform, *Simple, Fair, and Pro-Growth: Proposals to Fix America's Tax System* (Washington, November 2005), p. 243. Japan and the United Kingdom, however, have recently moved to a territorial system.

[4] According to IRS data for 2008, before-tax earnings and profits of foreign subsidiaries was $661 billion while branch gross income was $178 billion. The data are posted on the IRS website at http://www.irs.gov/uac/SOI-

[5] U.S. parent firms are permitted to claim foreign tax credits for foreign taxes paid by their foreign-chartered subsidiaries. Such "indirect" credits can be claimed by the parent when the foreign-source income is remitted as dividends.

[6] Jennifer Gravelle reports 62% of income in 2008 was earned by firms with excess credits in at least one basket; Presentation at National Tax Association Meetings, Providence, Rhode Island, November 2012. Similar shares were found in the past. See Rosanne Altshuler and Harry Grubert, 'Corporate Taxes in the World Economy: Reforming the Taxation of Cross-Border Income," *In Fundamental Tax Reform: Issues, Choices and Implications*, Ed. John W. Diamond and George R. Zodrow (Cambridge, MA: The MIT Press, 2008).

[7] For a more detailed discussion of this concept see CRS Report RS22445, *Taxes and International Competitiveness*, by Donald J. Marples. See also Jane G. Gravelle, "Does the Concept of Competitiveness Have Meaning in Formulating Corporate Tax Policy?" *Tax Law Review*, vol. 65, no. 3, 2012, p. 323-348.

[8] Comparative advantage is not a technical or unfamiliar concept; it is a common, everyday occurrence. A lawyer may be able to do his or her paralegal employee's work more efficiently, but that activity is not the best use of his or her time. A lawyer has an absolute advantage in both law practice and paralegal work, but a comparative advantage in practicing law.

[9] Mihir Desai and James Hines, Evaluating International Tax Reform, *National Tax Journal*, vol. 56, September 2003.

[10] Michael P. Devereux, "Capital Export Neutrality, Capital Import Neutrality, Capital Ownership Neutrality, and All That," Unpublished Paper, June 11, 1990.

[11] Daniel J. Frisch, "The Economics of International Tax Policy: Some Old and New Approaches," *Tax Notes*, April 30, 1990.

[12] Frisch, in "The Economics of International Tax Policy: Some Old and New Approaches," states, "In short, a major element of the CIN view would seem to possess a grain of truth," (p. 590) referring to the capital import neutrality framework. Devereux, in "Capital Export Neutrality, Capital Import Neutrality, Capital Ownership Neutrality, and All That," indicated that he originally attempted to redefine capital import neutrality to cover the capital ownership neutrality concept.

[13] The concepts were first developed by Peggy Musgrave. See, for example, her *United States Taxation of Foreign Investment Income: Issues and Arguments* (Cambridge MA: Harvard Law School, 1969), pp. 108-121.

[14] Calculated by reducing U.S. corporate equity issues by foreign stock holdings in the United States determining U.S. holdings of foreign stocks as a share. Data on corporate equities can be found in the Board of Governors of the Federal Reserve Flow of Funds Accounts, Table L213, which can be found at http://www.federalreserve.gov/releases/Z1/ Current/.

Historical series can also be found in the National Income and Product Accounts at http://www.bea.gov/ national/nipaweb/Ni_FedBeaSna/TableView.asp?SelectedTable=5&FirstYear=1998&Last Year=2005&Freq=Year.

[15] This optimality issue has also been addressed with the notion of National Ownership Neutrality, which indicates that it is both efficient and optimal to have source-based taxation.

[16] Congressional Budget Office, *Corporate Tax Rates: International Comparisons,* November, 2005.

[17] Data are from tax rates cited in Congressional Budget Office. *Corporate Tax Rates: International Comparisons, November, 2005,* and portfolio share data are from U.S. Department of Treasury *Report on U.S. Portfolio Holdings of Foreign Securities*.

[18] U.S. Department of Treasury, *Report on U.S. Portfolio Holdings of Foreign Securities*.

[19] Principal-agent costs occur when the objectives of the two parties are not identical. For example, the contract manufacturer (the agent) may want to increase the scale of the operation rather than maximizing profits for the firm authorizing the manufacturing (the principal).

[20] National Commission on Fiscal Responsibility and Reform, The Moment of Truth., Washington, DC, The White House, December 2010.

[21] Harry Grubert and John Mutti, *Taxing International Business Income: Dividend Exemption versus the Current System* (Washington: American Enterprise Institute, 2001), 67 pp; President's Advisory Panel on Tax Reform, *Simple, Fair, and Pro-Growth: Proposals to Fix America's Tax System* (Washington, 1985), pp. 239-244.

[22] Ibid., p. 11. Note, however, that cross-crediting also reduces current law's inefficient disincentive to invest in high-tax countries on the part of firms without excess credits, a feature not considered by the Grubert/Mutti analysis. Because income earned by firms with a deficit of credits outweighs that of firms with excess credits, it is plausible that an exemption system's loss of this easing of inefficiency would outweigh the gains from reduced investment in low-tax countries.

[23] Writing more recently, Grubert and his co-author Rosanne Altshuler note that if an exemption system is actively considered by policymakers, its adoption with its full panoply of deduction restrictions intact would be problematic. Rosanne Altshuler and Harry Grubert, *Corporate Taxes in the World Economy: Reforming the Taxation of Cross-Border Income*, unpublished paper presented at the James A. Baker II Inst. for Public Policy conference on tax reform, April 27-28, 2006, p. 4.

[24] Harry Grubert and John Mutti, *Taxing International Business Income*, p. 38.

[25] Report in U.S. Congressional Budget Office, *Budget Options* (Washington, February 2007), p. 319.

[26] Joint Committee on Taxation, *Estimates of Federal Tax Expenditures 2006-2010*, JCS-2-06, April 25, 2006.

[27] Edward D. Kleinbard, "Throw Territorial Taxation from the Train," *Tax Notes,* February 5, 2007, pp. 552-553.

[28] For a discussion of international tax avoidance, see CRS Report R40623, *Tax Havens: International Tax Avoidance and Evasion*, by Jane G. Gravelle. For a more detailed discussion of territorial tax proposals, see CRS Report R42624, *Moving to a Territorial Income Tax: Options and Challenges*, by Jane G. Gravelle.

[29] From 1954 to 1961, taxpayers were required to use a per-country limitation. For a synopsis of changes in limitation policy, see Thomas Horst, "The Overall vs. the Per-Country

Limitation on the U.S. Foreign Tax Credit," in U.S. Department of the Treasury, Office of Tax Analysis, *1978 Compendium of Tax Research* (Washington: GPO, 1978), pp. 213-214.

[30] The purest form of a separate limitation would require a separate limitation to be calculated for each investment a firm makes. Clearly, however, such a policy would present considerable administrative difficulties.

[31] Rosanne Altshuler and Harry Grubert, *Corporate Taxes in the World Economy: Reforming the Taxation of Cross-Border Income*, p. 17.

[32] Senate Finance Committee, Baucus Unveils Proposals for International Tax Reform, November 19, 2013, at http://www.finance.senate.gov/newsroom/chairman/release/?id=f946a9f3-d296-42ad-bae4-bcf451b34b14.

[33] *The President's Framework for Business Tax Reform: A Joint Report by the White House and the Department of the Treasury*, February 2012, http://www.treasury.gov/resource-center/tax-policy/

[34] The provisions of H.R. 3970 are discussed in CRS Report RL34249, *The Tax Reduction and Reform Act of 2007: An Overview*, by Jane G. Gravelle. The bill also contains a provision that repeals a planned liberalization of interest allocation rules for purposes of the foreign tax credit limit. This provision is discussed in CRS Report RL34494, *The Foreign Tax Credit's Interest Allocation Rules*, by Jane G. Gravelle and Donald J. Marples.

[35] U.S. Department of Treasury, General Explanations of the Administration's Fiscal Year 2013 Revenue Proposals (Green Book), Washington, DC, February, 2012, http://www.treasury.gov/resource-center/tax-policy General-Explanations-FY2013-Tables.pdf.

[36] U.S. Department of Treasury. General Explanations of the Administration's Fiscal Year 2010 Revenue Proposals (Green Book), Washington, DC, May 2009, http://www.treasury.gov/resource-center/tax-policy/

[37] See CRS Report R40623, *Tax Havens: International Tax Avoidance and Evasion*, by Jane G. Gravelle, for a summary of these enacted and proposed revisions.

[38] *The President's Framework for Business Tax Reform: A Joint Report by the White House and the Department of the Treasury*, February 2012, http://www.treasury.gov/resource-center/tax-policy/

[39] CRS Report R40623, *Tax Havens: International Tax Avoidance and Evasion*, by Jane G. Gravelle.

[40] Ibid., see Table 4.

[41] For more information, see CRS Report RL31444, *Firms That Incorporate Abroad for Tax Purposes: Corporate "Inversions" and "Expatriation"*, by Donald J. Marples.

[42] For a discussion of tax havens and illegal activities, see Martin A. Sullivan, "Sex, Drugs, and Tax Evasion," *Tax Notes*, June 18, 2007, pp. 1098-1100.

[43] 2002 Internal Revenue Service data on U.S.-controlled foreign subsidiaries show that subsidiaries pay, on average, a lower percentage of their pre-tax earnings in tax than do firms in the United States. This is true even for developed countries such as the United Kingdom and Canada.

[44] That tax havens actually stimulate investment in nearby higher-tax countries is argued in Mihir A. Desai, C. Fritz Foley, and James R. Hines, Jr., "Do Tax Havens Divert Economic Activity?" *Economics Letters*, vol. 90, 2006, pp. 219-224.

[45] Senate Finance Committee Chairman Max Baucus, for example, has observed that when tax havens are used for tax evasion "the honest American taxpayers who work hard, and do not have the ability to engage in offshore activity, are left holding the bill." Sen. Max Baucus, Hearing Statement Regarding Offshore Tax Evasion, May 3, 2007, available as a Finance Committee news release at http://www.finance.senate.gov/imo/media

[46] To illustrate, imagine a situation where country A has exchange of information agreements both with country B and tax haven H. Country B, however, has no exchange agreement with the tax haven. Conceivably, would-be taxpayers from country A could channel tax-saving tax haven transactions through country B.

[47] Jeffrey Owens, Director, OECD Centre for Tax Policy and Administration, "OECD's Work in Counteracting the Use of Tax Havens to Evade Taxes," unpublished paper presented at the American Enterprise Institute, December 11, 2006. Some U.S. critics of the OECD criticized what they saw as the initiative's underlying premise that low taxes are suspect. It was indeed partly on this basis that the Bush administration persuaded the OECD to focus on transparency and exchange of information rather than efforts to persuade targeted countries to change their tax practices toward nonresidents. See Hon. Paul O'Neill, Secretary of the Treasury, testimony before the Senate Committee on Governmental Affairs, Permanent Subcommittee on Investigations, July 18, 2001, available at the committee's website, at http://hsgac.senate.gov/071801_psioneil.htm.

[48] For a description of the proposal, see U.S. Congress, Joint Committee on Taxation, *Description of Revenue Proposals Contained in the President's Fiscal Year 2001 Budget Proposals* (Washington: GPO, 2000), pp. 500-509.

[49] See CRS Report R40623, *Tax Havens: International Tax Avoidance and Evasion*, by Jane G. Gravelle for descriptions.

[50] In 2004, taxable qualified dividends for individual income taxes were $104 billion according to the Statistics of Income data. Assuming a 15% rate differential, rolling back the provision for dividends would have raised revenues by $15.6 billion. The gain from raising the capital gains tax rate back to 20% depends on the behavioral response—how much individuals reduce their realizations, given tax increases. Based on the realization responses the Joint Tax Committee used in the past, and the Congressional Budget Office baseline, the gain for capital gains would be $9.2 billion. If the realizations response were based on the response used by the Congressional Budget Office in projecting the baseline, it would raise $12.7 billion. There is some evidence that even that response is too large as discussed in CRS Report R41364, *Capital Gains Tax Options: Behavioral Responses and Revenues*, by Jane G. Gravelle. If the revenue gain is to be used to reduce the corporate tax and raise after-tax profits, they need to be grossed up by (1-t) where t is the effective individual tax rate on an additional dollar of corporate after-tax profits. The estimate assumes an average tax rate of 25% and that half of the income goes to non-taxable recipients such as pension funds, for an overall rate of 12.5%. Corporate tax revenues were $189 billion in FY2004, but this value was unusually low because of bonus depreciation. Adjusting for bonus depreciation brings the revenue to $236 billion. (For a discussion, see CRS Report RL33672, *Revenue Feedback from the 2001-2004 Tax Cuts*, by Jane G. Gravelle.) The revenue gains divided by the gross-up factor and then by corporate tax receipts indicate the percentage reduction in the corporate tax (12% and 13.5% respectively), which are then multiplied by the 35% rate to determine the percentage point reduction.

[51] Taxing capital gains at full rates would have raised, for 2004, $7 billion to $20 billion, or even more, allowing a rate decrease of one to three percentage points. Accrual taxation would yield dramatically larger revenues. Two examples of corporate base broadening provisions include the production activities deduction for domestic manufacturing and certain industries, and the title passage rule, which is a rule allowing an arbitrary allocation of income from U.S. exports to be assigned to foreign-source income for purposes of the foreign tax credit limit (effectively an export subsidy). According to tax expenditure estimates, the production activities deduction (which is being phased in) will reach a cost of

$10 billion by FY2010. The title passage rule costs about $6 billion. These two corporate provisions should permit a three percentage point reduction, bringing the rate to between 27% and 28%.

[52] CRS Report R41743, *International Corporate Tax Rate Comparisons and Policy Implications*, by Jane G. Gravelle.

[53] Two reasons to provide relief at the individual level are (1) to focus tax cuts on marginal investment, which is more likely to be taxable investment to individuals rather than investment in pension funds and retirement accounts; and (2) to reduce the distortion that capital gains taxes impose on the willingness to realize gains and adjust assets. This latter distortion, however, would be improved if an accrual basis capital gains tax on corporate stock were adopted. Such a move would also raise a great deal of revenue that could be used to lower corporate tax rates. Doing so would also end concerns about using corporations with lower tax rates to shelter income.

In: Corporate Inversions
Editor: Fredrick White

ISBN: 978-1-63321-966-3

Chapter 3

INTERNATIONAL CORPORATE TAX RATE COMPARISONS AND POLICY IMPLICATIONS*

Jane G. Gravelle

SUMMARY

Advocates of cutting corporate tax rates frequently make their argument based on the higher statutory rate in the United States as compared with the rest of the world; they argue that cutting corporate taxes would induce large investment flows into the United States, which would create jobs or expand the taxable income base enough to raise revenue. President Barack Obama has supported a rate cut if the revenue loss can be offset with corporate base broadening. Others have urged on one hand, a revenue raising reform, and, on the other, setting deficit concerns aside.

Is the U.S. tax rate higher than the rest of the world, and what does that difference imply for tax policy? The answer depends, in part, on which tax rates are being compared. Although the U.S. statutory tax rate is higher, the average effective rate is about the same, and the marginal rate on new investment is only slightly higher. The statutory rate differential is relevant for international profit shifting; effective rates are more relevant for firms' investment levels. The 13.7 percentage point differential in statutory rates

* This is an edited, reformatted and augmented version of a Congressional Research Service publication R41743, prepared for Members and Committees of Congress dated January 6, 2014.

(a 39.2% rate for the United States compared with 25.5% in other countries), narrows to about 9 percentage points when tax rates in the rest of the world are weighted to reflect the size of countries' economies. (The OECD rates fell by slightly over one-half of a percentage point between 2010 and 2012.)

Regardless of tax differentials, could a U.S. rate cut lead to significant economic gains and revenue feedbacks? Because of the factors that constrain capital flows, estimates for a rate cut from 35% to 25% suggest a modest positive effect on wages and output: an eventual one-time increase of less than two-tenths of 1% of output. Most of this output gain is not an increase in national income because returns to capital imported from abroad belong to foreigners and the returns to U.S. investment abroad that comes back to the United States are already owned by U.S. firms.

The revenue cost of such a rate cut is estimated at between $1.2 trillion and $1.5 trillion over the next 10 years. Revenue feedback effects from increased investment inflows are estimated to reduce those revenue costs by 5%-6%. Reductions in profit shifting could have larger effects, but even if profit shifting disappeared entirely, it would not likely offset revenue losses. It seems unlikely that a rate cut to 25% would significantly reduce profit shifting given these transactions are relatively costless and largely constrained by laws, enforcement, and court decisions.

Both output gains and revenue offsets would be reduced if other countries responded to a U.S. rate cut by reducing their own taxes. Evidence suggests that the U.S. rate cut in the Tax Reform Act of 1986 triggered rate cuts in other countries.

It is difficult, although not impossible, to design a reform to lower the corporate tax rate by 10 percentage points that is revenue neutral in the long run. Standard tax expenditures do not appear adequate for this purpose. Eliminating one of the largest provisions, accelerated depreciation, gains much more revenue in the short run than in the long run, and a long-run revenue-neutral change would increase the cost of capital. Other revisions, such as restricting foreign tax credits and interest deductibility or increasing shareholder level taxes, may be required.

This report focuses on the global issues relating to tax rate differentials between the United States and other countries. It provides tax rate comparisons; discusses policy implications, including the effect of a corporate rate cut on revenue, output, and national welfare; and discusses the outlook for and consequences of a revenue neutral corporate tax reform.

Advocates of cutting corporate tax rates frequently make their argument based on the higher statutory rate observed in the United States as compared with the rest of the world.[1] Sometimes the higher rate alone is used as an argument, and in other cases the arguments include claims that cutting corporate taxes would induce large investment flows into the United States, which would create jobs or expand the base enough to raise revenue.

President Barack Obama has supported a rate cut if the revenue loss can be offset with corporate base broadening, while the Citizens for Tax Justice has urged a revenue raising reform and business leaders have urged setting deficit concerns aside.[2] House Majority Leader Eric Cantor has also proposed a 25% corporate rate in the context of tax reform and Ways and Means Chairman Dave Camp has proposed a 25% combined with a move to a territorial tax system.[3]

Many issues arise regarding the corporate tax outside of the global perspective addressed in other reports.[4] This report focuses on the global issue relating to tax rate differentials between the United States and other countries. The first section provides tax rate comparisons. The second section discusses policy implications, including the effect of a corporate rate cut on revenue, output, and national welfare; the possibility that a rate cut may induce reactions from other countries; and the outlook for and consequences of a revenue-neutral corporate tax reform.

EFFECTIVE TAX RATE COMPARISONS

Several important features affect the interpretation of the comparative tax rates: the type of rate, what taxes are included, and the use of weighted measures to adjust for size differences. A number of tax rate comparisons follow the discussion of these features.

Types of Tax Rates

Three basic types of tax rates are reported: the statutory rate, the effective rate, and the marginal effective rate. The statutory rate is the rate in the tax statute; in the case of the United States, it is the top marginal corporate tax rate of 35%. The effective rate is determined by the ratio of taxes paid divided by profits. The effective rate captures the tax benefits that reduce the taxable income base relative to financial profits. The marginal tax rate is calculated from a projected investment project: it estimates the share of the pre-tax return that is paid in taxes.

Each type of tax rate has its advantages and disadvantages, and is useful for considering certain types of behavior. For example, the statutory rate would potentially affect firms' attempts to shift profits by altering the source of borrowing or transferring assets or products at prices that are not arm's length.[5] Even the statutory rate, however, needs some adjustments for this purpose. For example, most multinational firms in the United States are eligible for the production activities deduction, which reduces the U.S. statutory tax rate by 9%, from 35% to 31.85%.

The effective tax rate is taxes paid divided by profits. The effective tax rate captures some of the tax benefits and subsidies, reducing the tax paid per dollar of profit. This measure can make a country with a high statutory rate but narrow base more comparable to a country with a low tax rate and broad base. It is probably more suited to assessing the true relative burdens on investment than the statutory tax rate. However, these types of tax rates may not capture timing effects (such as accelerated depreciation) very well and generally depend on accounting measures of profit that may vary across countries.

The marginal effective tax rate is, in theory, the appropriate measure for determining the effects of tax rate differentials on investment. However, in some cases marginal tax rates do not include all of the components of investment; frequently, they are restricted to investment in fixed assets or fixed assets and inventory. This report estimates an overall marginal effective tax rate that includes inventories and intangibles as well as buildings and equipment. Marginal tax rates also depend on estimates of economic depreciation, expected inflation, and rates of return.

Also briefly discussed is a measure referred to as the effective average tax rate. The implications of this tax rate, which combines statutory and marginal effective rates, are not clear.

Types of Taxes Included

Most tax measures reflect the effect of both national and sub-national corporate income taxes. Of the 31 Organisation for Economic Co-operation and Development (OECD) countries, 8 countries (Canada, Germany, Japan, South Korea, Luxembourg, Portugal, Switzerland, and the United States) have sub-national corporate taxes. In some cases, these sub-national taxes are more significant than those in the United States. In the case of the United States, these corporate income taxes imposed by the state increase the statutory rate (without the production activities deduction) to 39.2%. With the production activities deduction, the combined rate is 36.3%.[6]

Countries can also have other taxes that impose a burden on capital. In the United States, these taxes are imposed by the states and localities, and they include property taxes, franchise taxes, and retail sales taxes that apply to capital goods. These taxes are much more difficult to measure and are generally not included in comparative tax rate measures, although one study (discussed below) includes franchise, and transfer and sales taxes, but not property or wealth taxes.

Simple (Unweighted) versus Weighted Averages of Tax Rates

Another issue that affects the comparisons between U.S. and worldwide tax rates is whether tax rates are simple (unweighted) averages or whether they are weighted in some fashion to indicate their relative importance. If tax rates are not weighted, then a small economy, such as Iceland, can have the same effect on the average of international rates as a large economy, such as Germany or Japan. In general, smaller countries tend to have lower tax rates and thus unweighted averages are lower than weighted averages in most cases. In the results presented in this report, both weighted and unweighted averages are reported, but weighted averages are more relevant to making comparisons of measures of the tax burden on capital deployed around the world.

Tax Rate Comparisons: United States Compared with OECD and Large Economies

Table 1 reports the three measures of effective tax rates, with marginal rates restricted to equipment and structures separately, for the United States and the OECD excluding the United States. The statutory rate is reported with and without the production activities deduction.

The overall statutory rates in the OECD are slightly lower for 2013, with the rate in the OECD excluding the United States falling a little over a half to one percentage point. The U.S. rate is estimated at 39.1%, whereas the OECD weighted average is 28.4% and the unweighted average is 25.1%.[7]

The weighted rate was influenced by rate reductions in Japan and the United Kingdom.

The marginal tax rates do not reflect the effect of the production activities deduction that likely applies to most multinational corporations and would decrease these tax rates by 2-3 percentage points as of 2010. (The deduction was 3% in 2005-2006 and 6% for 2007-2009.) Thus while the difference between the statutory rate and the simple average—a difference of 13.7 percentage points—is frequently reported, a difference of about half that much—or 6.6 percentage points— occurs when the adjusted statutory rate of 36.2% is compared with the weighted average of 29.6%. The effective tax rate (which would automatically capture the production activities deduction and other provisions) is about the same. The marginal effective rate rates are also about the same when adjusted. Thus the tax rate most relevant for the purpose of incentives to invest is similar for the United States and the rest of the OECD with respect to equipment and structures investment.

Table 1. Corporate Tax Rates, United States and Rest of the OECD

Tax Rate Measure and Year	United States	OECD Excluding United States, GDP Weighted Average	OECD Excluding United States, Unweighted Average
Statutory (2010)	39.2	29.6	25.5
Statutory (2010) with Production Activities Deduction	36.3	29.6	25.5
Effective (2008)	27.1	27.7	23.3
Marginal Effective Equipment (2010)	23.6	21.2	17.3
Marginal Effective Equipment (2005)	23.0	21.1	18.7
Marginal Effective Buildings (2005)	29.0	26.4	23.4

Source: Statutory tax rates and gross domestic product (GDP), Organisation for Economic Co-operation and Development (OECD), http://www.oecd.org/dataoecd/26/56/33717459.xls and http://stats.oecd.org/Index.aspx? DatasetCode=SNA_TABLE1. Effective tax rate from Price WaterhouseCoopers, *Global Effective Tax Rate Comparisons—Methodology and Results*. Marginal tax rates, 2005, Institute for Fiscal Studies, http://www.ifs.org.uk/publications/3210.

Marginal tax rates 2010, Arparna Mathur and Kevin Hassett, *Report Card on Effective Corporate Tax Rates*, American Enterprise Institute, http://www.aei.org/outlook/101024. PriceWaterhouseCoopers reports similar effective tax rate data in their study Global Effective Tax Rates, April 14, 2011, at http://businessroundtable.org/uploads/studies-reports/downloads/Effective_Tax_Rate_Study.pdf.

The marginal tax rates do not reflect the temporary bonus depreciation in effect for 2008-2010 in the United States, which allowed 50% of the cost of equipment to be deducted. Aprovision allowing 100% of the cost to be deducted is in place for 2011. Because these are temporary provisions, it seems appropriate to exclude them. Whether these measures are captured in the effective tax rate depends on the treatment of deferred taxes, but measures from different years appear similar.

The OECD excludes some large countries, such as China and Brazil. **Table 2** provides the statutory and effective tax rate comparisons for the 15 largest countries, which account for three-quarters of world gross domestic product (GDP). The results are similar to those in **Table 1** with the weighted average about 1 percentage point higher. With the production activities deduction the rates differ by 5.6 percentage points. The effective rate is the same.

Tax rates have declined slightly, to a weighted average of 30 and an unweighted average of 29.2.[8]

Table 2. Corporate Tax Rates in the 15 Largest Countries

Tax Rate Measure and Year	United States	Remaining 14 Large Countries, GDP Weighted Average	Remaining 14 Large Countries, Unweighted Average
Statutory (2010)	39.2	30.7	29.8
Statutory (2010) Including Production Activities Deduction	36.3	30.7	29.8
Effective (2008)	27.1	27.2	25.3

Source: Statutory tax rates are at http://www.worldwide-tax.com/#partthree; effective tax rates are from same source as **Table 1**. GDP is from the World Bank http://siteresources.worldbank.org/DATASTATISTICS/ Resources/GDP.pdf.

Table 3. Effective Corporate Tax Rates, United States Compared with Six Countries

Tax Rate Measure	United States	Six Large Countries, GDP Weighted Average	Six Large Countries, Unweighted Average
Effective (2005-2009)	23.0	24.5	26.2

Source: Kevin S. Markle and Douglas A. Shackleford, "Cross-Country Comparisons of Corporate Income Taxes," working paper, February 2011.

Note: The six countries are Canada, France, Germany, India, Japan, and United Kingdom.

Table 3, **Table 4**, and **Table 5** provide results for effective tax rates from other studies. **Table 3** reports the Markle and Shackleford study that estimates the effective tax rate of domestic firms in different countries. Because a smaller number of countries are examined, **Table 3** compares the U.S. rate with that of the six large countries.

Table 4. Effective Tax Rates, United States and OECD

Tax Rate Measure	United States	OECD Excluding United States, GDP Weighted Average	OECD Excluding United States, Unweighted Average
Effective (2006)	29.5	28.4	23.7

Source: Charles Swenson and Namryoung Lee, "The Jury Is In: U.S. Companies are Overtaxed Relative to Their International Competitors," AICPA, July 17, 2008, at http://www.cpa2biz.com/Content/media/PRODUCER_CONTENT/Newsletters/Articles_2008/Tax/juryin.jsp. Rate table at https://media.cpa2biz.com/newsletter/2008/Tax/july/juryin_table.htm.

Table 5. Effective Tax Rates in the 15 Largest Countries

Tax Rate Measure	United States	Remaining 14 Large Countries, GDP Weighted Average	Remaining 14 Large Countries, Unweighted Average
Effective (2006)	29.5	28.7	27.3

Source: Charles Swenson and Namryoung Lee, "The Jury Is In: U.S. Companies are Overtaxed Relative to Their International Competitors, AICPA, July 17, 2008, at http://www.cpa2biz.com/Content/media/PRODUCER_CONTENT/Newsletters/

Articles_2008/Tax/juryin.jsp. Rate table at https://media.cpa2biz.com/newsletter/2008/Tax/july/juryin_table.htm.

Table 4 and **Table 5** report the Swenson and Lee study that estimated effective rates for firms headquartered in various countries for 2006 and 2007. The tables report for 2006 pre-dated the start of the recession and do not include years with bonus depreciation. Both results confirm the findings of other studies: effective tax rates in the United States and in other countries are similar.

Table 6. Marginal Effective Tax Rates, United States and Weighted OECD

	U.S. without Production Activities Deduction	U.S. with Production Activities Deduction	OECD Excluding United States, OECD, GDP Weighted	OECD Excluding United States, GDP Weighted, Adjusted by Statutory Rate Changes
Equipment	23.0	21.2	21.1	18.9
Structures	29.0	26.7	26.4	23.6
Inventories	39.2	36.2	29.6	29.6
Intangibles	-4.7	-4.7	-9.7	-9.7
Total	**22.2**	**20.2**	**18.3**	**16.4**

Source: Tax rates on equipment and structures from **Table 1**, Inventories taxed at statutory rates. Tax rates on intangibles, Department of Finance, Canada, *Tax Expenditures and Evaluations 2009: Part 2, An International Comparison of Tax Assistance for Investment in Research and Development*, http://www.fin.gc.ca/ taxexp-depfisc/2009/ taxexp0902-eng.asp. Weights are 24.2% equipment, 39.6% structures, 9.7% inventories, and 26.5% intangibles. For intangibles, 49% arise from R&D, which is taxed at rates of -10.1% in the U.S, -22.2% in the weighted OECD average, and -54.2% in the simple OECD average. The remaining intangibles arising from human capital investment and advertising are taxed at a 0 rate. Data on corporate equipment, structures, and inventories for 2003 from Flow of Funds Accounts 1995-2004, p. 96, http://www.federalreserve.gov/Releases/Z1/Current/annuals/a1995-2004.pdf.

Estimates of intangibles from Carol Corrado, Charles Hulten, and Daniel Sichel, *Intangible Capital and Economic Growth*, Finance and Economic Discussion Series, Division of Research and Statistics Federal Reserve Board, 2006-4, http://www.federalreserve.gov/releases/z1/20050921/z1.pdf.

Table 6 returns to the estimates of marginal effective tax rates, and expands the marginal rate analysis to reflect the other categories of assets, inventories, and intangibles. It provides a weighted average of these tax rates, using data on capital stock shares from the United States but applying the same shares to other countries. Note that intangibles are generally taxed at negative tax rates both in the United States and abroad. Expenditures on research, advertising, and human capital investment are generally deducted when incurred, which leads to a zero effective tax rate, and most countries (including the United States) have additional subsidies or credits for research expenditures.

As **Table 6** indicates, the overall marginal effective tax rates for the United States accounting for the production activities deduction and for the OECD countries weighted by GDP are similar, 20% and 18%. The differences are larger if the OECD rate is adjusted by average statutory rate changes that have occurred in these OECD countries since 2005, although base broadening could offset that reduction.[9] Marginal tax rates are also significantly lower than the statutory rates: the U.S. rate is about half the statutory rate and the weighted OECD rate is about 60% of the statutory rate.

The next measure is another marginal tax rate measure (Chen and Mintz). This measure has a number of differences from those in **Table 1** and **Table 4**. It includes equipment, structures, inventories, and land, but not intangibles. It also includes the effects of transfer taxes that fall on capital and debt finance. In the United States, these taxes are primarily state and local retail sales taxes that apply to capital goods purchases or inputs into construction and are quite large. It also includes franchise taxes. It does not, however, include wealth, capital stock, or property taxes. The measure also allows for debt finance and uses capital stock weights for Canada.

Table 7. Marginal Tax Rates Including Transfer and Franchise Taxes, United States Compared with the OECD

Tax Rate Measure	United States	OECD Excluding United States, GDP Weighted Average	OECD Excluding United States, Unweighted Average
Average Marginal Tax Rate 2010	34.6	23.6	18.4
Average Marginal Tax Rate Correcting for Additional Taxes	27.6	21.6	16.4

Source: Duanjie Chen and Jack Mintz, "New Estimates of Effective Corporate Tax Rates on Business Investment," CATO Institute, *Tax and Budget Bulletin*, no. 64, February 2011, http://www.cato.org/pubs/tbb/ tbb_64.pdf. Indications that transfer taxes added 7 points for the United States and 2 points for other countries on average is from the previous year's tax rates, "U.S. Effective Corporate Tax Rate on New Investments: Highest in the OECD," May 2010.

Table 7 reports these estimates for the OECD. Based on comments made in a previous analysis, indicating the size of these additional state and local taxes, the table reports a number with these additional taxes subtracted out to allow more comparability to other results. As compared with the numbers in **Table 6**, the discrepancy in the weighted OECD and the United States is larger. If the adjusted rates in **Table 6** are recomputed to exclude intangibles, they would be 28.7% for the United States and 23% for the OECD (weighted). This differential of 5.7 points shrinks to 3.8 points when intangibles are included. The only other differential is that these rates should be lowered to reflect the effects of debt finance. Normally, higher statutory tax rates result in a larger negative tax rate on debt, so the United States rate should fall more for this reason (although this effect can vary with inflation).

Table 8. Marginal Effective Tax Rates Including Transfer Taxes, 15 Largest Countries

Tax Rate Measure	United States	Remaining Large 14 Countries, GDP Weighted Average	Remaining Large 14 Countries Excluding U.S. – Unweighted Average
Average Marginal Tax Rate 2010	34.6	26.3	27.0
Average Marginal Tax Rate Correcting for Additional State and Local Taxes	27.6	24.3	25.0

Source: Duanjie Chen and Jack Mintz, "New Estimates of Effective Corporate Tax Rates on Business Investment," CATO Institute, *Tax and Budget Bulletin*, no. 64, February 2011, http://www.cato.org/pubs/tbb/ tbb_64.pdf. Indications that transfer taxes added 7 points for the United States and 2 points for other countries on average is from the previous year's tax rates, "U.S. Effective Corporate Tax Rate on New Investments: Highest in the OECD," May 2010.

The differential between the United State and the OECD as reported in the original study is 16.2 percentage points (34.6% minus 18.4%).

Out of that differential, 5.2 points are due to using an unweighted average, 5.0 points are due to including transfer taxes, 1.9 points are due to excluding intangibles, and the remaining 4.1 points are similar to the difference found in **Table 6**.

An updated study for 2012 shows similar relationships. The United States tax rate was 35.6%, the OECD excluding the United States was 24.0% weighted and 19.6% unweighted.[10]

Table 8 reports the comparative rates for the 15 largest countries. These rates are closer together, and quite close when adjusted for transfer taxes.

The Chen and Mintz study makes an important point, namely that other taxes outside of the corporate tax can affect the relative burden of tax in a way that could affect investment. (These types of taxes would not be relevant for profit shifting.) The main reservation about this finding is that the inclusion of these other capital taxes is partial. The other main capital tax in the United States is the property tax, which probably adds another 3 percentage points to the rate, but other countries also have property taxes as well as wealth taxes.[11]

Table 9 reports a fourth type of tax rate measure, which is named by its developers the "effective average tax rate." Estimates using this method differentiate between a normal (or riskless) return, which is taxed at an effective rate that reflects the various tax benefits such as accelerated depreciation, and the excess return, which is taxed at the statutory rate. Thus, it is a mix of marginal tax rates and statutory tax rates. This measure is reported because it is available and cited by some researchers. Some evidence suggests that it is a better predictor of location than other measures.[12] It shows U.S. taxes to be significantly higher than OECD rates, but the implications of such a measure for economic behavior are not clear.

Economists sometimes, when examining investment subsidies, differentiate between the normal and excess return. The normal return's tax burden is affected by items such as accelerated depreciation and investment subsidies, whereas the excess profit is subject to the statutory rate. In these views, however, it is the tax on normal return that would, in any case, affect economic behavior. The excess return is generally seen as bearing little or no tax burden because the reduction in expected return due to tax is offset by the reduction in variance of after tax return (i.e., the tax reduces gains and losses).

One reason that a combination of statutory and effective marginal rates might have an effect on location is that firms may locate some physical activity in a country to facilitate profit shifting associated with setting up subsidiaries to exploit developed intangibles.[13]

Table 9. "EffectiveAverage Tax Rate," United States and OECD

Tax Rate Measure	United States	Most OECD Excluding United States, GDP Weighted Average	Most OECD Excluding United States, Unweighted Average
Effective Average (2009)	37.4	29.8	24.3

Source: Michael P. Devereux, Christina Elschner, Dieter Endres, and Christoph Spengel, "Effective Tax Rates Using the Devereux-Griffith Methodlogy," ZEW Center for European Economic Research, October 2009, http://ec.europa.eu/taxation_customs/resources/documents/common/publications/studies/etr_company_tax.pdf. This research was focused on the European Union and selected additional countries; it excludes Australia, Chile, Iceland, New Zealand, Mexico, and Korea.

Summing Up

This comparison suggests some important precautions in comparing tax rates. First, it is important when forming a composite rate for the rest of the world to weight the tax rates by output or some other measure of economic importance. Because small countries tend to have lower rates than large ones, comparing rates using simple averages across countries exaggerates the differential between the United States and tax burdens elsewhere in the world. Second, weighted statutory tax rates differ but effective tax rates do not. Marginal effective tax rates have small differences. Third, in comparing the differences in statutory rates, the effect of the production activities deduction narrows the differential by close to half. Finally, although the role of subnational taxes outside of the corporate tax appears to be important for investment decisions, a full comparison has yet to be made. This analysis suggests that reform of state and local sales taxes could contribute to a more efficient system.

ECONOMIC EFFECTS OF A U.S. RATE CUT

The previous analysis has shown that U.S. statutory corporate tax rates are about 10 percentage points higher than a weighted average of the OECD or the large countries that account for most of output (7 percentage points when including the production activities deduction). Effective tax rates are about the same, and marginal effective tax rates are only slightly larger in the United States. The effects of including other capital taxes have not yet been explored on a comprehensive basis, although U.S. retail sales taxes on capital goods and franchise taxes are estimated to create an additional 5 percentage point differential.

This section explores the effects of a U.S. rate cut on the United States. The first subsection examines the effects on revenue, output, and national income for a corporate rate cut in isolation, only looking at capital flows. The second subsection discusses potential implications for profit shifting. The third subsection considers the possibility that other countries would react to a U.S. rate cut by cutting their rates as well. Finally, discussions of outlook for and consequences of a revenue neutral corporate tax reform are presented.

Effects on Revenue, Output, and National Welfare, Assuming No Tax Rate Changes by Other Countries or Offsetting Base Broadening in the United States

This section examines the effects of a corporate rate cut from 35% to 25% on revenues and international capital flows, and their effects on the U.S. economy (including feedback effects on revenues and effects on national welfare). It focuses on issues specific to global economy considerations of the corporate tax, not the traditional corporate tax issues that would also occur in a closed economy.

Revenues

The Congressional Budget Office (CBO) projected a 10-year corporate revenue of $4,360 billion from FY2013 to FY2022.[14] If this number were multiplied by 10/35 to estimate the revenue loss, the result would be $1,245 billion per year, on average.[15] The loss, however, is likely to be larger because net tax liability is the tax rate times taxable income, minus credits. Rate changes would not normally affect credits, and, if not, the revenue loss would be projected based on tax liability before credits. According to Internal Revenue Service (IRS) data, corporate tax before credits is 134% of corporate tax after credits.[16]

One of the major credits, the foreign tax credit, would be affected, in some cases, by a rate cut. The foreign tax credit is limited to the U.S. tax because of foreign source income, so as the U.S. rate falls, the limit on credits also falls.

In some cases, the credit would not be affected, or not affected proportionally, because the foreign tax credits are less than the limit and a change in the limit would not necessarily change foreign tax credits. (These firms are termed excess limit firms.) In other cases, firms have creditable taxes above the limit; with credits equal to the limit, a reduction in the limit would reduce foreign tax credits proportionally. (These firms are termed excess credit firms.)

Tax liability after the foreign tax credit but before other credits (general business credits and the alternative minimum tax credit) is 105.7% of tax liability after all credits. If foreign tax credits are reduced proportionally, the average loss is almost $132 billion. If foreign tax credits are not affected at all, the average loss per year is $168 billion.[17]

These estimates suggest that over the 10-year period, $1.3 trillion to $1.7 trillion would be lost in revenues due to the proposed rate cut. This number does not include any behavioral feedback effects, which could reduce the cost, but also does not include debt service or crowding out of private capital, which would increase the cost.

Estimates implied by this calculation are larger than projections based on a percentage point rate increase contained in CBO's Budget Options which, applying the percentage loss to the new baseline suggests revenue losses of about $1,113 trillion.[18] Some part of the discrepancy may reflect the fact that liabilities lag collections and that the first full year does not apply because estimates are based on fiscal years. In addition, to the extent that firms have unused foreign credits, a rate increase would raise less than reduction of the same size would cost. Other behavioral effects may occur as well.

Regardless of the precise estimate, a revenue loss in excess of $1 trillion and in excess of $100 billion a year would be expected over the next 10 years.

Effects on U.S. Output and Wages

What about the effects on the U.S. economy? The discussion sometimes focuses on job creation. Job creation is an important issue for the government to address during cyclical downturns. Standard economic theory suggests such policies should be temporary; in contrast, advocates of corporate rate cuts are proposing permanent cuts. In any case, temporary or permanent corporate rate cuts are unlikely to be very effective stimulus policies.[19]

Economic theory suggests that there is no reason to view general job creation as a long-run objective of government policies. The economy can generate the jobs needed by the natural process of growth and market adjustment. In 1961 and 1991, the unemployment rate was the same, 6.7%. Employment, however, rose from 66 million to 117 million. Employment tends to grow steadily; the unemployment rate fluctuates. Long-term jobs policies, according to economic theory, therefore, should not be aimed at increasing jobs, although they can be designed to reduce structural or frictional unemployment (such as improving the skills of disadvantaged workers).[20]

Rather, the capital flows induced by a corporate rate cut generally have effects on the level of output and on wage levels, rather than the number of workers. Despite the claimed effects of cutting the corporate tax on encouraging the flow of foreign-owned capital into the country from abroad (inbound capital) or discouraging the flow of U.S. capital to other countries (outbound capital), there are many forces that constrain the movement of capital. As capital flows into a country, its greater abundance coupled with a fixed amount of labor drives the wage rate up and the rate of return down, so that the pre-tax return to capital falls. If the economy is large enough to affect the rest of the world's returns, the proportional flow of capital is lessened further, because shift of capital from abroad (with no change in taxes) raises the after tax return abroad and draws some of the capital back. Capital flows are further reduced if there are significant non-corporate sectors (because a rate cut would draw capital from the unincorporated sectors of the economy as well as from abroad). Finally, the flow of capital would be further limited if capital is not perfectly mobile or products are not perfect substitutes.

A study by Gravelle and Smetters used a general equilibrium model to capture the effects of imposing a 35% tax, allowing for four sectors in the U.S. economy and a mirror foreign economy.[21] The estimated change in the capital stock, assuming the conditions most conducive to capital inflows, was 4.5%. (This scenario assumes that individuals and firms view investments in different locations as perfect substitutes and consumers view foreign and domestic products as perfect substitutes; these are referred to as the portfolio and product substitution elasticities and are set, effectively, at infinity.)[22] This effect implies a 4.7% increase from eliminating the tax (4.5/(1-4.5)). To convert a percentage change in the capital stock to a percentage change in output, multiply by the capital share of income, which was 0.29, to get a 1.36% increase in output. Because a partial change is proposed, multiply by 10/35 to obtain an estimated percentage change in output of 0.39%. With constant factor shares, which are assumed in this model, wages will also increase by this percentage.[23]

A similar magnitude of effects can be obtained by examining revenue reductions and incidence estimates for this same perfectly mobile case. CBO projects the corporate tax at 2% of GDP.[24] This revenue is as a percentage of gross output (which includes output that replaces capital and thus is not a part of an income concept). To convert it to a percentage of net of depreciation output (which is 82% of gross output[25]), divide by 0.82, for corporate revenues that are 2.27% of domestically generated income. To capture the effect of reducing the tax by 10 percentage points, multiply by 10/35, to obtain a tax cut of 0.65% of income. Incidence studies indicate that about 73% of the burden of the corporate tax falls on labor under this perfectly mobile assumption,[26] so this number is multiplied by 0.73 to obtain an increase in labor income of 0.47% of total income. Based on national income accounts, the share of labor income is 76%,[27] so dividing 0.47 by 0.76 yields a 0.62% increase in output and in wages.

Both estimates suggest a relatively small effect on output, of around 0.5%, but this estimate is too large. Perfect product substitution is not possible in a multi-good economy.[28] Moreover, empirical evidence suggests elasticities that are smaller. Gravelle and Smetters propose as a more reasonable case a model with portfolio and product substitution elasticities of 3. This assumption yields a 1.6% change in the capital stock. Following the methodology outlined above, the effect on output and wages is 0.13%, rather than 0.4%. These elasticities reduce the share of the burden borne by labor to 21% and, again, following the same methodology would cause an output and wage effect of about 0.18% rather than 0.62%.[29]

Two other aspects might make these effects even lower or perhaps reverse the sign. First, the effect of debt capital is not incorporated into any of these models. Because about a third of the capital stock is financed by debt, the magnitude of the first set of estimates (using capital stock estimates) should be reduced by about one-third to account for the presence of debt. This would be the expected outcome if returns to debt-financed investment were taxed at a zero rate, as would be the case if there were no inflation and no accelerated depreciation. However, since both of these conditions exist in the U.S. tax code, debt is subsidized at the corporate level because inflation is generally positive and the effective marginal tax rate is below the statutory rate. Lowering the statutory rate reduces these subsidies and discourages debt. This effect may be desirable for issues such as the debt-equity distortion, but can actually discourage capital inflows, as suggested in one study.[30]

Second, the estimates of capital stock assume that the United States has a territorial tax (i.e., the only tax due is on domestic profits). Although a relatively small share of foreign source income is taxed, the U.S. system is not fully territorial, but rather defers the tax until income is repatriated (except for branch income and some passive income that is easily shifted).[31] Under the U.S. system, the tax on income that is repatriated or currently taxed can be partially or fully offset by credits for foreign taxes paid. Most foreign source income is not taxed either because it is not repatriated or because credits are used to offset the tax; in addition to credits for tax paid in a country, unused credits from countries with higher taxes than the United States can be used to offset tax on income repatriated from low tax countries (called cross crediting).[32]

Effects on National Income and National Welfare

Even though output (or domestically generated income) increases by small amounts, that output gain does not represent a gain in U.S.-worldwide income. The gains that labor experiences are offset by the losses in the pre-tax return by the existing domestic capital, reducing the benefits of these firms. For example, in the case where labor income increases by 21% of the tax, existing capital, which absent capital flows would have had income increase by 100% of the tax cut, now has that increase offset roughly by 21% of the tax due to the lower pretax return. Although both labor and capital have higher after tax income, there is a transfer between the government and individuals, which must be offset by other tax increases or reduced spending either now or in the future.

Although there will be some gains in national welfare, they are likely to be only a small fraction of the revenue change. They would arise from income that transfers from foreigners to U.S. persons.[33] For thinking about this effect, consider separately inbound capital (capital owned by foreigners and invested in the United States) and outbound capital (capital owned by U.S. persons and invested abroad). The increase in inbound capital generates returns, but those returns are the income of the foreign investors. Thus, the only gain for the United States is the change in taxes, and the lower pre-tax rate of return on inbound investment. For outbound capital, the returns already belong to U.S. firms, and the gain is from moving capital back into the United States where taxes formerly paid to foreign governments are paid to the United States.

A recent study examined these effects, using data on foreign and domestic tax rates from a 2008 GAO study and estimates of inbound and outbound capital from the National Income and Product Accounts and found modest effects.[34] The estimated output effects in this study were larger than those calculated above because the study used a partial equilibrium framework with a simplified single sector model designed to distinguish between outbound and inbound capital flows. The purpose, however, was to consider the general magnitude of welfare effects. The estimates found that there was a slight *loss* (3% of the additional output) for inbound capital because the reduction in the tax rate on existing capital inflows was less than fully offset by taxes on induced capital flows and the small reduction in pre-tax returns. For outbound capital, the main source of increased capital, there was a gain of 12% of output because taxes on this capital were paid to the United States rather than foreign governments. Overall, only about 9% of the output increase was a benefit to the United States which, for the magnitude of effects calculated, is less than two-hundredth of 1% of output and less than 3% of revenue.

These findings are quite consistent with optimal tax theories. For inbound capital, the optimal tax rate should be 1/(1+e) where e is the elasticity of the flow of inbound capital.[35] Because the study used an estimated effective tax rate of 25% and the optimal tax rate is 25% when e is 3, a negligible effect on welfare would be expected. For outbound capital, the optimality rule is to tax foreign source income net of foreign taxes for a small country, with a slightly higher rate on outbound capital returns for a large country.[36] Because current tax rules impose taxes much smaller than this rate and cause too much capital to be allocated abroad, cutting the U.S. tax rate improves welfare. However, the effects are small compared with either the U.S. economy or revenue.[37]

Revenue Feedback Effects

A final issue is the magnitude of revenue feedbacks from the output increase. Recall that the corporate tax cut discussed is about 0.65% of net output.

This increase in output is taxed with a mix of both labor and capital taxes. The marginal tax rate on labor income is estimated by CBO at 28.4% and the capital income tax rate is estimated at 11.5%.[38] The 11.5% is further reduced by 2 percentage points to account for the reduction in the corporate rate, to 9.5%. The overall marginal tax rate is 23.7%. Multiplying the 0.13% and the 0.18% increases in output by 23.7% yields an offset of 4.7% to 6.6%. (If infinite elasticities were assumed and the output effects of 0.4% and 0.62% were considered the feedback effects would be from 14% to 23% of revenue.)

There are three reasons this feedback effect is probably too large (aside from the reservations about output effects due to debt finance discussed above). First, this tax on labor income does not account for the expectation that increases in labor income might be partially received through tax exempt employee fringe benefits or partially spent on tax favored purchases (such as charitable contributions). Second, absent other changes the share of individual taxes collected as payroll taxes would eventually lead to increased outlays for Social Security. Finally, the transition to the new capital stock will not be immediate.

In all the scenarios, these revenue offsets from behavioral changes would likely be smaller than the increase in revenue due to debt service, which is estimated at 25% on average over the 10-year period. In addition, if the increase in the debt displaces the capital stock, output would be reduced by 2021 enough to reduce revenues by 15% to 23% of the static cost. If revenues are not offset, and the increased debt crowds out the U.S. capital stock, output would be reduced about, 0.4% by 2021, an effect more than twice as large as the effects estimated from international capital inflows.[39]

Profit Shifting and Revenue Effects

Another aspect of behavior that is of concern for revenue is the possibility of profit shifting. It is more difficult to judge this effect. Because the evidence discussed above suggests that the revenue offset from corporate rate changes due to investment flows is likely in the neighborhood of 5%, real output effects do not appear large enough to make a corporate rate cut pay for itself in increased revenues, as some advocates claim.

Before examining profit shifting directly, consider the evidence cited to support the argument that there is a significant revenue shift. First, proponents point to studies that indicate a "Laffer curve" with a revenue maximizing tax rate of around 30%, using cross country panel data. These four studies were reviewed in a CRS report that found, due to both interpretation of the studies by proponents and statistical problems, these studies did not appear to support a gain in revenue from a cut in the U.S. tax rate.[40]

Proponents also make the general argument that the United States collects a smaller share of revenue relative to GDP than other countries, even though its rate is higher. For example, Hassett points out that the U.S. corporate revenue is 2% of GDP whereas the revenue of most other countries is 3%, and that the share has grown in some countries as rates have decreased.[41] Two factors other than profit shifting affect corporate revenues and their changes as a percent of GDP, the size of the base and the share of business income (and income in general) that is corporate source. Data shown earlier indicates that although the statutory rate is higher in the United States, the effective rate is not. Revenues patterns over time will reflect a combination of rate changes and base changes, and some countries financed some or all of their recent rate reductions with base broadening.[42] In addition, the size of the corporate sector will be affected by the ability of firms to operate in noncorporate form. A 2007 study by the U.S. Department of Treasury indicates that the U.S. rules allowing large firms to operate in noncorporate form are more generous than those of other countries. It also documented that the share of business income received by corporations in the United States had declined from 80% to 50% as more generous limits of the number of shareholders small corporations could have to elect taxation as unincorporated businesses were adopted and special forms of business such a limited liability corporations, taxed as partnerships, grew.[43] A recent OECD study indicated that corporate tax revenues, in addition to offsetting base changes, were increased by incentives to operate firms in corporate form and additional compliance measures.[44]

It is possible to consider the effect of profit shifting by examining direct estimates of the cost of profit shifting. These estimates of profit shifting suggest that they amount to 14% to 20% of total corporate tax revenue, which would not be enough to offset the revenue loss even if profit shifting disappeared entirely.[45] How much of a reduction in profit shifting might reasonably be expected? Because the profit shifting clearly occurs to the very low tax rate countries,[46] even a cut to 25% would leave a large benefit to profit shifting (it would lead to a combined federal and state rate of 29.8%, and 27.7% for eligible firms if the production activities deduction were retained). Recent discussions of a plan referred to as the double-Irish, Dutch sandwich showed two companies that, having moved profits to Ireland (with a 12.5% rate), took further steps to shift profits to Bermuda (with a 0% rate).[47] Because the cost in most cases is small, most firms would probably continue to shift profits to the limit currently allowed by law as interpreted by the courts, and probably considerably less than proportionally to the tax rate change.

As discussed below, reforms to the tax treatment of foreign source income, by eliminating deferral and by restricting the foreign tax credit, or by focusing on limiting profit shifting techniques, might reduce the ability or benefits of profit-shifting and raise revenues.

Other Countries' Reactions to a U.S. Rate Reduction

An important policy issue for the United States is whether other countries might react to a U.S. rate reduction. Evidence shows that the initial cut in corporate tax rates around the world may have been triggered by the cut in the U.S. corporate tax rate from 48% to 35% from 1986 to 1988 as a result of the Tax Reform Act of 1986. **Figure 1** shows the statutory tax rates, beginning in 1981, for the United States and for the remainder of the OECD. The U.S. combined state and federal tax rate was about 50% and fell to just below 40%

over those two years. Except for a slight rise in 1993, the tax rate has remained constant ever since. Two OECD numbers are provided: the unweighted numbers varying with the admission of new OECD members as well as tax rates and the GDP weighted tax rates of the OECD nations (outside the United States) in 1981. (Tax rates are shown in the **Appendix**, and they also indicate that the weighted average holding member country constant is about a percentage point higher.)

The tax rates for 2012 are similar to those for 2010: the unweighted average fell slightly from 25.5 to 24.9, but the weighted average was slightly higher, 29.8 compared to 29.6. The U.S. rate fell from 39.2% to 39.1%.[48]

While the simple (unweighted) average, which includes new entrants to the OECD, suggests a relatively continuous decline in rates, the weighted average indicates a more discrete pattern of tax cuts. As indicated by the graph, tax rates on average were close together before 1987 but rates of other countries began dropping in the next few years. For the weighted OECD average, the first drop followed the U.S. tax cut, but subsequently, rates were relatively constant over the next several years (and still slightly above U.S. rates). Tax rates then fell again, but stabilized around 2002 and were relatively unchanged until 2007, when Germany began cutting its tax rate. The fall beginning in the late 1990s may have been associated with the lower tax rates of the emerging former eastern bloc countries.

If one country cuts its tax rate, it attracts capital from other countries, which benefits labor and possibly overall national welfare, at the expense of other countries, as discussed above. However, if all countries cut their tax rates, none will gain capital but all will lose revenue. The observation of rate cuts in the rest of the world in the wake of the U.S. tax cut is not proof that countries will cut their rates again if the United States does, but it does provide some support for that expectation.

It is also possible that a smaller rate cut that does not move the United States to rates below those of other large countries would be less likely to trigger a response. For 2010, statutory tax rates for the next two largest countries in the remaining OECD, Japan and Germany, were 39.54% and 30.18% respectively, although Japan is proposing a 5 percentage point rate cut. The United Kingdom and France are respectively 28% and 34.4%, although the United Kingdom is planning further cuts to 24%. If the United States cut its federal rate to 25% its rate would be 29.8%; with the production activities deduction it would be 27.7%. A rate cut to 30% would result in a 34.5% rate (32% with the production activities deduction).[49] That rate would be similar to the rates in France, Japan, and Germany.

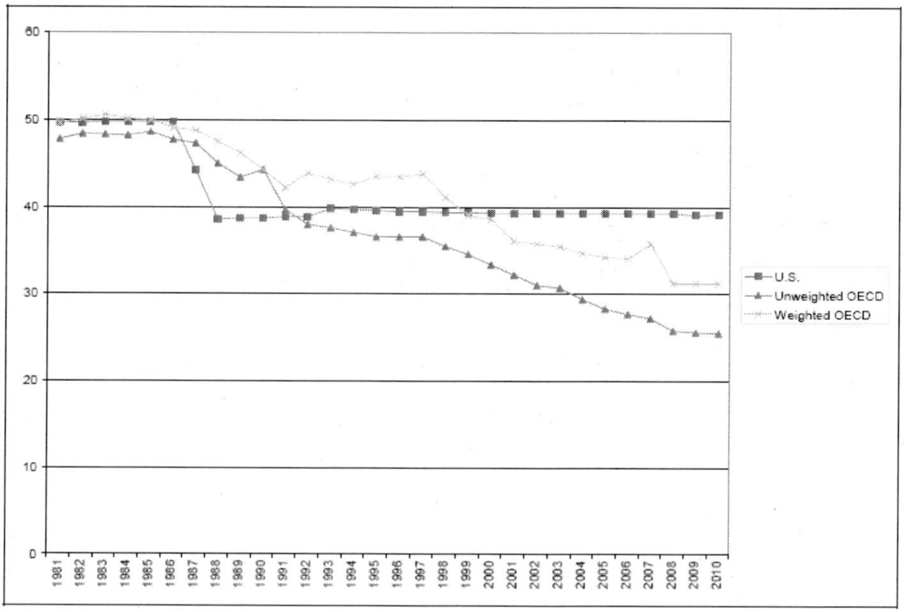

Source: CRS calculations based on tax rate data and GDP from the Organisation for Economic Co-operation and Development.

Notes: The weighted OECD measure provides for a constant set of initial countries, although this measure is only slightly different from that which covers all OECD countries with information available at any time. The unweighted measure includes the OECD countries in that year.

Figure 1. Statutory Tax Rates, United States and OECD (Excluding United States), 1981-2010.

Revenue-Neutral Rate Reduction and Corporate Reform

If revenue concerns require offsetting corporate base broadening, what changes might be made and what are the consequences for international capital flows and profit shifting? This section discusses base broadening options, focusing on the largest corporate tax expenditures. The base broadening provisions are listed in **Table 10**, along with the reduction in the corporate rate the revenue change would allow for. Note that while each proposal is stated in terms of the rate reduction its revision would permit, the rate reductions for several provisions taken together are slightly smaller than the sum of their individual rate reductions because the progressively lower rates make base broadening less valuable. (Note also that the Joint Committee recently increased the estimated revenue cost of deferral so that deferral is now estimated to lower the corporate rate by about 1.5 percentage points and the overall rate reduction to about 28.8%.)[50]

Table 10. Rate Reduction Permitted by Certain Options, 2016

Possible Change in Provision	Percentage Point Reduction in Corporate Tax Rate
Accelerated Depreciation for Equipment (steady state)	3.0
Accelerated Deprecation for Equipment (steady state, corporate revenue gain only)	2.2
Production Activities Deduction	0.7
Taxation of Foreign Source Income	
• End Deferral	3.1
• End Deferral Plus Per Country Foreign Tax Credit Limit	4.0
• President Obama's Proposals	0.9
• Territorial Tax with Deduction Allocation	0.5
LIFO and Lower of Cost or Market Inventory Accounting	0.7
Deferral of Gain on non-Dealer Installment Sales	0.4
Deferral of Gain on Like-Kind Exchanges	0.4
Expensing of Research and Experimental Expenditures	0.4
Low Income Housing Credit	0.4
Subsidies for Fossil Fuels	0.1
Graduated Rates for Corporations	0.2
Insurance Subsidies	0.1
Credit Union Exemption	0.1
Eliminate all Corporate Tax Expenditures	7.9
Eliminate Corporate Tax Expenditures Except for International Provisions	5.5
Disallow Deduction for Inflation Portion of Interest	1.1
Shifting Into Corporate Form[a]	2.3
Rolling Back 2003 Rates for Dividends and Capital Gains[b]	4.0

Source: CRS calculations, see CRS Report R41743, *International Corporate Tax Rate Comparisons and Policy Implications*, by Jane G. Gravelle, for a further discussion including estimation of the last two provisions in Table 15. The new tax rate is calculated by dividing the current rate (35%) by (1+the revenue gain divided by corporate tax revenue). Corporate tax revenue projections are from Congressional Budget Office (CBO), The Budget and Economic Outlook: Fiscal Years 2013 to 2023, February 5, 2013, at http://www.cbo.gov/publication/43907. The corporate base was increased by 20% to account for revenue prior to tax credits. Data on most tax expenditures are from Joint Committee on Taxation, Estimates of Federal Tax Expenditures For Fiscal Years 2012-2017, JCS-1-13. February 1, 2013, at https://www.jct.gov/publications.html?func=startdown&id=4503. The title passage rule estimate Estimates of accelerated depreciation cannot be taken from the tax expenditure estimates because they are affected by bonus depreciation. These estimates are from a Joint Committee on Taxation memorandum from Thomas Barthold, Revenue Estimates, October 27, 2011, updated and multiplied by 2/3 to adjust from the budget horizon to the steady state as indicated by James B. Mackie III and John Kitchen "Slowing Depreciation in Corporate Tax Reform," *Tax Notes*, April 29, 2013, pp. 511-521. Estimates for deferral plus foreign tax credit limit and for the interest deduction were from Joint Committee on Taxation, 2010b Estimates of the Revenue Effect of S. 3018, The Bipartisan Simplification Act of 2010, November 2, 2010, at http://wyden.senate.gov/imo/media/doc/Score.pdf. Estimates for President Obama's proposals were from U.S. Department of the Treasury, General Explanations of the Administration's Fiscal Year 2012 Revenue Proposals, April, 2013, http://www.treasury.gov/resource-center/tax-policy/Documents/General-Explanations-FY2014.pdf. Estimates for the territorial tax were adapted from estimates in CBO, Reducing the Deficit: Spending and Revenue Options, March 10, 2011, p. 187, at http://www.cbo.gov/sites/default/files/cbofiles/ftpdocs/120xx/doc12085/03-10-reducingthedeficit.pdf.

Notes: These provisions are all estimated beginning at a 35% corporate rate and the sum would be larger than the combined effect. If evaluated at the lower rate the reduction would fall proportionally for most base broadening provisions, so the reduction would be 86% as large (.30/.35) if evaluated at a 30% rate. Note that these tax expenditures do not include temporary provisions, the most important of which are the research credit and the deferral of active financing income.

a. Assumes income distributed as in the early 1980s, a starting corporate rate of 30% and an individual rate of 30%. See text of CRS Report R41743, *International Corporate Tax Rate Comparisons and Policy Implications*, for other calculations.

b. Assumes a lower realization elasticity consistent with more recent evidence. With elasticity currently in use by the Treasury Department, the reduction would be 2.3 percentage points.

Accelerated Depreciation

Of the items listed among corporate tax expenditures, the single largest provision outside of deferral, is accelerated depreciation for equipment which, abstracting from the effect of temporary bonus depreciation, would allow a rate reduction of about 2 percentage points.[51] This measure is based on an alternative depreciation system. (Much more revenue would be raised in the short run, but revenue neutrality based on a 10-year budget window would lead to a long-run loss, because slowing depreciation leads to much larger revenue gains in the short run compared with the long run.) Equipment, in particular, is taxed at rates well below the statutory rate, at least at current inflation rates. Nevertheless, the desirability of restricting depreciation is unclear. A revenue neutral revision that cuts the rate in exchange for higher taxation of new investment would raise the marginal effective tax rate, because the rate reduction would apply to the return to existing capital. Moreover, estimates suggest that the value of depreciation under the alternative system would be too small and would tax investments at effective rates in excess of the statutory rates.[52] This provision would also raise revenues on unincorporated businesses, equivalent to about 30% of the corporate loss, which would permit a larger corporate rate reduction, by 3.3 percentage points.

In addition, there is some accelerated depreciation for buildings, primarily rental housing, but the revenue losses are largely for unincorporated businesses.

The Senate Finance Committee has released discussion drafts on cost recovery and accounting that relate to corporate taxation as well as a draft on international corporate tax issues.[53] These proposals have not been scored. The cost recovery provisions would introduce a new depreciation system that would slow depreciation and approximate the present value of economic depreciation. Assets would be added to general pools rather than each vintage of investments being depreciated separately. Real property would be depreciated over 43 years. Research and development expenses would be deducted in equal increments over five years, as would half of advertising expenditures (the remainder would continue to be deducted when incurred). Oil extraction expenses would be recovered over five years and percentage depletion would be repealed. LIFO and lower of cost of market inventory would be repealed (see discussion of LIFO below).

Production Activities Deduction

One of the larger tax expenditures outside of deferral is the production activities deduction, which allows a deduction of 9% of taxable income for domestic production for certain industries, primarily manufacturing, electricity and natural gas production, and construction. This provision would allow a corporate tax rate reduction of 0.7 percentage points. This provision has been criticized as distorting the tax treatment of different industries by granting differential tax rates. In addition, it creates administrative and compliance problems in both distinguishing domestic content and identifying eligible activities. About a quarter of the cost benefits unincorporated businesses and these revenues are included in the above estimate; without those revenues the reduction would be under a percentage point.[54]

The only reservation about this deduction is that it is more likely to apply to multinationals because of the industry restrictions and a revenue neutral substitution could raise the true statutory rate. For example, a 0.7 percentage point reduction in the federal rate would allow, after interacting with state taxes, a reduction from 39.2% to 38.5%, whereas firms with the production activities deduction have a rate of 36.3%. One option would be to tailor the provision more closely to the characteristics of multinationals, including disallowing the deduction for unincorporated businesses and further restricting the eligible activities (e.g., disallow electricity production as a qualified activity), and use those revenues to cut the rate, while retaining the deduction. If restricted to corporate manufacturing most than half of revenues would be recouped.[55]

Tax Treatment of Foreign Source Income

The largest tax expenditure is the deferral of tax on foreign source income, which would permit a corporate tax rate reduction of 0.8 percentage points. This move toward worldwide tax would also, independently, increase the amount of capital in the United States by discouraging outbound capital and would reduce the benefit of profit shifting mechanisms, perhaps significantly. A larger reduction would be possible, by about 4 percentage points or more if the foreign tax credit were limited to offsetting tax only on income earned in that country as was proposed in S. 3018, 111th Congress.[56] This change would eliminate most cross-crediting and raise more revenue; it would also be projected to gain a similar amount in welfare gain to the rate cut itself.[57]

Other revenue raising alternatives affecting taxation of foreign source income have been proposed. President Obama has proposed a set of revisions that is estimated to raise $157 billion over 10 years: the major proposals are disallowing interest and certain other deductions of the parent company to the extent income abroad is not taxed currently ($37 billion), limiting foreign tax credits that can offset income to the same share as the share of income repatriated ($66 billion), a provision to tax excess returns of intangibles ($26 billion), and limiting foreign tax credits for certain extractive companies ($10 billion). These provisions would allow a rate cut of about a percentage point.[58] An alternative would be to move to an actual territorial tax that exempts all active income earned abroad but disallows part of overhead expenses of parent companies, which is estimated to raise $76 billion[59] and allow a rate cut of 0.5

percentage points. There are many other revisions to the treatment of foreign source income that would raise varying amounts of revenue.[60]

House Ways and Means Chairman Camp has proposed a territorial tax (revenue neutral) that would preclude any revenue gains from the tax treatment of foreign source income.[61] The Senate Finance Committee has released d a discussion draft on international corporate tax issue. All foreign source income would be subject to tax (equivalent to repealing deferral) but some income would be taxed at a lower rate than the statutory rate (i.e., a minimum tax would be imposed).[62] This proposal has not been scored but could raise revenue, depending on the minimum tax rate.

Revenue offsets that increase the taxation of foreign source income can be significant and reinforce the capital flow and welfare effects of a rate cut in a global economy. Whether revenue increases from the treatment of foreign source income can be used as revenue offsets is unclear. Most proponents of rate reductions are also strong opponents of increasing the tax on foreign source income, and indeed favor lowering that tax burden, perhaps by moving to a territorial system without cost allocation, which would likely lose a small amount of revenue.[63] Such a change would reduce capital investment in the United States, although probably slightly, and offset the capital flow and welfare gains of a rate cut.

The estimate in **Table 10** does not include the effect of deferral of active financing income, which is a temporary provision but has been extended for many years. It would increase the cost of deferral by about 10%.

LIFO Inventory Accounting

Another option is the repeal of LIFO (last in, first out) accounting, which allows firms to treat goods sold as the latest acquired; eliminating this provision would raise $97.5 billion over 10 years[64] and allow a 0.8 percentage point reduction in the corporate rate. Most firms do not use LIFO because they must conform tax and book methods.[65] There is, however, a justification for LIFO, in that, on average, it eliminates the tax on inflationary gains.[66]

Other Tax Expenditures and Base Broadening Provisions[67]

There are several remaining tax expenditures but most are either small or would be questionable as offsets for a variety of reasons.[68] If every corporate tax expenditure were repealed, including those mentioned previously, the corporate rate could be cut by 7.9 percentage points, to 27.1%, assuming no behavioral responses.[69] (In the category addressing the treatment of foreign source income, only the deferral provision is a tax expenditure.) Larger cuts could occur if the repeal of benefits for unincorporated businesses were used to cut corporate rates. Without revenue from the repeal of deferral, the rate would fall by approximately 5.5 percentage points, or to 29.5%

The Joint Committee on Taxation estimates a rate of 28% for repeal of corporate preferences excluding deferral, but this estimate allows for higher gains from depreciation and expensing of research and development during the budget horizon. (They note this rate would not be revenue neutral in the long run).

The incentives for research and development are popular provisions that have some economic justification, and, in the case of expensing, would be extremely difficult to administer. Only the expensing provision is reflected in **Table 10**, but the research credit, which is temporary (and which the President proposes to make permanent, is actually larger. Special provisions for insurance companies are almost the size of the title passage rule, and would be an option as would the relatively smaller provisions for fossil fuels. The President's budget proposals would restrict insurance company provisions for a $14 billion gain (0.1 percentage point) and benefits for fossil fuels for a $43.6 billion gain (0.3 percentage points).[70] Provisions such as tax-exempt bonds or the low-income housing credit are, however, designed to benefit others (state and local governments or low-income tenants) and if the corporate benefit were removed, these activities would largely migrate to the unincorporated sector. Lower rates for small corporations would allow a 0.3 percentage point reduction. Taxing income of credit unions would allow less than 0.1 percentage points. There are a number of energy subsidies that are directed at conservation whose repeal is not generally considered, as is the case for corporate charitable deductions.

In addition, there are also some tax reform possibilities that are not in the tax expenditure budget. For example, a tax reform bill introduced by then-Chairman of the Ways and Means Committee Rangel in the 110th Congress (H.R. 3970) included a provision extending the write period for acquired intangibles that raised $20 billion over 10 years.[71]

Limits on Interest Deductions

Restricting the deduction of interest would permit a significant reduction in rates. Although the benefits vary with expected inflation, disallowing the deduction for the inflation portion of interest is estimated to allow a reduction of the tax rate in the neighborhood of 2.5 percentage points and, in a closed economy, would be an efficient reform.[72] It might also reduce the use of debt as a method of profit shifting (by borrowing in high tax countries).

There is, however, a reservation about this change when considering international capital flows: a revenue neutral change could decrease the net inflow of capital if debt is more mobile than equity.

Shifts between Individual and Corporate Taxes: Restrictions on Using the Non-Corporate Form, and Shifting Tax Burdens to the Shareholder Level

According to a Treasury study, the share of business income that is in corporate form has declined from 80% to 50% since the early 1980s, primarily through the increase in the number of shareholders for small corporations that are allowed to elect partnership treatment (Subchapter S corporations) and the growth in new organizational forms such as limited liability corporations that are taxed as partnerships.[73] Using the tax rates currently in effect, if all business owners moving to this form are in the top 35% tax bracket, and if dividends and capital gains are distributed and realized based on economy wide averages as well as being subject to the current 15% rate, returning to the early 1980s share would allow a rate cut of 3 percentage points without altering overall individual and corporate revenue.[74] Note, however, that the contribution to rate reduction declines rapidly as the corporate rate is cut. For example, a base broadening provision, such as those discussed above, that allowed a 3 percentage point rate cut starting at a 35% rate would allow a 2.6 percentage point reduction applying to a 30% rate and a 2.3 percentage point reduction starting at a 25% rate. The effect of moving operations to corporate form depends on the differential between the individual and corporate tax, and would reduce the rate by 1.3 percentage points starting at a 30% corporate rate, and actually raise the corporate rate if starting at a 25% rate.

This potential rate reduction is larger, however, if the individual rate is lower. According to estimates, the average tax rate for all partnership and Subchapter S income is 30%.[75] In that case, the percentage point reductions are 5, 2.3, and 1.5, respectively, beginning at a 35%, 30%, and 25% corporate tax rate. Because these shifts into the noncorporate sector are driven by new forms of large companies, it is likely that the tax rate is higher than average for partnership and Subchapter S income (many partnerships, for example, are no different from proprietorships except they have two owners instead of one), but probably lower than the top rate.

In a global economy, it is better to allow tax cuts within the corporate sector at the corporate rather than the individual level. One option is rolling back the 2003 cuts in dividends and capital gains, which would allow a rate cut of about 2.5 percentage points, and perhaps as much as 4 percentage points.[76] These increases in rates are scheduled to occur after 2012 when the Bush tax cuts expire, however, and whether they can be counted as revenue raisers depends on scoring options.

The last two options interact, however. The more taxes are collected at the individual level by raising taxes on dividends and capital gains, the larger a rate reduction from shifting income into the corporate sectors. If dividends were taxed at full rates and capital gains at 20%, then at a 30% individual tax rate and a 35% corporate rate, the reduction is 6.5 percentage points. These effects depend as well, of course, on how the individual tax rate on ordinary income develops, which is currently scheduled to rise.

SUMMING UP

This section has identified enough provisions to allow the corporate tax rate to be reduced to 25% without losing revenue over the long run (i.e., that do not depend on large short-run gains, such as those from reducing accelerated depreciation), but that would require going beyond corporate tax expenditures (which would account for only 5 percentage points) to business preferences associated with unincorporated businesses, foreign tax credit restrictions, or more fundamental reforms.

APPENDIX. STATUTORY TAX RATES, 1981-2010

Table A-1. Statutory Tax Rates in the United States and the Rest of the OECD Countries, 1981-2020

Year	United States	OECD Unweighted	OECD Weighted	OECD Weighted Fixed Countries
1981	49.7	47.8	49.6	49.6
1982	49.7	48.4	50.1	50.2
1983	49.8	48.3	50.5	50.6
1984	49.8	48.2	50.2	50.2
1985	49.8	48.6	50.0	50.0
1986	49.8	47.7	49.0	49.1

Table A-1. (Continued)

Year	United States	OECD Unweighted	OECD Weighted	OECD Weighted Fixed Countries
1987	44.2	47.3	48.7	48.8
1988	38.6	45.0	47.4	47.5
1989	38.7	43.4	46.2	46.2
1990	38.7	44.3	43.2	44.3
1991	38.9	39.7	44.1	42.2
1992	38.9	38.0	43.8	43.9
1993	39.8	37.6	43.1	43.2
1994	39.7	37.1	42.4	42.6
1995	39.6	36.6	43.1	43.5
1996	39.5	36.6	43.1	43.5
1997	39.5	36.6	43.3	43.8
1998	39.4	35.5	40.8	41.1
1999	39.4	34.6	38.8	39.1
2000	39.3	33.4	37.6	38.6
2001	39.3	32.2	35.5	36.1
2002	39.3	31.0	35	35.8
2003	39.3	30.7	34.6	35.5
2004	39.3	29.4	33.8	34.7
2005	39.3	28.3	33.1	34.3
2006	39.3	27.7	32.5	34.1
2007	39.3	27.2	32.0	35.8
2008	39.3	25.8	29.8	31.2
2009	39.1	25.6	29.6	31.2
2010	39.2	25.5	29.6	31.2

Source: Statutory tax rates and GDP, Organisation for Economic Co-operation and Development (OECD), http://www.oecd.org/dataoecd/26/56/33717459.xls and http://stats.oecd.org/Index.aspx?DatasetCode= SNA_TABLE1.

Note: The table provides the data incorporated into Figure 1; the OECD weighted line in that figure uses fixed countries.

End Notes

[1] These advocates include several economists. For example, see Kevin Hassett, "Let's Cut Corporate Taxes to Create More Jobs," *Bloomberg*, January 9, 2006, http://www.bloomberg.com/apps/news?pid=newsarchive&cid=hassett&sid=aZDVcYUY1j2c and

"Laffer Curve Pays Billions If Obama Just Asks," *Bloomberg Business Week*, February, 13, 2011, http://www.businessweek.com/news/2011-02-13/laffer-curve-pays-billions-if-obama-just-asks-kevin-hassett.html; Robert Carroll, "Comparing International Corporate Tax Rates: U.S. Corporate Tax Rate Increasingly Out of Line by Various Measures," Tax Foundation, *Fiscal Facts*, no. 143, August 28, 2008, http://www.taxfoundation.org/publications/show/23561.html; Duanjie Chen and Jack Mintz, "New Estimates of Effective Corporate Tax Rates on Business Investment," *CATO Institute Tax and Budget Bulletin*, no. 64, February 24, 2011, http://www.cato.org/pubs/ tbb/tbb_64.pdf, and Curtis Dubay, "Corporate Tax Reform Should Focus on Rate Reduction,"The Heritage Foundation, February 11, 2011, http://www.heritage.org/Research/ Reports/2011/02/Corporate-Tax-Reform-Should-Focus-on-Rate-Reduction.

[2] See "Obama Backs Corporate Tax Cut If Won't Raise Deficit," *Bloomberg*, January 25, 2011, http://www.bloomberg.com/news/2011-01-26/obama-backs-cut-in-u-s-corporate-tax-rate-only-if-it-won-t-affect-deficit.html.

[3] See "Leader Cantor Unveils Pro-Growth Economic Plan at Stanford University," press release, March 21, 2011, http://majorityleader.house.gov/newsroom/2011/03/embargoed-leader-cantor-unveils-pro-growth-economic-plan-at-stanford-university.html. See CRS Report R42624, *Moving to a Territorial Income Tax: Options and Challenges*, by Jane G. Gravelle, for a discussion of the Camp proposal.

[4] See CRS Report RL34229, *Corporate Tax Reform: Issues for Congress*, by Jane G. Gravelle, for a more general discussion of corporate tax issues. In general, the corporate tax contributes revenue and progressivity to the tax system as well as protecting the individual income tax base by preventing or limiting the use of the corporation as a tax shelter. It imposes costs in distortions in the allocation of capital between the corporate and noncorporate sector, the use of debt versus equity finance, and savings behavior. Although the tax creates a savings distortion, it probably has a limited effect on the size of the domestic capital stock, because of income and substitution effects.

[5] An arm's length price is the price that would occur for sales or asset transfers between unrelated firms.

[6] The combined rate without the production activities deduction is 0.392 which implies a state tax rate of 0.0646 (solving the equation 0.35+x(1-.0.35) = 0.392). With the production activities deduction the U.S. rate is 0.3185 and the combined rate is.3185+.0646*(1-.3185) = 0.363, or 36.3%.

[7] Calculated from OECD data. Corporate rates at http://www.oecd.org/ctp/taxpolicyanalysis/oecdtaxdatabase.htm#C_CorporateCaptial; GDP at http://stats.oecd.org/Index.aspx?DataSetCode=SNA_TABLE1.

[8] Tax rates are at http://www.kpmg.com/Global/en/services/Tax/tax-tools-and-resources/Pages/corporate-tax-rates-table.aspx.

[9] Rate changes between 2005 and 2010 largely reflect the reduction in the German tax rate, although the U.K. rate also fell. However, these measures do not reflect changes in the base, which apparently provided some offsetting revenue. See Simon Kennedy, "Tax Cut War Widens in Europe," *New York Times*, May 28, 2997, http://www.nytimes.com/2007/05/28/business/worldbusiness/28iht-tax.4.5899993.html?_r=1.

[10] Calculated from data in Duanjie Chen and Jack Mintz, "Corporate Tax Competitiveness Rankings for 2012," CATO Institute, *Tax and Budget Bulletin*, no. 65, September 2012, http://www.cato.org/sites/cato.org/files/pubs/pdf/ tbb_65.pdf.

[11] According to Jennifer Gravelle, "Empirical Essays on the Causes and Consequences of Tax Policy: A Look at Families, Labor, and Property" (Ph.D. diss., George Washington University, January 2008), the effective property tax rate, which applies almost solely to buildings, is 1.59%. Multiplying this rate by the share of buildings in the capital stock (39.6%) and by one minus the tax rate of 36.2%, because these taxes are deductible, results in an overall rate of 0.4%. Assuming a pre-tax equity return of 12%, it adds about 3 percentage points to the rate. For information on property and wealth taxes in the European

Union, which can be quite significant in some countries, see the documents at http://ec.europa.eu/taxation_customs/taxation/gen_info/economic_analysis/tax_structures/index_en.htm.

[12] Michael Devereux and Rachel Griffith, "Taxes and the Location of Production: Evidence from a Panel of US Multinationals," *Journal of Public Economics*, vol. 68, June 1998, pp. 335-367.

[13] For example, newspaper reports have indicated that Google and Forest Labs set up sales and production facilities in Ireland as part of a measure that ultimately caused profits to be realized in Bermuda. See Jesse Drucker, "Google 2.4% Rate Shows How $60 Billion Lost to Tax Loopholes," *Bloomberg*, October 21, 2010, at http://www.bloomberg.com/news/2010-10-21/google-2-4-rate-shows-how-60-billion-u-s-revenue-lost-to-tax-loopholes.html and Jesse Drucker, "U.S. Companies Dodge $60 Billion in Taxes in Global Odyssey," *Bloomberg*, May 13, 2010, at http://www.bloomberg.com/news/2010-05-13/american-companies-dodge-60-billion-in-taxes-even-tea-party-would-condemn.htm.

[14] See Congressional Budget Office, *The Budget and Economic Outlook, Fiscal Years 2013-FY2022*, January 2013, p. 85, at http://www.cbo.gov/sites/default/ files/cbofiles/attachments/01-31-2012_Outlook.pdf.

[15] For a roughly flat tax rate, the percentage reduction in revenues would be the same as the percentage reduction in rate, so multiplying by the ratio of the percentage point reduction, 10 percentage points, to the original rate, 35, provides an estimate of the revenue loss.

[16] Internal Revenue Service, Statistics of Income, Corporate Income Tax Returns for 2007, http://www.irs.gov/taxstats/ article/0,,id=170726,00.html.

[17] The lower number multiplies $125 billion by 1.057 and the higher number multiplies $125 billion by 1.34.

[18] See Congressional Budget Office, Reducing the Deficit: Spending and Revenue Options, p. 173 at http://www.cbo.gov/sites/default/files/cbofiles/ftpdocs/120xx/doc12085/03-10-reducingthedeficit.pdf. The estimate for 2012-2021 was $100.6 billion while the baseline was $3.923 billion.

[19] Corporate rate cuts are not likely to be effective as a short-run stimulus. Several CRS Reports discuss the effectiveness of alternative tax provisions. See CRS Report R40104, *Economic Stimulus: Issues and Policies*, by Jane G. Gravelle, Thomas L. Hungerford, and Marc Labonte; CRS Report RS21136, *Government Spending or Tax Reduction: Which Might Add More Stimulus to the Economy?*, by Marc Labonte; CRS Report R41034, *Business Investment and Employment Tax Incentives to Stimulate the Economy*, by Thomas L. Hungerford and Jane G. Gravelle; CRS Report RS21126, *Tax Cuts and Economic Stimulus: How Effective Are the Alternatives?*, by Jane G. Gravelle; and CRS Report R41006, *Unemployment: Issues and Policies*, by Jane G. Gravelle, Thomas L. Hungerford, and Marc Labonte.

[20] If labor supply were responsive to wage increases, increased wages induced by capital flows could increase the size of the labor force, but evidence suggests that labor supply is relatively inelastic. See CRS Report RL31949, *Issues in Dynamic Revenue Estimating*, by Jane G. Gravelle, for a review of labor supply elasticity research.

[21] Jane G. Gravelle and Kent A. Smetters, "Does the Open Economy Assumption Really Mean That Labor Bears the Burden of a Capital Income Tax?" *Advances in Economic Analysis and Policy*, vol. 6, iss. 1, 2006, pp. 1-40. Results of simulations are on p. 25.

[22] An elasticity is the percentage change in quantity divided by percentage change in price and a substitution elasticity is the percentage change in the ratio of two quantities divided by the percentage change in the ratios of their prices. For the portfolio elasticity the ratio is between domestic and foreign assets relating to their relative after tax returns, while for the product substitution elasticity it is the ratio of the domestic and imported traded good as it relates to the relative prices. Other elasticities also appear in the model, which are generally set at 1; these include substitution between factors of production and products produced by the different sectors.

[23] This correlation requires a Cobb-Douglas production function, which has a unitary factor substitution elasticity.

[24] Congressional Budget Office, *The Budget and Economic Outlook, Fiscal Years 2012-FY2021*, January 2011, p. 87. http://www.cbo.gov/ftpdocs/120xx/doc12039/01-26_FY2011Outlook.pdf.

[25] *Economic Report of the President*, February 2010, p. 360, data are for 2006, the year before the recession began.

[26] This finding was reported by William Randolph, *International Burdens of the Corporate Income Tax*, Congressional Budget Office, Working Paper 2006-09, August 2006, http://www.cbo.gov/ftpdocs/75xx/doc7503/2006-09.pdf as well as by Jane G. Gravelle and Kent A. Smetters, "Does the Open Economy Assumption Really Mean That Labor Bears the Burden of a Capital Income Tax?" *Advances in Economic Analysis and Policy*, vol. 6, iss. 1, pp. 1-40. An earlier general equilibrium study found 84% of the burden fell on labor under these circumstances: John Mutti and Harry Grubert, "The Taxation of Capital Income in an Open Economy: The Importance of Resident-Nonresident Tax Treatment," *Journal of Public Economics* 27 (August 1985): 291-309. Their study assumes a production function with a much lower elasticity, so that the change in wage rate would be much larger than the change in overall output. This type of function allows a smaller percentage change in the capital stock to have a larger effect on labor income. Although their effects on wages are larger, their effects on capital inflows and total output are smaller. Another study sometimes mentioned is Arnold C. Harberger. Harberger's paper, "Corporate Tax Incidence: Reflections on What is Known, Unknown, and Unknowable," in John W. Diamond and George R. Zodrow, eds., *Fundamental Tax Reform: Issues, Choices, and Implications* (Cambridge, Mass.: MIT Press, 2008). That paper reports 130% of the tax falling on labor income, but the analysis is not really a model of the U.S. economy calibrated to observed values, but an illustration. The illustration assumes a much higher capital intensity in the corporate traded sector relative to the economy as whole than evidence suggests. For a discussion of these four models and their underlying differences, see Jennifer Gravelle, *Corporate Tax Incidence: Review of General Equilibrium Estimates and Analysis*, Congressional Budget Office, Working Paper 2010-03, May 2010, http://www.cbo.gov/ftpdocs/115xx/doc11519/05-2010-Working_Paper-Corp_Tax_Incidence-Review_of_Gen_Eq_Estimates.pdf.

[27] *Economic Report of the President*, February 2010, p. 362, data are for 2006, the year before the recession began. The share is calculated as the sum of compensation of employees plus 75% of proprietor's income, divided by the sum of compensation of employees, proprietor's income, corporate profits, rental income and interest income.

[28] In economics parlance, the result would be a corner solution where a country produces only one, or a few traded goods.

[29] The only other study that examines lower elasticities is that of John Mutti and Harry Grubert, "The Taxation of Capital Income in an Open Economy: The Importance of Resident-Nonresident Tax Treatment," *Journal of Public Economics* 27 (August 1985): 291-309. Their study still finds a large share of the burden falling on labor, but assumes a very low factor substitution elasticity that dominates the outcome and also makes it not possible to generalize about output effects from their incidence results. For a discussion of the role of the factor substitution elasticity as well as a review of the literature on elasticities, see Jennifer Gravelle, *Corporate Tax Incidence: Review of General Equilibrium Estimates and Analysis*, Congressional Budget Office, Working Paper 2010-03, May 2010, http://www.cbo.gov/ftpdocs/115xx/doc11519/05-2010-Working_Paper-Corp_Tax_Incidence-Review_of_Gen_Eq_Estimates.pdf. This paper finds the portfolio and product substitution elasticities of 3 to be consistent with the evidence but suggests that the factor substitution elasticity should be somewhat lower, leading to a share of the tax falling on labor of around 40% but a smaller capital flow and a smaller total change in output.

[30] Harry Grubert and John Mutti, "International Aspects of Corporate Tax Integration: The Role of Debt and Equity Flows," *National Tax Journal*, vol. 47, March, 1994, pp. 111–133.

[31] If dividends are eventually to be taxed, then there is no obvious benefit to deferral because the income will either be taxed currently or taxed with interest in the future (and the present value of the tax will be the same). However, some income can be indefinitely deferred in the steady state to allow for growth, firms have developed techniques for repatriating without paying tax, and firms can use excess foreign tax credits from high tax countries to shield income from tax.

[32] The residual tax rate on foreign subsidiaries of U.S. parents is 4%. See U.S. Government Accountability Office, *U.S. Multinational Corporations: Effective Tax Rates are Correlated With Where Income is Reported*, GAO-08-950, 2008.

[33] To the extent that taxes in the United States are higher than elsewhere, there could be efficiency gains as well, although Gravelle and Smetters find these to be small. They find an efficiency gain of 3% of revenue for eliminating the tax entirely. Because the excess burden rises with the square of the tax rate, about half the gain, 1.5% of revenue, would occur with the first 10 percentage points. However, this gain accrues to the world (and the United States would presumably get only a share equal to its share of world GDP, or about one-half of a percent of revenue) and is measured assuming there are no other taxes. Given other countries have similar tax rates, the effect could disappear entirely or be negative. But in any case, it is small enough to be disregarded.

[34] Jane G. Gravelle, "International Tax Policy: Are We Heading in the Right Direction?," December 2010, Forthcoming in the Proceedings of the National Tax Association.

[35] This result is derived by maximizing the benefit to inbound capital K: $F(K) - r(1-t)K$ with respect to t, the U.S. tax rate, where F(K) is a production function and recognizing that r and K are functions of t and r is the marginal product of capital.

[36] This optimality rule maximizes the benefit to outbound capital, K, with respect to the foreign tax rate $(F(K) + r(1-t^f)K$, where t^f is the foreign tax rate.

[37] As mentioned earlier, this study focuses on the income effects of international capital flows. Reductions in the corporate tax rate could produce welfare gains, largely through reduction in the debt-equity distortion and changes in the composition of consumption, effects that would occur in a closed economy. In CRS Report RL34229, *Corporate Tax Reform: Issues for Congress*, by Jane G. Gravelle, these costs are estimated at about 10% to 15% of the corporate tax. Based on revenues of 2% of GDP and the rule of thumb that the excess burden rises with the square of the tax rate, the gain would be 0.1% to 0.15% of output from 10 percentage point rate reduction. These welfare tradeoffs do not rely on global economy considerations, and would largely not be experienced by an increase in income, but rather a decrease in risk and a more optimal composition of consumption.

[38] The rates are for 2009, which better reflect current tax rates. See Congressional Budget Office, *Analysis of the President's Budget*, March 2010, Tables 2.2 and 2.3, at http://www.cbo.gov/ftpdocs/112xx/doc11280/03-24-APB.pdf.

[39] This calculation uses the 2021 GDP of $24 trillion projected by 2021 and assumes capital is 3.5 times output, for a total capital stock of $84 trillion. The cumulative revenue loss of $1.2 trillion is 1.4% of this capital stock, and multiplied by 0.3 would reduce output by 0.42%. Multiplied by the tax rates of 0.237 and divided by the static loss of 0.65% indicates an increase in the revenue loss of 15%. Using the $1.5 trillion estimate, the calculation yields an additional revenue loss of 20% and adding debt service net of the feedback effects from capital inflows yields 23%. Projected GDP is from CBO data at http://www.cbo.gov/ftpdocs/120xx/doc12039/Year-by-YearForecast_110125.xls.

[40] See CRS Report RL34229, *Corporate Tax Reform: Issues for Congress*, by Jane G. Gravelle. All of the studies were had methodological deficiencies due to lack of country fixed effects. One study did not find statistically significant effects in any case. The most sophisticated study actually found a much higher rate of 57% for a country like the United States. That

study and another study were re-estimated using fixed effects and the statistical significant disappeared. This final study had an extremely short panel.

[41] See Kevin Hassett, "Laffer Curve Pays Billions If Obama Just Asks," *Bloomberg Business Week*, February, 13, 2011, http://www.businessweek.com/news/2011-02-13/laffer-curve-pays-billions-if-obama-just-asks-kevin-hassett.html.

[42] See Steven Matthews, "Tax Reform: An International Perspective," Power Point presentation at the American Enterprise Institute, February 25, 2011, http://www.aei.org/docLib/MatthewsTaxReform.pdf.

[43] United States Department of the Treasury, "Treasury Tax Conference on Business Taxation and Global Competitiveness: Background Paper," July 30, 2007, at http://www.ustreas.gov/press/releases/hp500.htm.

[44] OECD, *Tax Policy Reform and Economic Growt*h, OECD Publishing, 2010, http://dx.doi.org/10.1787/ 9789264091085-en.

[45] For reviews of profit shifting, see CRS Report R40623, *Tax Havens: International Tax Avoidance and Evasion*, by Jane G. Gravelle. The estimates used include those of Christian and Schultz of $30 billion compared with corporate revenues of $151 billion in 2001, those of Sullivan of $26 billion compared with revenues of $187 billion, and those of Clausing and Avi-Yonah of $60 billion compared with revenues of $370 billion. Corporate revenue numbers are from CBO, http://www.cbo.gov/ftpdocs/120xx/doc12039/ HistoricalTables[1].pdf. Because the rate cut reduces revenues by 31% to 38%, the offset is less than 100% even if all profit shifting ended. A more recent estimate by Clausing indicates a loss of 20% to 30% depending on the method used. See Kimberly A. Clausing, "The Revenue Effects of Multinational Firm Income Shifting," *Tax Notes*, March 28, 20011, pp. 1581-1586.

[46] See, for example, Government Accountability Office, *U.S. Multinational Corporations: Effective Tax Rates are Correlated With Where Income is Reported*, GAO-08-950, August 2008. Other evidence is discussed in CRS Report R40623, *Tax Havens: International Tax Avoidance and Evasion*, by Jane G. Gravelle.

[47] See Jesse Drucker, "Google 2.4% Rate Shows How $60 Billion Lost to Tax Loopholes," *Bloomberg*, October 21, 2010, at http://www.bloomberg.com/news/2010-10-21/google-2-4-rate-shows-how-60-billion-u-s-revenue-lost-to-tax-loopholes.html and Jesse Drucker, "U.S. Companies Dodge $60 Billion in Taxes in Global Odyssey," *Bloomberg*, May 13, 2010, at http://www.bloomberg.com/news/2010-05-13/american-companies-dodge-60-billion-in-taxes-even-tea-party-would-condemn.htm.

[48] Calculated from OECD data. Corporate rates at http://www.oecd.org/ctp/taxpolicyanalysis/oecdtaxdatabase.htm#C_CorporateCaptial; GDP at http://stats.oecd.org/Index.aspx?DataSetCode=SNA_TABLE1.

[49] Calculations are made by dividing revenues by an estimate of corporate taxes adjusting for the credits, so the revenue base of $3,293 billion for FY2012-FY2021 is increased to $4,728 billion. This number divides corporate revenues by the ratio of $112 billion to $135 billion per year, which relates the estimate of the rate cut without considering the effects of credits to the midpoint between allowing foreign tax credits and not allowing them (recall those estimates were $120 billion and $150 billion on average).

[50] The Joint Committee on Taxation has recently increased the cost of deferral substantially.

[51] Estimates of depreciation as a percentage of revenues are from Jane G. Gravelle, "Practical Tax Reform for a More Efficient System, *Virginia Tax Review*," vol. 30, fall 2010, pp. 389-406.

[52] See Jane G. Gravelle, "Reducing Depreciation Allowances to Finance a Lower Corporate Tax Rate," National Tax Journal, vol. 64, December 2011, pp. 1039-1053; "Practical Tax Reform for a More Efficient System, *Virginia Tax Review*," vol. 30, fall 2010, pp. 389-406;. Statement Before the Senate Committee on Finance, Tax Reform Options: Incentives for Capital Investment and Manufacturing, March 6, 2012, at http://www.finance.senate.gov/imo/media/doc/ Testimony%20of%20Jane%20Gravelle.pdf.

[53] Senate Finance Committee, Baucus Works to Overhaul Outdated Tax Code, November 21 at http://www.finance.senate.gov/newsroom/chairman/release/?id=536eefeb-2ae2-453f-af9b-946c305d5c93.

[54] See CRS Report R41988, *The Section 199 Production Activities Deduction: Background and Analysis*, by Molly F. Sherlock. Statement Before the Senate Committee on Finance, Tax Reform Options: Incentives for Capital Investment and Manufacturing, March 6, 2012, at http://www.finance.senate.gov/imo/media/doc/ Testimony%20of%20Jane%20Gravelle.pdf.

[55] Jane G. Gravelle Statement Before the Senate Committee on Finance, Tax Reform Options: Incentives for Capital Investment and Manufacturing, March 6, 2012, at http://www.finance.senate.gov/imo/media/doc/ Testimony%20of%20Jane%20Gravelle.pdf.

[56] Estimate from Joint Committee on Taxation scoring of S. 3018, 111th Congress, at http://www.wyden.senate.gov/ download/joint-committee-on-taxation-estimated-score-of-the-bipartisan-tax-fairness-and-simplification-act-of-2010. This estimate could be larger, since it was prepared before JCT increased the revenue effect of deferral.

[57] For revenue estimates and analysis of this provisions, see Jane G. Gravelle, "International Tax Policy: Are We Heading in the Right Direction?," December 2010, Forthcoming in the Proceedings of the National Tax Association. This provision should raise about $60 billion of revenue a year, much more than eliminating deferral alone. Note that further measures might need to be taken to prevent corporations from inverting (moving their headquarters abroad), although current rules are already in place that appear to have been effective in preventing these inversions.

[58] U.S. Department of the Treasury, General Explanations of the Administration's Fiscal Year 2012 Revenue Proposals, April, 2013, http://www.treasury.gov/resource-center/tax-policy/Documents/General-Explanations-FY2014.pdf.

[59] Estimates by the Joint Committee on Taxation as reported in Congressional Budget Office, *Reducing the Deficit: Spending and Revenue Options*, March 10, 2011, http://www.cbo.gov/ftpdocs/120xx/doc12085/03-10-ReducingTheDeficit.pdf.

[60] See CRS Report R40623, *Tax Havens: International Tax Avoidance and Evasion*, by Jane G. Gravelle, for a discussion. Other options include eliminating deferral and limiting tax credits for tax haven or low tax countries, requiring a share of foreign income to be repatriated, and formula apportionment.

[61] See CRS Report R42624, *Moving to a Territorial Income Tax: Options and Challenges*, by Jane G. Gravelle.

[62] Senate Finance Committee, Baucus Unveils Proposals for International Tax Reform, November 19, 2013, at http://www.finance.senate.gov/newsroom/chairman/release/ ?id=f946a9f3-d296-42ad-bae4-bcf451b34b14.

[63] See "Obama Backs Corporate Tax Cut If Won't Raise Deficit," *Bloomberg*, January 25, 2011, http://www.newsmax.com/Newsfront/ALLTOP-BB-BNALL-BNSTAFF/2011/01/25/id/383906.

[64] Ibid.

[65] Ibid.

[66] This proposal would also repeal another method, the lower of cost or market, which is more difficult to justify.

[67] Table 15 does not include an item for the title passage rule (inventory source sales rule) that allows a reduction of tax on foreign source income for firms with excess foreign tax credits. Indications are that this estimate has been reduced significantly, based on data in the most recent CBO options study, See Congressional Budget Office,(2011) Reducing the Deficit: Spending and Revenue Options, http://www.cbo.gov/ftpdocs/120xx/doc12085/03-10-ReducingTheDeficit.pdf.

[68] Most of these are discussed in Jane G. Gravelle, "Practical Tax Reform for a More Efficient System, *Virginia Tax Review*," vol. 30, fall 2010, pp. 389-406.

[69] Based on sums for FY2012-FY2014, reported in U.S. Committee on the Budget, *Tax Expenditures: Compendium of Background Material on Individual Provisions*, December

2010, compared with revenue projections as adjusted, for the same years. See http://www.gpo.gov/fdsys/pkg/CPRT-111SPRT62799/pdf/CPRT-111SPRT62799.pdf. Using these years avoids the effects of bonus depreciation.

[70] *General Explanations of the Administration's Fiscal Year 2012 Revenue Proposals*, U.S. Department of Treasury, February 2011.

[71] See CRS Report RL34229, *Corporate Tax Reform: Issues for Congress*, by Jane G. Gravelle, for a list of provisions in H.R. 3970.

[72] See CRS Report RL34229, *Corporate Tax Reform: Issues for Congress*, by Jane G. Gravelle.

[73] United States Department of the Treasury, "Treasury Tax Conference on Business Taxation and Global Competitiveness: Background Paper," July 30, 2007, at http://www.ustreas.gov/press/releases/hp500.htm.

[74] To be revenue neutral, the new corporate tax plus the tax on after tax earnings of shareholders, which is t(B+dB) +ts(1-t)dB, where t is the corporate tax, ts is the tax at the shareholder level, B is the base and dB is the change in the base, must be equal to the current corporate tax less the individual tax on the change in base. The calculations assume that four-seventh of the corporate steady state return is paid in dividends, that half of capital gains is realized and that none of the earnings are in tax exempt forms such as IRAs, 401(k)s or pension funds.

[75] Weighted marginal tax rate based on data by the Tax Policy Center, Table T10-0211, http://www.taxpolicycenter.org/numbers/displayatab.cfm?DocID=2787.

[76] Based on estimates provided in the FY2011 budget proposals, indicating a revenue gain of $344.4 billion, $233.3 billion for dividends and $111.1 billion for capital gains. See "General Explanations of the Administration's Fiscal 2011 Revenue Proposals," February 2010, at http://www.treasury.gov/resource-center/tax-olicy/Documents/ greenbk10.pdf. Because these changes do not affect the corporate base and interact with the corporate rate change, the estimate is the percentage of revenue times the tax rate. This estimate was for a year earlier, so was increased by 5% to reflect economic growth. These estimates assume a large realizations elasticity, and would be considerably higher if that elasticity were reduced to levels consistent with recent empirical research. Based on data in CRS Report R41364, *Capital Gains Tax Options: Behavioral Responses and Revenues*, by Jane G. Gravelle, Table 2, the capital gains revenue would increase from $13.9 billion in 2019 to $33.1 billion, if lower elasticties are used. That implies the $111.1 billion would be higher and would permit a reduction of 3.6 percentage points.

In: Corporate Inversions
Editor: Fredrick White

ISBN: 978-1-63321-966-3

Chapter 4

MOVING TO A TERRITORIAL INCOME TAX: OPTIONS AND CHALLENGES*

Jane G. Gravelle

SUMMARY

Among potential tax reforms under discussion by Congress is revising the tax treatment of foreign source income of U.S. multinational corporations. Some business leaders have been urging a movement toward a territorial tax, which would eliminate some U.S. income taxes on active foreign source income.

Under a territorial tax, only the country where the income is earned imposes a tax. Territorial proposals include the Grubert-Mutti proposal (included in President Bush's Advisory Panel on Tax Reform proposal in 2005) and, more recently, a draft Ways and Means Committee proposal and a Senate bill, S. 2091. The Fiscal Commission also proposed a territorial tax. Proposals have, however, also been made to increase the taxation of foreign source income, including S. 727, and proposals by President Obama.

Although the United States has a worldwide system that includes foreign earnings in U.S. taxable income, two provisions cause the current

* This is an edited, reformatted and augmented version of a Congressional Research Service publication, CRS Report for Congress R42624, from www.crs.gov, prepared for Members and Committees of Congress, dated July 25, 2012.

system to resemble a territorial tax in that very little tax is collected. Deferral delays paying taxes until income is repatriated (paid as a dividend by the foreign subsidiary to its U.S. parent). When income is repatriated, credits for foreign taxes paid offset the U.S. tax due. Under cross-crediting, unused foreign tax credits from high tax countries or on highly taxed income can be used to offset U.S. tax on income in low tax countries.

Some proponents of a territorial tax urge such a system on the grounds that the current system discourages repatriations. Economic evidence suggests that effect is small, in part because in normal circumstances a large share of income is retained for permanent reinvestment. Amounts held abroad may have increased, however, as firms lobbied for another repatriation holiday (similar to that adopted in 2004) that allowed firms to exempt most dividends from income on a one-time basis.

Opponents are concerned about encouraging investment abroad. A territorial tax is generally not viewed as efficient because it favors foreign investment, but that increased outflow of investment is likely to have a small effect relative to the U.S. economy. Artificial shifting of profits into tax havens or low tax countries is a current problem that could be worsened under some territorial tax designs, and proposals have included measures to address this problem.

Proposals also address the transitional issue of the treatment of the existing stock of unrepatriated earnings. The Ways and Means proposal would tax this stock of earnings, but at a lower rate, and use the revenues to offset losses from other parts of the plan, which would lead to a long-run revenue loss. S. 2091 has a similar approach. The Grubert-Mutti proposal does not have a specific transitional tax, but would raise revenue largely due to its disallowance of parent overhead expenses aimed at reducing profit shifting. The other two proposals also contain provisions to address profit shifting.

In addition there are complicated issues in the design of a territorial tax, such as how to treat branches and dividends of firms in which the corporation is only partially owned. A number of issues arise from the ending of foreign tax credits, with perhaps the most significant one being the increased tax on royalties, which are currently subject to tax, have low or no foreign taxes, and would lose the shield of excess credits.

The final section of the report briefly discusses some alternative options, including those in S. 727 and in the Administration proposals. It also discusses hybrid approaches that combine territorial and worldwide systems in a more efficient way, including eliminating the disincentive to repatriate.

One such approach is a minimum tax on foreign source income, which is proposed by the President in the context of current rules, but could be combined with a territorial system.

INTRODUCTION

Tax reform is a perennial issue before Congress. One area of increasing attention is the taxation of U.S. companies on the income they earn abroad. Recently, proposals have been made to, in some cases, decrease taxes and in others to increase these taxes.

Businesses leaders have been urging a movement toward a territorial tax, which would generally eliminate U.S. income taxes on active foreign source income. Such a proposal (presumably based on one developed by Grubert and Mutti) was included in the President's Advisory Panel on Tax Reform in 2005,[1] more recently in a draft proposal by Ways and Means Committee Chairman Dave Camp,[2] and in a bill, S. 2091, introduced by Senator Enzi. The National Commission on Fiscal Responsibility and Reform (referred to as the Fiscal Commission) also proposed a territorial tax in general terms.[3]

Proposals have also been made to move in the opposite direction and increase the taxation of foreign source income, including S. 727, introduced by Senators Wyden and Coats, which would use the significant revenues gained to help finance a corporate income tax rate cut. President Obama has included increased taxes on foreign source income in his budget outlines and, more recently, in his framework for business tax reform, as a revenue source for rate reduction.[4] Because of various features in the current tax system, the U.S. tax system already bears a close resemblance, in terms of revenue collected, to a territorial tax. Tax on the income of foreign subsidiaries is deferred until repatriated (paid as dividends to the U.S. parent) and tax can be avoided by not repatriating income. The system limits credits claimed for foreign taxes paid to U.S. tax on foreign income. The limit, however, is on an overall basis, permitting unused credits from high-tax countries to shield income from low-tax countries, or income that bears little foreign tax, from being taxed in the United States. Because firms have flexibility in timing repatriations, the residual effective tax rate on foreign income is estimated at only 3.3%.[5] Some types of income, such as royalties, are treated more favorably under the current system than they would be under a territorial tax.

Economists have traditionally analyzed the foreign tax system in terms of economic efficiency. Economic theory tends to support, on efficiency grounds, a worldwide system in which income from U.S. investment earned abroad is subject to the same tax, or as close to the same tax as possible, as that on domestic investment. It does not support a territorial tax, and most proposals in the past were to move closer to an effective worldwide tax (see *Appendix*). At the same time, if such a change is not feasible, another question becomes whether moving to an explicit territorial tax would be better or worse than the present system. The fundamental issues are

- the effects on disincentives to repatriate income,
- to what extent the revision will divert investment from the United States,
- the effects on artificial profit shifting,
- transition issues,
- administrative and compliance considerations, and
- the revenue consequences.

There is no single blueprint for a territorial tax and the answers to these questions depend, to some extent, on specific design choices.

This report first explains how the international tax system works and describes the magnitude and distribution of foreign source income and taxes. The report then focuses on alternative features of a territorial tax and their consequences. It also contains, in a final section, a brief discussion of options that move in the opposite direction and other alternatives that do not fit into either the territorial or worldwide approach (such as current taxation of foreign source income but at a lower rate).[6]

How the International Tax System Works

The current U.S. tax system is a hybrid. It has some elements of a residence-based or worldwide tax, where income of a country's firms is taxed regardless of its location. It also has some elements of a source based or territorial tax, where all income earned within a country is taxed only by that country regardless of the nationality of the firms. The provisions that introduce territorial features are deferral and cross-crediting. There are a number of complex interactions that will affect both the design of a territorial or other tax revision and the consequences of those changes.

Deferral

Deferral allows a firm to delay taxation of its earnings in foreign subsidiaries until the income is paid as a dividend to the U.S. parent company.

Although a territorial tax is often focused on exempting foreign source income that under current law is taxed when repatriated, there are four basic categories of foreign source income, three of which are not eligible for deferral. They are profits of foreign incorporated subsidiaries; current payment income, such as royalties and interest payments; branch income; and Subpart F income.

Profits of Foreign Incorporated Subsidiaries

U.S. multinationals are not currently taxed on the profits of their subsidiaries incorporated abroad (except for "Subpart F Income" discussed below). Rather they defer payment of taxes until the income is received by the parent as a dividend (repatriated). U.S. tax is then due on the dividend and, because the dividend is after foreign tax, an additional amount (called a gross-up) is added to taxable income to reflect the foreign taxes paid and place the income on a pre-tax basis.[7] A foreign tax credit is then allowed against this U.S. tax.

Current Payment Income

Current payment income is income that is received as a direct payment, such as royalties and interest. It is taxed currently. This income is usually deductible as an expense in the foreign country and, indeed, may not constitute true foreign source income, at least in the case of royalties that could be viewed as more like export income.

Branch Income

Branch income is income from operations that are carried out without a separately incorporated foreign subsidiary. Income of operations organized as foreign branches rather than as separately incorporated subsidiaries is also taxed currently. For tax purposes, branch gross income and deductions are combined with parent income just as if the operation were taking place in the United States. Although branch income is not eligible for deferral, it can be a beneficial form of organization in some cases. If a firm is experiencing a loss, which may be the case with start-ups or mineral or exploration companies, the losses can only reduce U.S. income if the operation is in branch form. In some cases, dividends may attract an additional withholding tax, although for most trading partners these taxes are eliminated or minimized through tax treaties. Non-tax reasons may also cause a firm to choose the branch form; this form, for example, may be particularly beneficial for financial firms in which the branch operation is backed by the assets of the worldwide firm.

Subpart F Income

Subpart F income, named after the section of the Internal Revenue Code that imposes the rules, is income that can easily be shifted to low tax jurisdictions. Subpart F income includes passive income, such as interest and dividends, and certain sales and service income flowing between A variety of tax rules can affect the degree and nature of cross-crediting: separating income and credits into baskets with cross-crediting only allowed within the basket; characterizing certain royalty and export income as foreign source; restricting the use of excess credits generated from oil and gas extraction; and interest and other expense allocation rules. In addition, a provision that effectively allowed claiming of foreign tax credits when the associated income was not subjected to U.S. tax, termed foreign tax credit splitting, may have affected past practices and data. This provision was restricted in 2010.

Firms whose foreign tax payments are larger than those permitted to be credited under the foreign tax credit limit rules are said to be in an excess credit position. Firms whose tax payments are smaller are in an excess limit position.[10]

Foreign Tax Credit Limit Baskets

While the United States has had a variety of limit rules in the past,[11] it currently has an overall limit that allows cross-crediting, separated into two significant baskets based on the type of income: an active or general basket and a passive basket. About 95% of income is in the general basket so there is much scope for cross-crediting.[12] Therefore, companies that have paid taxes higher than the U.S. rate can still (within each basket) offset U.S. taxes on income earned in low-tax countries. Higher tax rates can also offset taxes on income generally taxed at low or no rates; one example is royalties associated with active operations, which fall in the active basket and may be shielded from U.S. tax by excess foreign tax credits. Another is foreign source income from export sales, discussed below under the "Title Passage Rule."

Separate Limit on Oil and Gas

The law also contains separate restrictions on certain other types of income, one of importance, as measured by foreign income affected, being oil and gas extraction income. A separate provision disallows credits paid on oil and gas extraction income in excess of the U.S. tax due, although they can be carried over to future years. This treatment has the effect of placing oil and gas extraction income in a separate basket, because generally this income is subject to high foreign taxes. For example, if the U.S. tax on foreign oil and gas extraction income is 35% and the foreign tax is 50%, the extra 15% credit cannot be used to offset tax on other income. This treatment has the same effect as placing this oil and gas extraction income in a separate basket. If the tax on oil and gas extraction income were lower than the U.S. tax, this income would be eligible to have the additional U.S. tax offset by excess credits on other income because income from oil and gas extraction income is not actually in a different basket.

Allocation of Deductions

Another feature that may contribute to the generation of excess foreign tax credits is the allocation of overhead and other deductions that are not taken for foreign tax purposes. While many deductions can be traced to a particular source of income, the parent firm's costs for interest, research, and other overhead (e.g. administration) is allocated between domestic and foreign uses for purposes of the foreign tax credit limit. This allocation lowers the amount of foreign source income. Because these reductions in income are not recognized by the foreign jurisdiction, the result could be to generate excess credits, even in countries whose general effective tax rate is actually lower than that of the United States.

These allocations are necessary for determining net income by source. Borrowing is generally done at the parent level. In addition, the interest allocation limits the ability of firms who are in the excess credit position to avoid U.S. tax by borrowing in the United States rather than in low-tax countries where the deduction is less valuable.

The rule, however, has some imperfections. Foreign subsidiaries may also have overhead costs, particularly interest, which are not recognized in income because dividends are received net of deductions. In 2004, a revision that would have allowed elective allocation of worldwide interest, was adopted but did not go into effect immediately. This elective worldwide interest allocation rule has been delayed on several occasions; currently it is scheduled to take place in 2021.

Title Passage Rule

There is a special rule called the title passage rule (or the inventory sales source exception rule) that allows half of manufacturing export income (and all of sales of inventory) to be sourced as income in the country in which the title passes. Because this title passage can be arranged in foreign countries, this income is foreign source income and thus eligible for cross-crediting. This provision is effectively an export subsidy for firms with excess foreign tax credits. The title passage rule is important in considering a territorial tax because cross-crediting, at least for active income, would, in theory, disappear. Export income, as well as royalties, would be subject to higher tax rates in some cases with elimination of foreign tax credits.

Foreign Tax Credit Splitting (Now Restricted)

Prior to 2010, there was also a possibility of claiming foreign tax credits for income that had not actually been subject to tax due to differing rules across countries as to entity status.[13] P.L. 111-226 disallowed any consideration of a foreign tax credit unless the underlying income was reported. Although this provision was estimated to gain relatively little revenue (about $0.4 billion annually), 14 it is hard to be certain how prevalent these activities were. These arrangements may affect the data currently available by increasing the ability of firms to offset, for example, royalties with excess credits.

THE MAGNITUDE AND DISTRIBUTION OF FOREIGN SOURCE INCOME AND TAXES, ACTUAL AND POTENTIAL

Before discussing the issues and consequences of reforms, it is useful to get a "lay of the land." How important are the various sources of foreign income, how much tax do they generate currently, and how much might they generate with various reforms? Because individual tax return data are not available, this issue can only be explored by combining aggregate data available and various analyses that have been done by researchers with access to tax returns. This section discusses the current sources of foreign income, the potential magnitude of foreign income not reported, the sources of tax liability, and the potential size of foregone taxes due to deferral and cross-crediting.

Current Sources of Realized Foreign Income

Table 1 shows the distribution of foreign source income by type for firms claiming and receiving foreign tax credits for 2007 and 2008, to the extent that sources can be identified. This data set should capture most of foreign source income reported by U.S. multinationals on their tax return (i.e., not deferred). (Although some data are available for 2009, these data may be skewed because of the economic slowdown that spread abroad). Total foreign source net income was $392.5 billion in 2007 and $413.4 billion in 2008. In the data, oil and gas extraction income is reported separately, so that dividends do not include that income.

Table 1. Distribution of Foreign Source Income Realized in the United States by Type, 2007 and 2008

Type of Income	Share of Taxable Income, 2007 (%)	Share of Taxable Income, 2008 (%)
Dividend Payments	19.2	22.2
Includable Income (Subpart F)	16.6	16.5
Deemed Taxes (Gross Up)	12.9	16.9
Export Income	3.7	3.5
Royalties, and License Payments (Gross)	26.0	25.7
IC-DISC	2.3	0.0
Other	19.4	15.2

Source: Statistics of Income, International Statistics, Returns With Foreign Tax Credits, http://www.irs.gov/ taxstats/bustaxstats/article/0,,id=210069,00.html; Royalties and License Payments adjusted to eliminate rents based on data from Bureau of Economic Analysis, Trade in Services, 1999-2010, http://www.bea.gov/scb/pdf/2011/07%20July/0711_itaq-tables.pdf. Foreign taxes withheld as reported in the IRS data are added to royalties. Total taxable income for royalties from the Commerce Department data was increased by withholding taxes of approximately $4 billion.

Notes: Newly provided data for 2008 and 2009 separate the deemed tax gross up; for 2008, 73% of these taxes were associated with dividend payments and the remainder with Subpart F. See Internal Revenue Service http://www.irs.gov/pub/irs-soi/08colinecount.pdf.

Note that the third item in the table is related to the first two. Because dividends and Subpart F income are on an after-tax basis, the dividends must be increased by the taxes paid for corporate taxpayers electing a foreign tax credit. Most of the deemed paid taxes are probably associated with dividend payments (73% for 2008 when data first because available)[15] because Subpart F income is usually subject to lower foreign taxes. Accordingly, the data suggest an estimate of 30% to 35% of foreign source income that arises from these dividends.

The table also shows that royalties are significant parts of foreign source income, accounting for about a quarter of foreign source income, suggesting that the consequences of changes in the law for this income might be significant.

In *Table 1*, the measure of net income was income net of all deductions (but before adjustments). Some of these deductions were overhead costs that are allocated based on formulas. In *Table 2,* shares are calculated based on income before these allocated deductions. With this approach, it is also possible to calculate the share of interest income and oil and gas extraction income. In *Table 2*, foreign source income before non-allocable deductions is $615.4 billion in 2007 and $614.6 billion in 2008. Non-allocable deductions accounted for 36% of this income in 2007 and 33% in 2008.

Table 2. Distribution of Realized Foreign Source Income Before Non-Allocable Deductions, 2007 and 2008

Type of Income	Share of Taxable Income, 2007 (%)	Share of Taxable Income, 2008 (%)
Dividend Payments	12.2	14.9
Includable Income (Subpart F)	8.3	11.1
Deemed Taxes (Gross Up)	10.6	11.4
Export Income	2.3	2.3
Royalties, and License Payments (Gross)	16.6	17.3
IC-DISC	1.4	0.0
Oil and Gas Extraction Income	10.2	15.9
Service Income	2.8	3.2
Interest	21.3	18.4
Other (rents, other branch income)	14.3	5.3

Source: Statistics of Income, International Statistics, Returns With Foreign Tax Credits, http://www.irs.gov/ taxstats/bustaxstats/article/0,,id=210069,00.html; Royalties and License Payments adjusted to eliminate rents based on data from Bureau of Economic Analysis, Trade in Services, 1999-2010, http://www.bea.gov/scb/pdf/ 2011/07%20July/0711_itaq-tables.pdf. Foreign taxes withheld as reported in the IRS data are added to royalties. Total taxable income for royalties from the Commerce Department data was increased by withholding taxes of approximately $4 billion.

Notes: Newly provided data for 2008 and 2009 separate the deemed tax gross up; for 2008, 73% of these taxes were associated with dividend payments and the remainder with Subpart F. See Internal Revenue Service http://www.irs.gov /pub/irs-soi/08colinecount.pdf.

Dividend payments and their related tax gross ups are smaller as a share (25% to 30%) when pretax income is considered. Their true importance probably lies somewhere between the shares in *Table 1* and *Table 2* given the imperfections in allocation rules. Note however, that oil and gas extraction income can arise from a subsidiary and is simply reported separately. Including oil and gas income in dividends would bring the totals back up toward 35% to 40% of income. Oil and gas extraction income, however, has little or no reason not to be repatriated because the taxes due on these earnings are generally larger than the U.S. tax (which is why they are treated separately in a way that effectively results in a separate basket). *Table 2* also shows the importance of interest income in the totals for foreign source income (although a full measure of the importance of interest would require information on income of financial institutions through branches).

Deferred Income

Table 1 and Table 2 report realized income (direct, repatriated, branch, and Subpart F). Total foreign source income also includes deferred income. How large is this deferred income on an annual basis? Estimates in this section indicate that close to half of foreign source income is subject to U.S. tax, but less than a quarter of active income of foreign subsidiaries of U.S. firms that can be deferred is currently repatriated.

There are no precise data sources to estimate this effect. Based on IRS statistics for controlled foreign corporations, available for 2008, which accounted for $177 billion of distributions out of pre-tax income to U.S. parents (about 78% of the total distributions), total deemed and distributed income was 27% of total pre-tax income. Subpart F income was 12.1% of pre tax income and dividends were 14.7%.[16] As a share of after tax income, dividends were 18.1% of income and Subpart F 14.3% income, for a total of 32.4%. These ratios might be somewhat understated because of the possibility of non-U.S. shareholders, but that is likely to be unimportant.

Commerce Department data (Table 6.16D: Corporate Profits by Industry) reports $511 billion and $582 billion of rest of world corporate profits in 2007 and 2008, on an after-tax basis.[17] Considering distributions after foreign tax in 2007, the ratios are 14.7% for dividends and 12.7% for Subpart F income, for a total of 27.4%. These ratios are 15.7% for dividends, 12.0% for Subpart F, and 27.8% for the total for 2008.

These numbers do not capture deemed taxes. Using IRS data on controlled foreign corporations and based on the ratios of deemed taxes to distributions in Table 1 (with 73% of deemed taxes associated with active dividends), the share of pre-tax profits including taxes for 2008 was 19.7% for dividends and 14.7% for Subpart F. Because Subpart F is not voluntary, the share of dividends out of pre-tax profits net of Subpart F income is 23%.

A study of the new M-3 form that reconciles tax and book income finds that for firms with positive taxable and book income, 9% of the foreign source income is actively paid as a dividend and 47% is subject to U.S. tax (including royalties and other direct). Dividends as a share of total income are 19%, the same share as in Table 1. The ratios would be similar to those above if deemed taxes were included.

Overall, it appears that close to half of foreign source income is reported as taxable income in the United States, but less than a quarter of the income over which firms have discretion, active income of foreign subsidiaries, is subject to U.S. tax. Rates of deferral vary significantly by location. For 2008, in the aggregate 33% of after tax income of controlled foreign corporations was distributed, 18% as discretionary dividends and the remaining 15% as Subpart F income. Canadian subsidiaries, however, distributed 44%, with 36% as discretionary payments and the remaining 8% as Subpart F. However, for Switzerland, a significant tax haven country, 19% was paid out, 10% as dividends and the remaining 9% as Subpart F. These shares are not available for 2007, and 2006 is probably not very representative, at least for tax haven countries, because it was immediately after the repatriation holiday enacted in 2004 that permitted a one-time dividend payment with an 85% exclusion.[18]

In determining the consequences of present and proposed systems, it is also important to note the repatriated income is not random. Firms presumably choose to repatriate income that can be most easily shielded by foreign tax credits. Some evidence of this effect can be found in the M-3 study, in which the residual U.S. tax on foreign source income was only 3.3% even though half of income was reported and a significant share was in royalties that had little foreign tax (to be used for credits) attached.

Sources of Tax Liability

To examine this issue, consider the data in *Table 3* on foreign tax credits, which indicate the foreign taxes paid, and credits claimed.

Table 3. Foreign Tax Payments and Credits, 2007 and 2008

Item	2007 ($ billions)	2008 ($ billions)
Current Foreign Taxes Paid	99.1	156.2
Minus Reduction (Largely for Oil and Gas Taxes)	10.3	14.7
Plus Carryover	29.2	49.7
Equals Total Foreign Tax Credits Available	117.9	191.2
Foreign Tax Credit Limit	114.0	122.5
Foreign Tax Credits Claimed	86.5	100.4
Residual U.S. Tax (Limit Minus Claim)	29.5	22.1

Source: Statistics of Income, International Statistics, Returns With Foreign Tax Credits, http://www.irs.gov/ taxstats/bustaxstats/article/0,,id=210069,00.html.

Even though a significant share of the income was royalties and other direct income that should have been taxed, the effective U.S. residual tax rate on foreign source income as measured for tax purposes was only 7% in 2007 and 5% in 2008.[19] Moreover, the size of the tax suggests that royalties were being shielded from tax by excess credits. The royalties were $101.9 billion and $106.4 billion. Had they been fully subject to a 35% tax rate the tax on this source of income (offset by approximately $4 billion in withholding taxes) would have been around $32 billion and $33 billion respectively, larger than total taxes paid.

The indication that royalties are shielded from tax is reinforced by evidence from 2000 tax returns, which traced the $12.7 billion of U.S. residual taxes to foreign sources.[20] *Table 4* shows the distribution of the shares paid. In 2000, there were nine foreign tax credit limit baskets. Only three accounted for a significant share: passive (4.6% of the total), financial services (21.3% of total), and the residual general limit basket (71.3% of the total).[21] Active dividends in the general basket accounted for only 10.2% of total taxes and dividends in financial services accounted for 2.4%. The largest share was due to royalties, interest, and branch income in the active basket. Financial branch income and financial interest each accounted for 18% so that the financial income basket bore a share of taxes out of proportion to its share of income, presumably in part because interest income was subject to tax. The remainder, 16.5% was due to the passive basket, which was largely composed of Subpart F income.

Table 4. Estimated Sources of Tax Revenue on Foreign Source Income, 2000

Type of Income	Share of Taxes Paid (%)
Dividends Non-Financial Services	10.2
Dividends Financial Services	2.4
Active Royalties, Interest and Export (Non-Financial)	33.9
Financial, Branch Income	18.1
Financial, Interest	18.1
Passive (Largely Subpart F)	16.5

Source: Harry Grubert and Rosanne Altshuler, "Corporate Taxes in the World Economy: Reforming the Taxation of Cross-border Income," in Fundamental Tax Reform: Issues, Choices, and Implications, Ed. John W. Diamond and George R. Zodrow, Cambridge, MIT Press, 2008, pp. 326-327.

If current taxes were distributed in the same manner now as they were in 2000, then taxes on active dividends for 2007 would have been responsible for a residual U.S. tax of around one-half of 1% on total foreign source active income potentially paid out as dividends.[22] The combination of selective deferral and cross-crediting appears to have essentially eliminated any U.S. tax on active income of foreign subsidiaries.

The same study that estimated data for *Table 4* estimated that two-thirds of royalties were shielded by tax credits. It is possible, however, that more tax is collected on royalties currently because of the declines in foreign tax rates and the elimination of foreign tax credit splitting.

Current and Potential Tax Collections

To consider a year that should be more normal (i.e., past the effects of a slow recovery from the recession) *Table 5* estimates three components of potential foreign taxes for FY2014: foreign taxes projected to be collected, additional taxes collected as a result of the repeal of deferral, and additional taxes collected if, in addition to repealing deferral, a per country foreign tax credit were imposed.

Those provisions taken together should result in a close approximation of a true worldwide system that eliminated deferral and largely eliminates cross-crediting.

Table 5. Current and Potential Tax Collections on Foreign Source Income, FY2014

Provision	Effect on Revenues ($billions)	Share of Current Total U.S. Corporate Tax (%)
Current Tax	32.1	7.5
Gain from Ending Deferral	18.4	4.3
Additional Gain from Per Country Foreign Tax Credit	45.9	10.9
Limit		
Total Share of All	96.4	22.5
Addendum: Eliminate Title Passage Rule	6.3	1.6
Addendum: Repeal Worldwide Interest Allocation	3.6	0.8

Source: Current Tax extrapolated from 2007 data based on changes in corporate tax revenues. Gain from Ending Deferral and Title Passage Rule from Joint Committee on Taxation, Estimates Of Federal Tax Expenditures For Fiscal Years 2011-2015, January 17, 2012, JCS-1-12. Gain from Per Country Foreign Tax Credit Limit from Joint Committee on Taxation estimates at http://wyden.senate.gov/imo/media/doc/Score.pdf; Worldwide interest allocation based on FY2019 cost adjusted to FY2014 based on projected corporate tax revenues; FY2019 cost at Joint Committee on Taxation, General Explanation Of Tax Legislation Enacted In The 111th Congress, JCS-2-11, March 24, 2011.

This table shows the importance of cross-crediting, by showing the effects of moving to a per country foreign tax credit limit given deferral is eliminated. Because of this importance, a territorial tax, which would eliminate foreign tax credits, can have consequences beyond the active income it is designed to remove from the U.S. tax base, since excess credits currently shield royalty and export income from U.S. tax.

Table 5 also shows the separate revenue consequences of two other provisions: the title passage rule and the effect of worldwide allocation of foreign source income.

Issues in Considering Territorial Taxation

Several issues arise when considering moving from the present hybrid tax system to a territorial tax: the effect on repatriations, the effect on the location of real investment, the consequences for artificial profit shifting, transition, administrative and compliance issues, and the revenue consequences.

Effect on Repatriations

One criticism of the current system is that while collecting very little revenue from foreign subsidiaries, it nevertheless discourages repatriations. The negative effect of the current system on repatriations is the major economic rationale cited by the Ways and Means Committee's press release proposing a territorial tax.[23] This argument also ties the lower repatriation rates to less investment and fewer jobs in the United States.

Before discussing the potential effects, however, note that the repatriation argument alone is not a sufficient justification for a territorial tax. The tax effect on repatriation could be eliminated by moving in the opposite direction, ending deferral. Or it could be achieved by a variety of hybrid approaches such as taxing a fixed share of profits currently and exempting the remainder, or allowing an exemption combined with a minimum tax that is smaller than the U.S. tax rate. All of these approaches create a system where taxation is not triggered by repatriation.

Would the elimination of the tax triggered by repatriations (which could be achieved by either a territorial tax or elimination of deferral) increase repatriations significantly? And if so, would those increased repatriations result in more investment and jobs in the United States?

Although the projections vary with data source and with shares of pre-tax and after-tax income, estimates in the previous section suggest that about a third of foreign subsidiaries' earnings was repatriated, with discretionary distributions net of Subpart F income around 23%. Does that imply that the remaining two thirds of income (or 77% of income net of Subpart F distributions) would be repatriated? It is unlikely that much of an increase would occur, as discussed below, and even more unlikely that it those repatriations would be translated into investment.

Several considerations suggest that the increase in repatriations would be limited. First, regardless of tax considerations, much of foreign source earnings would be retained abroad to be reinvested in the enterprises there. Historical evidence on corporate rates of return and growth rates in the United States suggest that about 60% of nominal income is typically retained to maintain the real capital stock and allow it to grow normally at a steady state.[24] The remainder, 40%, would be distributed. Thus we might expect, using the estimates above, at best to see an increase of 7% of earnings, or 17% of earnings net of Subpart F income.

Second, these repatriation rates are probably at an unusually low level because they followed the large one time repatriation (generally in 2005) from the temporary repatriation holiday enacted in 2004. Not only had large sums been repatriated to take advantage of a one time tax exemption which reduced the need for repatriations immediately after the holiday, but more might have been retained abroad than usual in anticipation of another holiday.[25] Historical data indicate that repatriation rates fell towards the end of the 1990s and continued to be low from 2000 to 2008.[26] Data were provided every other year and did not include 2005, the year most repatriations occurred under the repatriation holiday. Over the period 1968-2008, the average repatriation rate was 40%; for 2000-2008 it was 20%. In addition to the anticipation and aftermath of repatriation holidays, the growth of high-tech and dot.com firms that were expanding rapidly and not initially paying dividends may also have affected these payout ratios.[27] The evidence from tax data is also consistent with studies examining repatriation rates over an earlier period of time using financial data that found rates of around 40%.[28] Since a 40% rate is about the rate that might be expected in a no-tax world, these results suggest that the repatriation tax has had relatively little effect on a permanent basis. If firms came to believe another repatriation holiday or territorial tax were not in store, and the high-tech industries achieved a steady state growth, repatriation rates might rise to more normal levels.

Third, there is direct evidence that shifting to a territorial tax would not have large effects. Some initial evidence indicates that the Japanese shift to a territorial tax increased repatriations in the first year by about 20%.[29] Applied to current realizations rates, it would increase realizations by about 4% of total earnings; compared to the 40% rate it would increase realizations by about 8% of earnings. Since a larger first year effect might be expected, as pent up earnings are returned, such an increase is quite modest. Preliminary results from a study of the UK territorial tax shift, while subject to revision, suggest an increase of 6% of earnings.[30] A statistical study of U.S. affiliates in different countries facing different taxes suggested that repatriations would increase by about 13%, which would be 2.5% to 5% of earnings.[31]

Moreover, some theory and research suggests the effects would be negligible on a permanent basis. Theoretical considerations indicate that the repatriation tax should not matter because firms will eventually have to repatriate earnings. This theory, referred to as the "new view" is related to a similar theory about why domestic firms pay dividends to their individual shareholders even though it triggers a dividend tax. In both cases, the idea is that eventually shareholders will want to receive their dividends in excess of amounts needed for steady state reinvestment and dividends will be paid either currently, or in the future with interest. In either case, the same present value of tax will occur. While this "new view" for dividends paid in the U.S. to its individual shareholders could be rejected on the grounds that firms can return cash to the economy by repurchasing shares, such an option is not available for dividend payments between a multinational affiliate and its parent.

If the theory correctly describes behavior, then one would expect that, regardless of the repatriation tax a similar share of earnings would be paid in dividends with or without a repatriation tax. A large empirical literature has developed to study repatriation behavior, finding a variety of results. For example, some early evidence suggested that repatriation rates are sensitive to tax, but subsequent research showed that it might be due to transitory effects.[32] Evidence that repatriations were more likely from highly taxed subsidiaries (where taxes generated would be offset by foreign tax credits) relative to low taxed ones suggested that taxes have effects on repatriations.[33] However, another study found that the repatriations tax became less important given alternative strategies for returning cash for the United States.[34] These strategies included making passive investments abroad with the parent company borrowing against them, or having low tax subsidiaries make equity investments in high tax subsidiaries which in turn repatriated income with attached foreign tax credits.[35] These strategies would indicate differential repatriation rates exist between high and low tax subsidiaries but they are not necessarily meaningful. Most recently, a study suggested taxes had some effect, but a limited one, on repatriations; this study also showed over a long period of time payout shares of about 40%.[36]

The recent pressure for a repatriation holiday and reports of large amounts of accumulated unrepatriated earnings probably comes largely from firms that have intangible assets, have been growing rapidly abroad and thus retaining earnings for that purpose, and perhaps shifting profits arbitrarily.[37] They may have also been delaying repatriations in anticipation of another holiday. As affairs settle into more of a steady state, there may be a greater need to distribute to pay shareholders, so this phenomenon may be largely transitory.

Even if repatriations increase under a permanent territorial tax, those repatriations may not result in additional investment, but are likely to be paid out as dividends, or substitute for borrowing by the parent company.[38] Job creation is not the primary focus here in any case, as in the long run, reduce jobs. The economy will tend to create jobs naturally. As an illustration, consider that in 1961 and in 1991 the unemployment rate was the same, 6.7%. Employment, however, rose from 66 million to 117 million, as the economy accommodated the baby boom and the entry of women into the labor force.

Permanent provisions that encourage capital to move abroad can change the types of jobs and reduce wages, but not overall employment.[39]

Location of Investment

Historically, the central issue in evaluating a foreign tax regime has been the effect on the allocation of investment. Economic theory seeking efficiency objectives supports taxing investments at the same rate wherever they are invested; this approach would maximize worldwide output by investing capital where it earns the highest pre-tax return. For example, if the after tax return is 7% and the U.S. tax is an effective 30% while the foreign tax rate is zero, and investments are perfect substitutes, the total pre-tax return at the margin on an investment in the United States is 10% (0.07/(1-0.30) while the return in the foreign location is only 7%. Allowing foreign source income to be exempt causes capital to move to a less productive use, where it earns a pre-tax return of 7%, when it could earn a 10% return in the United States.[40]

The equating of taxes on a firm's investment is most closely associated with a residence based tax system. Given the need for limits on foreign tax credits, this system would be most closely approximated by a system that eliminates deferral and imposes a foreign tax credit limit on a country by country basis. If the objective were not worldwide optimization or efficiency, but maximizing U.S. welfare, the rules would be more stringent by allowing foreign taxes as a deduction rather than a credit.[41]

Assessing Arguments for A Territorial Tax

What, then, is the justification for moving in the opposite direction, to a territorial tax? One may be that if, for political or other reasons, it is not possible to move closer to a residence-based system, it is possible to design a territorial tax system that is an improvement over the current rules. This argument is made by Grubert and Mutti,[42] and their proposal was incorporated in President Bush's Advisory Commission's tax reform proposals.[43] Grubert and Mutti proposed, along with exempting active dividends from tax, to provide for an allocation of overhead costs of the firm (such as interest) between taxable and tax exempt income. For example, if 10% of income is exempt because of the dividend exemption then 10% of interest and other overhead costs would be disallowed. They also note that that the elimination of foreign tax credits would mean that royalty, export and other income would not be shielded from U.S. tax with excess foreign tax credits. As a result, this proposal is projected to raise revenue, a result also found by the Joint Committee on Taxation, and the overall tax rate on foreign source income would rise.[44] Grubert and Mutti also note that repatriations would not trigger a tax and that such a change would reduce the cost of tax planning to avoid the repatriation tax.

The argument that a territorial tax that could improve economic efficiency, or at least make it no worse, should be distinguished from arguments that do not stand up to economic reasoning. For example, moving to a territorial system because other countries have generally done so does not mean such a system is desirable either for them or for the United States. Many policies exist in other countries, such as a value added tax or national health insurance, policies that many oppose and that have not been adopted in the United States. The issues may differ as well. European countries, for example, are geographically and politically closer than the United States is to other countries. The European Union also has provisions on freedom of capital movement and establishment that prevent the type of anti-inversion laws that the United States has, to prevent U.S. firms from relocating their headquarters.[45] These rules may influence decisions to adopt territorial systems as well as decisions to lower corporate tax rates, which has occurred in the United Kingdom recently.

Similarly, the argument that because most other countries do not tax their foreign subsidiaries, the United States also should not do so in order to allow its firms to compete abroad does not stand up to economic analysis. A country does not compete in the manner that a firm does, because its resources (labor and savings provided by its citizens) do not disappear if another firm undercuts prices; they are simply used in a different way. That is, a country does not compete with the rest of the world, it trades with them, both its products and its capital. It can generally be shown that the United States would still be better off, or at least no worse off, if it taxes foreign and domestic investments by its firms at the same rate, even if other countries do not.[46]

Finally, arguments made based on empirical studies that indicate that increased foreign investment of multinationals is correlated with more, not less, domestic investment do not show that overall U.S investment is not reduced by more favorable foreign treatment, and may simply identify firms that are growing.

In any event, the aggregate amount of capital owned by U.S. citizens and the allocation of that capital are separate issues. Even if savings responds to the overall U.S. tax burden, of two revenue neutral regimes, the one that taxes capital equally in both locations would be more efficient.

There are some arguments that have been made that bear consideration. Perhaps the most important of these is that U.S. firms can change their nationality by moving their headquarters abroad, merging with foreign companies, or incorporating abroad. However, anti-inversion rules adopted in 2004 are likely to prevent large-scale shifting of headquarters of existing firms, while mergers and incorporating abroad are probably largely determined by non-tax factors and could be addressed with legislative revisions.[47] Evidence suggests that very little incorporation of true U.S. firms occurs abroad[48] and this effect could be addressed with legislation (such as basing taxation on where effective management occurs) if necessary.

Arguments have also been made that the higher taxes on returns to capital investments would prevent U.S. firms from exploiting intangible assets abroad.[49] However, there are many ways of exploiting intangibles without engaging directly in manufacturing or other activities, such as licenses, franchises, and contract manufacturing.[50] Products embodying U.S. innovations could also be produced in the United States and exported.

Likely Effects of International Tax Revision on Investment

What are the likely effects of altering the international tax system on investment? There are several reasons that these effects would probably be modest, although they would depend on the particular design features of the reform.

First, most countries where physical investment might take place, such as manufacturing, tend to have taxes that are not much different from those that apply in the United States: average effective rates of 27% and marginal effective rates of about 20%.[51] The average effective tax rate on foreign subsidiaries of U.S. parents is estimated to be lower than that of U.S. firms in general (about 16% versus 26% with a 3% residual U.S. tax on foreign earnings), but that partially reflects profit shifting to low tax countries, since the effective rate in tax haven countries was 5.7%.[52] Overall effective tax rates abroad for foreign subsidiaries of U.S. companies also vary by industry. Industries with a lot of intangible assets have lower tax rates. For example, computer and electronic product manufacturing had an effective tax rate of 8.7% and finance 11.3%.[53]

Second, to the extent that firms expect largely to avoid U.S. taxes under the current system, either through permanent reinvestment of profits or tax planning, moving to a territorial tax would not make much difference in inducing outflows of capital, especially if anti-base erosion provisions (such as treating income earned in tax haven countries as Subpart F Income) are adopted. Nevertheless, since firms' investments are only observed under the current deferral and foreign tax credit system, it is possible that significantly more capital would be invested abroad, especially in lower tax jurisdictions.

Moving in the opposite direction, by ending deferral and possibly cross-crediting (with a per country foreign tax credit limit) would reduce capital investment abroad by retaining more outbound capital in the United States.

Nevertheless, effects from either revision are unlikely to be important to the overall U.S. economy or to U.S. welfare; estimates of the effect of cutting the U.S. corporate tax rate by ten percentage points, which would presumably have larger effects by attracting inbound capital as well is estimated to increase U.S. output by only about 2/10^{ths} of 1% and U.S. income by 2/100^{ths} of 1%.[54] The effects of moving to a territorial tax would be negative (decrease U.S. output) because they increase the return on outbound capital, but would be smaller in magnitude because the effects are smaller. Based on relative sizes of revenue effects, a ten percentage point rate reduction would lose about 29% of corporate revenue, while, based on the estimates in *Table 5*, eliminating all taxes on foreign source income would lose about 7.5% of corporate revenue, or a quarter of the amount. Eliminating deferral alone would gain revenue equal to about 15% of the absolute change from a ten percentage point rate reduction, while eliminating deferral and cross-crediting would be about 53% of the change. This last change could be more significant than the domestic rate reduction but nevertheless not large relative to the U.S. economy.

All of these effects are small, relative to output, for several reasons. First, although capital flows respond to differential tax rates, capital is not perfectly mobile.[55] Even if it were, the large size of the U.S. domestic economy and capital stock and the constraints of production (capital must combine with labor to be productive) limit the effect to 1/2 of 1% of output and a negligible effect on income.[56] The corporate tax itself is also small as a cost factor: about 2% of GDP. Thus even a 10 percentage point rate reduction would be slightly over 1/2 of 1% of GDP, while most international revisions would be even smaller. Finally, most of these gains would not accrue to U.S. income: for inbound capital most of the gain would be profit to foreign investors, and for outbound capital drawn back, profits were already in existence and merely change location.

The analysis in this section suggests that while there may be concerns about the effects of international reforms on investments, either reducing U.S. investment in the case of a territorial tax or increasing it by moving towards a residence based tax (e.g., eliminating deferral and cross-crediting) these effects are likely quite modest.

Treatment of Royalties and Export Income

One effect of the current system that might be changed by moving to a territorial system is the reduction in the beneficial treatment of royalties and export income through the use of excess foreign tax credits. The current benefits for royalties encourage firms to exploit intangibles in foreign operations rather than in the United States, while the export subsidy causes prices and magnitudes of exports to be too large.

Royalties, in particular, are a difficult issue to address because increased taxes on royalties paid from foreign subsidiaries would encourage manufacturing of goods in the United States but, as will be discussed in the next section, also creates an incentive to understate royalties and artificially shift intangible income into untaxed active earnings of foreign subsidiaries that are exempt. Ideally, such profit shifting should be addressed by anti-abuse provisions.

Artificial Profit Shifting

The third issue, which primarily involves revenue, is artificial profit shifting—that is, shifting profits into low-tax jurisdictions that are then exempt from U.S. tax. Profit shifting also exists under the current system because of deferral. Evidence of profit shifting is clear from the distribution of shares of U.S. subsidiary profits as a percentage of GDP, where profits as a percentage of output were typically less than 1%-2% in the G-7, were significantly larger in the larger tax-haven countries (7.6% in Ireland and 18.2% in Luxemburg), and were more than 600% and 500% respectively in Bermuda and the Cayman Islands.[57] The estimates of magnitude vary substantially reaching up to $90 billion and ranging from about 14% to 29% of corporate revenues.[58] They have been growing as well.[59]

In general, most of this profit shifting apparently arises from either leveraging (borrowing in high-tax jurisdictions) or shifting of the location of profits from intangibles. It is not surprising, therefore, that low-tax rates tend to be associated with manufacture of drugs and electronics, and the information and communications industries.

Profit shifting is a policy problem even without a move to a territorial tax. One of the concerns about moving to a territorial tax is the possibility that it will increase the already significant and growing estimated level of profit shifting. Under current law, firms that have shifted profits to low-tax jurisdictions may still have to face eventual taxation. The considerable lobbying for a repatriation holiday such as that in 2004 may be a sign of this concern.[60] With a simple territorial tax with no anti-abuse provisions, profit shifting could increase substantially. There is little to clarify the likely magnitude of this effect. Evidence for European countries has also indicated significant profit shifting, benefiting most European countries largely at the expense of Germany.[61] Germany has since lowered their corporate tax rate (and profit shifting may have played a role in that decision). However, it is difficult to draw conclusions from the experiences of these very different countries, who already have territorial systems but also have in most cases had measures to address base erosion.

If the new view of dividends is correct, and companies expect to pay taxes on excess profits with interest when deferred, then the move to a simple territorial tax (without any anti-base erosion measures) could increase profit shifting, perhaps considerably. However, if this view is not correct and firms expect to escape tax indefinitely, then going to a territorial tax might not make much difference. Unfortunately, while there is a relatively powerful theoretical justification for the new view, the empirical evidence has been mixed. At the same time, however, as noted above, the lobbying for a repatriation holiday supports the new view and the expectation that profit shifting might increase insignificantly.

One particular potential effect on profit shifting involves royalties. Because royalties are protected to some extent by excess foreign tax credits, moving to a territorial tax would eliminate that protection and increase the tax on royalties. This change in taxation would create a further incentive to shift intangible income into the earnings of foreign subsidiaries and out of royalties.

Aside from the issue of the effect of a territorial tax (and of its particular design features) on profit shifting, other reforms might be considered that might address profit shifting either in the current system or in a system revised in ways other than moving to a territorial tax. These reforms might include provisions reforming the current system proposed by President Obama (and earlier by former Ways and Means Committee Chairman Rangel), which would tax excess earnings from intangibles as subpart F income and rules that would disallow some portion of overhead expenses to the extent income is not taxed.

Fundamentally, as long as a system allows for differential taxes, whether between the U.S. and foreign source income or between types of foreign source income, there is likely to be profit shifting. Companies appear willing to exploit relatively small differentials in tax as illustrated by the double-Irish, Dutch sandwich technique that allowed firms to not only avoid the U.S. tax, but to avoid the 12.5% Irish tax as well, and establish taxation in Bermuda, with a zero tax rate.[62] The only tax system that eliminates differential taxes is the elimination of deferral, possibly combined with a separate tax credit limit basket for royalty income.

Transition

An important issue in moving to a territorial tax is how to treat accumulated unrepatriated earnings, which were generated under a worldwide system. One approach would be to deem all accumulated earnings as repatriated and pay taxes, with a number of years allowed to pay these taxes. The provision might create a hardship for firms to the extent that income is tied up in non-liquid form, unless the period of time for paying the tax were extensive. In addition, it would be a retroactively harsh tax compared with the present system, because a significant portion of earnings need never be repatriated. During normal times, estimates suggest that more than half of retained earnings abroad is probably reinvested in the firms activities. Note also that while perhaps 60% or so of the flow of income would be retained abroad, a much larger share of the stock of unrepatriated earnings would be likely to be permanently reinvested abroad.

Another option is to treat these earnings the same as newly generated earnings and exempt them in the same way. This approach would create a windfall benefit, especially to the degree that firms have been holding off repatriating and engaging in aggressive profit shifting because of a potential tax holiday.

A third option would be to treat dividends as paid out of accumulated earnings until these earnings are exhausted, while applying the full tax rate and foreign tax credit rules. This approach, however, would continue the disincentive to repatriate for some time.

None of these approaches may be entirely satisfactory. Intermediate proposals that are under consideration would tax this income but at a lower rate. One, in the Ways and Means proposal, is to deem all this earnings repatriated prior to the law changes, apply the provisions of the 2004 tax holiday (85% exclusion of income with proportional foreign tax credits), which would impose a small tax, and allow it to be paid over a period of time.

On average this may be a reasonable compromise, because, although a significant fraction of income is exempt, a significant fraction of this income would probably never have been repatriated.

A second intermediate option is to allow firms to elect the holiday (with an extended pay out period) and to tax any remaining dividends at the full tax rate until all of the remaining earnings is paid out as dividends. This voluntary approach allows firms to avoid undesirable forced payouts, but prolongs the effective movement to a territorial tax.

Striking a balance between limiting the windfall benefits and the associated revenue loss compared with a baseline, providing firms with terms that allow the funds to pay (since a lot of accumulated earnings are not liquid) and avoiding prolonged coverage of dividends under the old system is one of the most difficult problems in crafting a shift to a territorial tax. As will be discussed subsequently, the proposals have included a variety of approaches.

While accumulated untaxed earnings are an important issue, there are other transition issues relating to the shift from the current system to a territorial tax. These include unused foreign tax credits associated with previously taxed income and foreign loss carryovers. How credits and losses might be treated may depend largely on the treatment of existing earnings accumulated abroad and how other features of the foreign tax credit are modified.

Administration and Compliance

Arguments have often been made that moving to a territorial tax would simplify administration and compliance. Grubert and Mutti, in their proposal for a territorial tax, stressed the cost of tax planning associated with repatriating income while paying minimal tax. Thus a territorial tax would add value by simplifying repatriation policy. U.S. parents could receive dividends from their subsidiaries without concerns about the tax consequences. However, the same simplification would occur if deferral were ended, because firms would have no choice about paying taxes or arranging for optimal cross-crediting. Hybrid approaches such as taxing a share of income currently would also eliminate the scope for tax planning around repatriation.

Although repatriation tax planning would be eliminated, if a territorial tax increased profit shifting incentives, tax planning in that area could increase. And, as will be shown in the discussion of design issues, provisions considered to combat income shifting can add considerable complexity to the tax code.

Revenue Issues

A shift to a territorial system could potentially gain revenue, in part because relatively little tax is collected on foreign operations. In any case, it is unlikely that large revenue losses would occur unless the move to a territorial tax includes other provisions (such as lower tax rates on royalties) or induces pronounced income shifting responses. If *Table 4* shares of income are applied to estimates of current taxes paid on foreign source income listed in *Table 5*, the taxation of dividends of foreign subsidiaries is quite small, a little over $4 billion in FY2014, or about 1% of corporate revenues. Branch income is slightly under $6 billion, so if this income is also exempted in a move to a territorial tax, the total effect would be about $10 billion. The two together are about 2% of corporate revenues. Taxes on royalties and export income (which along with nonfinancial interest would be somewhat over $10 billion, or about 2% of revenues) could increase with the loss of foreign tax credits, leading to a relatively small net loss or possibly a small gain.

There is considerably more revenue to be gained by moving in the opposite direction, as some proposals do. Eliminating deferral and providing a per country foreign tax credit limit could triple the revenue collected on foreign source income, raising $64 billion or about 15% of corporate taxes, according to the estimates in *Table 5*. Other intermediate changes could raise revenues; eliminating deferral alone would raise about $18 billion in revenue, and the combination of President Obama's budget proposals for international taxation would raise $16 billion.[63]

Some proposals for moving to a territorial tax aim for revenue neutrality, but also propose to use transitional revenues (from taxes on accumulated untaxed earnings) to achieve this revenue neutrality in the budget horizon. Because transitional gains are temporary, this approach results in a long-run revenue loss.

DESIGN ISSUES IN A TERRITORIAL TAX

Moving to a territorial tax goes far beyond a simple matter of exempting foreign source income from U.S. tax. There are issues of transition, the treatment of current flow through income, and the retention and perhaps revision of anti-abuse rules. In this section, three proposals are outlined: the Grubert Mutti proposal, the discussion draft provided by Ways and Means Committee Chairman, and Senator Enzi's bill, S. 2091. The latter two proposals are similar in general approach. Note that the Grubert Mutti proposal is a general outline, while the Ways and Means Discussion Draft and S. 2091 are in legislative language and are more detailed.

The Grubert Mutti Proposal

This proposal has been circulating for some time as a general proto-type of a move to a territorial tax, and has been estimated to raise revenue, primarily due to increased taxes on royalties and allocation of parent company expenses between taxable and exempt income.[64] A proposal of this nature was included in President Bush's Advisory Panel Proposal in 2005.[65]

- Exemption of dividends for active foreign income by U.S. shareholders with a 10% or more interest and eliminate foreign tax credits.
- Foreign branches treated the same as subsidiaries.
- Royalties and interest paid to the U.S. parent are taxable.
- Current anti-abuse rules for passive income (Subpart F) would be retained, although some aspects would become obsolete (primarily the inclusion of dividend payments between subsidiaries).
- Parent's overhead expenses, such as interest, would be allocated in proportion to untaxed income and disallowed.
- Active foreign losses could not offset domestic income.
- Capital gains and losses from the sale of productive assets would be exempt.
- Income from U.S. exports would not be classified as foreign source income.

The proposal does not address the treatment of existing accumulated earnings abroad or profit shifting via intangible assets, although one of the proposal's authors has indicated that their plan should probably include a tax on accumulated earnings, but at a lower rate.[66]

This proposal has been estimated to raise revenue of approximately $6.9 billion in 2014.[67] If the shares of revenue in *Table 4* remain the same for 2014, about 30% of current tax on foreign source income or slightly under $10 billion (based on aggregates from *Table 5*) is collected on active dividends and branch income. The additional taxes on royalties and export income plus limits on the deduction of overhead expenses presumably raise about $17 billion (replacing the lost revenue and generating additional amounts).

Ways and Means Chairman Camp's Discussion Draft

In October 2011, Ways and Means Chairman Dave Camp released a discussion draft outlining an approach to a territorial tax (hereafter Discussion Draft). This proposal includes some options and unsettled issues, and there is not as yet a revenue estimate. Note also that the intention expressed in press releases at that time was to couple the move to a territorial tax with a general tax reform that would reduce the top corporate rate from 35% to 25%. This rate matters since some provisions allow a proportional tax benefit. Since the other changes that might be needed to achieve this reduction have not been yet spelled out, no observations on the effects if any remaining revision will be included, outside of noting the consequences of the rate change for specific territorial provisions.

The following summary of these provisions does not include all of the detailed nuances of the proposal, which are contained in a technical draft discussion.[68]

- Allows a 95% deduction for the foreign source portion of dividends for 10% U.S. corporate shareholders of foreign subsidiaries that are controlled foreign corporations (CFCs). A holding period of one year for stock in foreign corporations is required. If the rate is reduced to 25%, dividends would be taxed at 1.25%; at the current rate, they would be taxed at 1.75%. (CFCs are those where 50% of the stock is owned by five or fewer 10% U.S. shareholders.)
- 10% corporate shareholders of non controlled corporations (where 50% of the stock is not owned by five or fewer 10% U.S. shareholders, called 10/50 corporations) can elect the same treatment as CFCs.
- Foreign branches are treated the same as subsidiaries; the draft also considers the possible inclusion of partnerships in this treatment.
- Anti-abuse (Subpart F) provisions are retained, although these rules would be revised in light of the other changes; these details are to be considered subsequently. Dividends paid between CFCs are exempt.
- Capital gains on sales of stock in active eligible subsidiaries are also eligible for a 95% exclusion.

- Accumulated untaxed earnings will be taxed with an 85% exclusion and apportionment of associated foreign tax credits in the same fashion as the 2004 repatriation holiday, except that all earnings will be taxed rather than earnings that are voluntarily repatriated. No actual repatriation is necessary. Firms can pay the tax in installments with interest over eight years. Assuming this provision applies before changes in the statutory tax rate, the effective rate is 5.25% less any apportioned foreign tax credits.
- The foreign tax credits associated with active dividends and with foreign branch income are disallowed (those for Subpart F are retained). All foreign tax credits would be in one basket, presumably because the active basket would no longer be relevant. The proposal also eliminates the allocation of parent interest that presently applies to determine the foreign tax credit limit: only directly associated expenses will be applied to determine foreign income. It would also repeal the provision preventing the splitting of foreign tax credits.
- A provision that requires the inclusion in income of investments of deferred income (income that is not taxed because it is not distributed) in U.S. property is repealed. This provision exists to prevent firms from effectively repatriating earnings without declaring dividends that are subject to the tax.
- Three anti-base-erosion options, two directed at intangible income, are considered. Option A is similar to a proposal made by President Obama in his budget proposals, that would tax excess earnings on intangibles (in excess of 150% of costs) in low tax jurisdictions as Subpart F. The inclusion would be phased out between a 10% and a 15% rate. Option B would tax income that is subject to an effective foreign tax rate below 10% unless it qualifies for a home country exception. The home country exception applies when a firm conducts an active trade or business in the home country, has a fixed place of business, and serves the local market. Option C would tax all foreign income from intangibles (whether earnings by the foreign subsidiary or royalty payments) but allow a deduction for 40%, resulting in a tax rate of 15% at a 25% statutory tax rate.
- Additional base-erosion provisions (sometimes call thin-capitalization rules) relating to interest would restrict the deduction for interest if the company failed to meet either of two tests: if debt to equity ratios in the U.S. differed from the total debt to equity ratio worldwide and if interest expenses exceed a certain share of adjusted income (generally

taxable income before the deduction of interest and depreciation). The smaller of the excess interest under either test would be disallowed, but the percentage has not been specified.

- The draft indicates that the two extenders, exception from Subpart F of active financing and active insurance income and the look-through rules, would be considered separately.

Senator Enzi's Bill (S. 2091)

Senator Enzi has introduced S. 2091 which is similar in many respects to the Ways and Means Discussion Draft. His bill is a separate bill that does not include a general tax reform or lowering of the corporate rate.[69]

- The Enzi proposal provides the same 95% dividend exemption and election option for 10/50 companies as the Discussion Draft.
- Foreign branches would not be treated as subsidiaries.
- Anti-abuse rules (Subpart F) would be retained, but the inclusion of foreign base company sales and service income would be eliminated.
- Capital gains on the sale of stock would be eligible for the exclusion to the extent they would be treated as a dividend under Section 1248 (which treats gains as dividends to the extent of earnings and profits).
- Firms could elect to tax accumulated earnings with a 70% exclusion (a 10.5% tax) and no foreign tax credits; otherwise accumulated earnings would be taxed at full rates with foreign tax credits allowed when paid out as dividends and these pre-existing earnings would be deemed to be paid out first.
- Foreign tax credits (and deductions for these taxes) associated with exempt income would be disallowed.
- The Enzi bill does not repeal the provision taxing investments of deferred income in U.S. property.
- For anti-base-erosion provisions a version of Option B in the Discussion Draft along with a version of the first part of Option C would be included. Income in countries with tax rates of half or less than the U.S. rate (17.5%) would be subject to tax. However, operations that conduct an active business, with employees and officers that contribute substantially, would be excepted except to the extent the income is intangible income of the CFC. The CFC's

intangible income would be Subpart F income. These rules provide more scope for exemption as compared to the rules in the Discussion Draft which would require exempt income to carry out activities serving the home country market. The bill also includes the first part of Option C, allowing a 17.5% tax rate on intangible income (such as royalties) earned by a domestic corporation. Intangible income would be placed in a separate foreign tax credit basket.

- The bill does not contain the thin capitalization rules (such as allocating interest between U.S. firms and their foreign subsidiaries).
- The bill makes the two extenders, the exception from Subpart F for active financing and active insurance income and the look-through rules, permanent. It also applies the worldwide interest allocation for purposes of the foreign tax credit in 2013, rather than 2021.

Analysis and Commentary on the Proposals

Some insights into issues and trade offs may be noted by observing the difference between these proposals. In addition, the Discussion Draft proposals invited commentary, which has appeared in a number of venues including testimony before a Ways and Means Subcommittee on Select Revenue Measures hearing on November 27, 2011. This section examines the alternative approaches in light of the issues discussed earlier and general design considerations.

Repatriation Incentives

While the Grubert-Mutti proposal has no tax that is triggered by repatriation, the other two territorial proposals do, due to the 5% "haircut" resulting from the proposed 95% exemption. In addition, the Discussion Draft also allows firms to choose an alternate completely tax free method of repatriation since investment in U.S. assets is not taxed, even at a 5% share. Presumably, the expectation is that the tax due to the 5% inclusion in income (1.25% at a 25% rate and 1.75% tax at a 35% rate) is too small to matter. At least one commentator, however, has singled this issue out as a potentially serious one indicating that as long as tax planning to avoid even a small tax is costless, firms will undertake it.[70] One option for the Discussion Draft, which would not eliminate the small repatriation tax but would eliminate the costless avoidance, would be to continue to tax these transactions, or to tax 5% of them. An approach that could eliminate the repatriation tax trigger arising from the 5% exclusion altogether is to include 5% of income whether repatriated or not, and make dividends entirely exempt.

S. 2091 also has an additional temporary repatriation trigger arising from its transition rule, which allows firms to elect to repatriate under a 70% exclusion without credits, but would tax dividends until any remaining accumulated funds are exhausted. Presumably, firms would repatriate funds voluntarily from low tax jurisdictions, and then repatriate funds from countries with high foreign taxes until the backlog is exhausted.

The Grubert Mutti proposal does not have any special provision for accumulated untaxed earnings and dividends paid out of those earnings. Basically this provision was not addressed although, as noted above, the authors would expect some transition rule similar to the other proposals; this treatment was not incorporated into their revenue estimates.

Effects on Tax Burden and Investment

Although the Discussion Draft leaves a number of options open, its objective to be revenue neutral indicates that it is more beneficial to U.S. multinational firms than the Grubert-Mutti proposal that raises revenue. Moreover the Discussion Draft proposes to finance part of the revenue loss through the one time revenue gain from the tax on existing accumulated earnings. Senator Enzi has indicated an intention for his bill to be revenue neutral as well, although it has not been scored.[71]

Some elements that increase the tax burden on foreign source income (offsetting the loss from exempting dividends and in some cases branch income) are the allocation of deductions and taxation of royalties in the Grubert-Mutti proposal and the 5% inclusion of dividends in the other two proposals. The base erosion provisions may or may not increase taxes depending on which option is chosen and the extent to which firms can use the active trade or business exception to avoid the tax. Some of the reason for these differences in revenue effect is that the 5% inclusion appears to be significantly smaller than overhead costs (even excluding interest). One comment also noted that the 5% inclusion does not take account of a firm's individual circumstances.[72]

Altshuler and Grubert estimate that overhead expenses outside of interest and research expenditures are 10% of pretax earnings.[73] Moreover, their proposal would disallow the deduction regardless of whether dividends are paid out, while the 5% inclusion would apply only to dividends paid. Assuming that about 40% of earnings are paid out in a steady state the 5% provision would be 2% of total earnings. Thus the provision in the Grubert-

Mutti proposal would be about five times the size of the provision in the Discussion Draft and S. 2091.

Presumably interest would also be significant. The Grubert-Mutti proposal has a direct allocation rule for the parent's interest presumably based on allocations of assets.[74] The proposal does not spell out specifics, but interest allocation could be net or gross, and it could involve only the parent interest or worldwide interest. Turning to years of 2006 and 2007, net interest as a share of combined interest and pretax earnings of nonfinancial corporations in the National Income and Product Accounts was 15% in 2006 and 21% in 2007.[75] The 2006 measure may be more appropriate as a steady state guide since profits had begun to decline in 2007. According to tax statistics, for manufacturing the share was 13% in 2006 and 18% in 2007.[76] Gross interest, the basis of the current allocation rules for the foreign tax credit limit, would be much larger, ranging from 34% to 39% of profits plus interest payments. In a related article, by Altshuler and Grubert, the analysis assumes that debt accounts for a third of the capital stock.[77] The Discussion Draft has thin capitalization rules that are based on two alternative tests: an allocation provision for net interest based on parent versus subsidiary debt-equity ratios taking into account worldwide debt and an alternative based on an as-yet-unspecified share of adjusted income, so that the effects on interest are uncertain. S. 2091 has no allocation rule.

Grubert and Mutti could have an allocation for research and development expenditures but apparently do not.[78] Thus, they have no provision that addresses profit shifting from intangibles.

If these costs were included, for 2006 for manufacturing they were 18% of the total of earnings and research costs.[79] Neither the discussion draft nor S. 2091 have such an allocation, although they have some options that affect base erosion that could address intangibles.

Without more specific guidelines, it is difficult to determine the share of income that would be taxed under the Grubert Mutti proposal. Using net interest, the ratio for manufacturing in 2006 relative to net income is about 15% and the overhead costs add another 10%, taxing about 25% of income, whether paid as a dividend or not. In contrast, assuming 40% of income is paid as a dividend, the 5% inclusion in the Discussion Draft and S. 2091 would tax about 2%. At a 35% rate, these effects would impose additional taxes of 8.75% (0.25 times 0.35) under the Grubert Mutti plan and 0.7% (0.05 times 0.35 times 0.40).

If the allocation of interest is made based on worldwide costs (and not just U.S. parent costs), the allocation could be smaller and firms could shift interest costs to their foreign subsidiaries and deduct them so that the effect would be only the difference between the U.S. and foreign rate. In addition, with an overall allocation, this interest cost would presumably be shifted to high tax countries. The United States would still gain revenue but some of it would be offset (from the firm's point of view) by lower tax payments to foreign countries. At the extreme, only the overhead allocation of 10% would affect taxes, leading to a 3.5 percentage point tax increase.

Both the Discussion Draft and S. 2091 include specific anti-base erosion measures which are not included in the Grubert Mutti proposal and these may to some extent substitute for cost allocation provisions. These provisions relate less to investment than to profit shifting and are discussed in the next section.

Incentives could also be affected by the treatment of royalties whose tax burden would rise as excess foreign tax credits disappear. This higher tax on royalties could encourage both more exports of products with technology embodied (as the cost of exploiting intangibles abroad increases). It could also encourage more research to be performed abroad in low tax CFCs although this effect is unclear since such research would not have a benefit as an investment (expensing and the R&D credit) as is the case in the United States.

S. 2091 also provides that royalty income will be taxed at a 17.5% rate, which reduces the additional taxes that would arise from the loss of foreign tax credits on other incomes. A lower tax on royalties is an option in the discussion draft. Under S. 2091, intangibles that fall under the anti-base erosion rules would be taxed at the full rate, 35%.

As noted earlier, none of the shifts in investment are likely to be large relative to the U.S. economy. Thus, even if the provisions induce more research to be performed abroad, the consequences would not be likely to be significant.

Artificial Profit Shifting

There are several different anti-profit shifting regimes discussed in the proposals: the full allocation of deductions in Mutti and Grubert, the interest allocation rules plus one of three options in the Ways and Means Draft, and the combination of components of two of the three options for S. 2091. Although a more detailed discussion is presented below, Table 6 summarizes the discussion. Grubert and Mutti address artificial profit shifting by allocating deductions, including overhead administrative costs and interest. For interest deductions, this allocation method should address the shifting facilitated through leveraging, although their proposal may only allocate parent company expenses.

Table 6. Summary of Discussion in Text of Base Erosion Provisions of the Proposals

Grubert and Mutti	
Allocation of Deductions	Allocation of overhead costs and interest is simple. It might be desirable to employ worldwide allocation. Allocation would automatically impose an additional tax on shifted profits. Grubert and Mutti have no provisions to address profit shifting through intangibles.
Ways and Means Discussion Draft	
Interest restrictions	Worldwide allocation of interest may be effective in dealing with leverage. The ability to meet an alternative less restrictive test may undermine the effects; it is not clear what the purpose of this alternative is.
Plus Option A	Provisions to tax as U.S. connected income intangible earnings in excess of 150% of costs for countries with rates below 15% (phased out between 10% and 15%) would discourage profit shifting of this nature. It creates an incentive to shift costs to low tax countries and could encourage firms to relocate. Measuring effective tax rates and identifying affected income would be complicated.
Or Plus Option B	Provisions to tax income in countries with rates below 10% as U.S. income would exclude Ireland, and would encourage firms to shift to slightly higher tax rate countries, or perhaps encourage tax havens to increase taxes, both of which would increase taxes paid to foreigners. Measuring effective tax rates could be complicated. Firms may be able to avoid the U.S. tax through the home country exception.
Or Plus Option C	This provision, which taxes all intangible income as U.S. income at a lower rate is not triggered by the country's tax rate and effectively imposes a minimum tax of 15% on intangible income. It thus imposes a lower tax rate on income in low tax jurisdictions but does not induce shifting to other countries. It also imposes the same tax rate on royalties, reducing the incentive to shift these profits into a subsidiary, but compared to a plan without this feature, encouraging production abroad. Distinguishing intangible income would be difficult. This royalty provision might violate WTO rules against export subsidies.

Grubert and Mutti	
S. 2091 (Enzi)	
No Deduction Allocation	This bill has no provision for restricting leveraging directly.
Option B Version	Income in countries with taxes less than half the U.S. rate (17.5%) are subject to U.S. tax, unless there is an active trade or business. A higher rate encompasses more countries, including Ireland. However, it also has an incentive for affected firms to move income to slightly higher tax rate countries and involves complications in measuring effective tax rates. The provision excepts firms that are making a substantial contribution to a business, a more easily avoided rule than the one in the Discussion Draft which allows an exception only for production for the home market.
Plus Part of Option C	Would also tax royalties at 17.5%, which could in some cases encourage income to be received as royalties. It would encourage exploitation of intangibles abroad and might violate the WTO.

Source: CRS analysis of proposals.

A more comprehensive approach is to allocate world wide expenses.[80] They discuss this world wide approach as well, which would lose revenue compared to allocating only parent company costs and could potentially cause an overall revenue loss. For intangible profits, they do not address the tax on income shifted abroad. Rather they disallow a portion of the associated investment costs (research and development costs and other overhead costs such as marketing). Their anti-abuse program has the virtue of simplicity and because an increase in profits abroad triggers a tax (in the form of foregone deductions) it reduces the incentive to shift profits through that effect as well.

The Ways and Means Discussion Draft addresses the shifting due to leveraging by restricting interest deductions. They impose the lesser of two restrictions. The first is an allocation of interest based on worldwide interest and assets, much like the Grubert and Mutti approach. The second is a limit on interest relative to modified income, and since the limit is not spelled out, the extent of that restriction is yet to be determined. If a high enough ratio of interest to modified income is allowed then the interest allocation would not be very effective and since modified income is prior to not only interest but depreciation and some other production expenses, the ratio would have to be relatively low to be broadly effective. The effectiveness would need to be explored once a percentage is determined. The value of this alternative is not readily apparent given that the first restriction, the allocation rule, provides a reasonable method. The Enzi bill has no interest allocation provisions.

A specific base erosion provision outside of interest has not been chosen in the discussion draft, and it is difficult to determine how effective the base erosion proposals are likely to be. Both Options A and Option B hinge on being in a low tax country and the tax rate is relatively low, only 10%. Option A, which phases out the U.S. taxation of excess intangibles between 10% and 15% may only partially affect Ireland, for example, which has a statutory tax rate of 12.5% and Option B would miss it altogether. These tax rates are effective rates, which is appropriate, but which could be difficult to measure.[81] Options A and C require the identification of intangible income, which is not necessary for B; this problem has been identified as an important complicating factor in several comments.[82]

By triggering current taxation of intangibles when the return exceeds 150% of costs, Option A provides an incentive to push deductible development and marketing costs into the CFC, a point made in Ways and Means hearing.[83] Once a firm falls into the excess profit class a dollar of cost moved to the CFC will decrease income subject to U.S. taxation by $1.50, while increasing taxable income in the United States by $1.00 (although if the tax code retained the production activities deduction and income were eligible for it, this additional dollar would increase taxable income by $0.91).

tion B, which triggers full U.S. taxation of some income in countries with tax rates below 10% would create incentives to move profits to countries with tax rates higher than the 10% level but lower than the U.S. 25% level. Ireland is a possibility, but there are many potential locations which might not currently be used as tax havens which would become so, including a number of former eastern block countries. It is also possible that jurisdictions that cater largely to U.S. multinationals would raise their own taxes to prevent U.S. firms from leaving. In either case, total U.S. income (the sum of taxes and company profits) would be reduced because a third party (the other countries) would collect a higher share of U.S. firms profits. Option B also is formulated as a cliff: once the country reaches a trigger level all income is subject to full U.S. taxes. Option B exempts from inclusion income derived in the home country (an active trade or business with income derived from the sale of property for use in the country or services provided in the country). These rules may be exploited by firms to avoid the tax.

The drawbacks of option B could also potentially affect option A as well. Since the lower taxes would apply to profits equal to 150% of costs, the lower taxes paid in countries with rates below 10% on this portion of profits would have to be traded off against higher taxes on the excess profits. However, in countries where the costs are small relative to profits firms might also have incentives in this case to shift locations.

Option C, which applies this system only to intangibles and is not triggered by a specific tax rate would also have the merit of not inducing undesirable behavioral changes. Option C would also apply this lower tax to royalties, although at least one analysis has suggested that a lower tax rate on royalties might violate WTO rules on export subsidies.[84] Several critics have pointed out the complication of measuring intangible income which would be a drawback. However, it would still require the measurement of affected income, adding complexity.

The purpose of option B could be accomplished is a way that does not encourage these undesirable behavioral responses by imposing a minimum (combined U.S. and foreign) tax on all foreign source income. Consider, for example, the 60% share of income taxed that comprises the second half of Option C. If a 15% minimum tax were imposed, it would only affect income in those countries with effective tax rates of below 15% but it would not produce incentives to move to a higher tax country.

Option B does appear to have relatively effective provisions defining an active operation that can avoid the tax in the Ways and Means Discussion Draft, although whether companies could work around them remains to be seen. The Enzi bill has a weaker rule, which would might more easily allow firms to justify an exception to the tax authorities and to the courts. The Enzi bill provision is triggered by a higher tax rate, which should capture Ireland.

One witness at the Ways and Means Hearing also noted that there is no distinction in the Discussion Draft between intangibles created in the United States and in other foreign countries: any intangible income could trigger a U.S. tax even if developed outside the United States.[85]

Option C of the Ways and Means Discussion Draft and S. 2091 also contains a reduced tax rate for royalties. Under Option C, royalties would be taxed at the same rate as intangible income generated inside the CFC which would eliminate the incentive to shift newly taxed royalties into tax exempt CFC income. If two thirds of royalties were exempt before due to sheltering by foreign tax credits, this change would be a slight relative tax increase (since 40% is taxed), but if the share is lower due to small excess credits and elimination of the splitter rules it could be a tax cut. Similar points could be made about S. 2091.

Transition

The Grubert-Mutti proposal appears to exempt dividends regardless of their source, a view that is probably consistent with their emphasis on reducing tax complexity, such as planning around repatriation. This approach provides a windfall benefit. However, as the Grubert and Mutti study is a general outline, the authors may simply not have addressed transition issues. One of the authors has indicated that it would be appropriate to impose a lower tax on the accumulated unrepatriated earnings in an approach similar to the Ways and Means Discussion Draft.[86]

The Ways and Means Discussion Draft would tax all accumulated earnings before implementation of the reform, but with an 85% exclusion, which may or may not provide a windfall since it might largely apply to earnings that would probably never be repatriated. These earnings would not have to be actually repatriated, but could be deemed repatriated, a benefit that is important if these funds are tied up in illiquid investments. Taxes would be offset by a proportional share of foreign tax credits. In a steady state, most accumulated earnings, based on past evidence and new view theory would be earnings that are permanently reinvested. However, since earnings may have accumulated at higher rates through anticipation of another repatriation holiday, more of these earnings may be planned for distribution.

One critic suggests that the deemed repatriation provision which is extended to individuals as well may not be appropriate for taxpayers not eligible for the dividend exemption.[87] Another suggests that firms may have trouble measuring the total amount of unrepatriated earnings.[88]

S. 2091 has a repatriation tax that differs from the Ways and Means provision in that it is elective on a CFC by CFC basis, the exclusion is smaller at a 70% exclusion and no foreign tax credits would be allowed. However, for income that is not elected to be taxed, the dividend relief would not occur until these accumulated earnings are exhausted. Since firms might eventually wish to repatriate earnings, this rule should create an incentive to repatriate, however, the elective aspect allows firms not to repatriate if their conditions are such that a move of this nature would be difficult (i.e., lack of funds to pay the tax).

Current tax treatment is governed in some respects by tax treaties and these treaties may now come into conflict with the new proposed rules. Interactions with treaties would need to be addressed.

An issue to be determined is the treatment of foreign tax credits and losses that have been carried over. For the Grubert-Mutti proposal and the Ways and Means Discussion Draft, which are aimed at a full break from the old system, it seems appropriate to allow foreign tax credit carryovers to lapse (if any foreign tax credit carryovers remain after the taxation of accumulated earnings). That is apparently the intent of the deemed repatriation tax.[89] S. 2091 would presumably continue carryovers for entities not covered (such as branches) and tax credits associated with accumulated income not yet taxed. Treatment of losses under the Discussion Draft has not been addressed, but presumably would continue under S. 2091 which continues aspects of the pre-existing system.

Administrative and Technical Issues

Many of the major rules discussed above would complicate tax administration. The Grubert-Mutti proposal appears to involve the least amount of complication as it has a simple exclusion, somewhat reduces the scope of Subpart F, and has a straightforward anti-abuse provision in the form of the allocation of deductions. There is no scope for a repatriation tax. Although the Ways and Means Discussion Draft is not fully fleshed out, it retains a small repatriation tax that could lead to tax planning (the 5% inclusion of dividend income), and its anti-abuse provisions could be quite complicated. S. 2091 could also potentially lead to a continued repatriation incentive.

This section addresses some other specific issues that have technical and administrative implications.

Including Branches

Including branch company income under the territorial rules is contained in two of the proposals, Grubert and Mutti and the Ways and Means Discussion Draft, but not in S. 2091. There is a good reason for including branches in the scope of the territorial tax, since, if branch income is not allowed or if firms can opt out, then firms could continue to use branches versus subsidiaries for tax planning, to allow the recognition of losses but not positive earnings. Moreover, while there are non-tax reasons for operating as a branch, including branches would equalize the treatment of branch and subsidiary operations.

Nevertheless, one comment suggests that the approach in the Discussion Draft, which treats branches as if they are CFC's subject to all of the other provisions of the proposal comes with additional complications. It is difficult to: measure income of an entity that does not legally exist as if it were separate, determine when a foreign branch exists as designed in the proposal, determine the formation or liquidation of an operation that is not a separate entity, and address the rules that apply to intra-company payments. In addition, firms might shift to operating as a partnership. This comment suggests that branch income simply be exempt from the tax without defining them as CFCs[90] Another comment raises a number of specific tax issues that need to be addressed when branches are included, including whether taxes will be triggered by reorganization and the treatment of inter-branch payments.[91]

10/50 Election

The Grubert Mutti proposal includes 10/50 corporations in their exemption system, while the Ways and Means Discussion Draft and S. 2091 allow it as an election. (Recall that a 10/50 company is one where the corporation has a 10% or more share but the company is not controlled by five or less 10% U.S. shareholders). Presumably companies would prefer to elect the exempt treatment especially as they will lose the foreign tax credits associated with dividends.

One comment suggested that 10/50 corporations that wish to elect inclusion may have difficulties because they will become subject to Subpart F rules but may not be able to obtain the information on Subpart F income because they do not control the firm. In addition, 10/50 firms may not be able to compel the cash dividend payments needed to pay tax given the tax on accumulated earnings under the Ways and Means Discussion Draft,[92] and may not be able to determine the size of those accumulated earnings.[93] A concern was also expressed that the tax on accumulated deferrals would include income generated before the taxpayer purchased shares in the company.[94] In S. 2091, a similar argument could be made about the elective repatriation, which these firms may not be able to take advantage of.

Foreign Tax Credit Revisions

The Ways and Means Discussion Draft eliminates foreign tax credits for CFC's, branches, and 10/50 corporations except for those associated with Subpart F income. It also eliminates the foreign tax credit baskets, splitter rules, and allocation of indirect expenses to foreign source income (including interest allocation rules).

One comment suggests that these changes are problematic because individuals will still be eligible for foreign tax credits.[95] Another adds that these changes in the foreign tax credit would encourage countries to reinstate foreign withholding tax and abrogate treaties because the changes effectively eliminate the limits of current law that credits are limited to foreign source income.[96]

Thin Capitalization Rules and Interest Allocation

One comment raised the question of whether strengthened thin capitalization rules that limit debt would be extended to U.S. subsidiaries of foreign parents (where presumably weaker rules already apply), or at least that intentions in this area might need to be made clear.[97] Although the legislation is focused on U.S. multinationals and their foreign operations, profit shifting can also occur across foreign parents and their U.S. subsidiaries, the current focus of thin capitalization rules.

Another comment pointed out that with more restrictive interest allocation rules firms might want to shift borrowing abroad so that interest could be deducted in other jurisdictions, but that this change might increase borrowing costs.[98] One option that might be considered is to allow loans from the parent to foreign subsidiaries at the borrowing rate of the parent or allow the parent to guarantee subsidiary loans without triggering effective dividends.

Continuing Subpart F

Some discussion of the treatment of the existing anti-abuse rules under Subpart F has occurred. At least one commentator questions why Subpart F, which was developed as a general anti-deferral provision, should continue as is with respect to certain types of income, when income is now generally exempt. One example is foreign to foreign base company income relating to sales and services, which is active income.[99]

Grubert and Mutti suggest that Subpart F should be retained to address profit shifting but modified by eliminating taxes on dividends and also on deemed dividends from investments in the United States. The Ways and Means Discussion Draft makes these two changes although they do not account for the 5% inclusion in income for either. They indicate a further consideration of Subpart F will be made. Grubert and Mutti suggest that the case for other rules such as the foreign base company rules relating to sales and services and interest would be strengthened under a territorial tax. Presumably they are referring to income shifted out the United States. S. 2091, however, specifically excludes this income from Subpart F.

Grubert and Mutti prepared their analysis before check-the-box rules (and the look-through rules) that allow CFC's to disregard their related foreign subsidiaries, which have undermined Subpart F, became so important. The Ways and Means Discussion Draft indicates that these issues will be considered separately and S. 2091 would make the look-through rules (as well as the exclusion of active financing income), currently part of extenders and having expired after 2011, permanent One comment suggested that tax reform should address the leakage in Subpart F including checkthe-box and the look-through rules[100] At the same time, one of the concerns about check the box and look through rules is that the result would not be greater U.S. tax collections but an increase in taxes paid to other countries. For example, if a subsidiary's interest payments from loans to its own high tax subsidiary could not longer be disregarded for purposes of Subpart F with an end to these rules, the response could be to no longer make the loan causing additional tax to be collected by the higher tax foreign country. This outcome would not be beneficial for the U.S. overall since it would reduce the sum of U.S. private profits and U.S. taxes. One comment, for example, notes that exemption would cause firms to have every incentive to reduce foreign taxes paid, and broadening of Subpart F rules should not undo that incentive.[101]

A final comment about Subpart F income is that, since this income is deemed repatriated and not actually paid out, there will be an additional tax under the Discussion Draft and S. 2091 on 5% of income when these earnings are actually paid out as dividends.[102] Thus, 5% of income would be subject to double taxation.

Revenue Consequences

The Grubert-Mutti proposal is projected to raise revenue on a permanent basis, although the gain is small, less than 2% of corporate revenues. Both the Ways and Means Discussion Draft and S. 2091 aim to be revenue neutral over the budget horizon. However, both also rely on a one time revenue gain from taxing existing accumulated earnings. Since this gain is transitory, these proposals will lose revenue on a permanent basis. Since the proposals have not been scored, there is no way to determine how large the permanent revenue loss would be, but it is likely to also be small.

ALTERNATIVES TO A TERRITORIAL TAX

As noted in the prior discussion, there are alternatives to a territorial tax that could address issues associated with repatriation and profit shifting as effectively or perhaps more effectively than the territorial tax provisions. These alternatives fall into three main groups: ending deferral and possibly limiting cross-crediting to move closer to a true worldwide system, reforming the existing system in more limited ways, particularly to address profit shifting, and a hybrid between ending deferral and a territorial tax, such as a minimum tax, which would eliminate the repatriation tax trigger. By traditional theory all of these approaches would probably attract capital back to the United States and improve efficiency in the allocation of capital, although they may create a need to further address shifting of headquarters.

These proposals are summarized briefly. Many of them are addressed in more detail in other CRS reports.[103] Note that many of the same issues that arise with a territorial tax would need to be addressed in some cases, such as dealing with the transition, and dealing with operations outside of CFCs.

Ending Deferral

Ending deferral, as shown in *Table 5,* is estimated to raise $18.4 billion in FY2014. A deferral option is also included in the CBO budget options study and is estimated to raise $11.1 billion in revenue in FY2014.[104] The smaller revenue gain may reflect a provision that eliminates the current interest allocation provision for purposes of the foreign tax credit limit. It would tax income of foreign subsidiaries, while allowing foreign tax credits as in current law. Current taxation would eliminate any disincentive to repatriate, and would also reduce the benefits and scope for profit shifting. Cross-crediting would still be available. It would be more consistent with efficient resource allocation, although issues of shifting headquarters might need to be addressed further. As with territorial tax proposals, transition issues would arise which could be addressed in a fashion similar to that in the Ways and Means Discussion Draft. The revision would require the measurement of earnings under U.S. law, which could add complexity, although such measurement would also be needed for most base erosion measures as well. As with the territorial tax, issues would arise in extending the treatment to 10/50 corporations that have a large U.S. shareholder but are not controlled by a group of large U.S. shareholders, since information on earnings may not be available. This change would, however, permit the elimination of Subpart F.

Ending Deferral and Ending Cross-Crediting via a Per Country Limit

A greater level of taxation and a more effective provision to discourage artificial profit shifting, which would also eliminate disincentives to repatriate, is to combine ending deferral with a per country limit on foreign tax credits, preventing tax haven income from being shielded by foreign tax credits. This proposal is part of S. 727, the Wyden and Coats general tax reform plan, and is combined with a repatriation holiday similar to that enacted in 2004. This provision was estimated to raise $64.3 billion in FY2014 (see *Table 5*). This larger revenue gain aided in the reduction of the corporate tax rate in that bill to 24%. This provision would require country-by country measures of foreign taxes paid as well as income (focusing on income earned within that country and not adjusting for intercompany dividends). Provisions would need to be enacted to prevent firms from using holding companies to avoid the per country limit and check the box and look through rules would probably need to be revised.

Measures to Modify the Current System: The President's Proposals

The President has made several proposals that address international tax issues.

The FY2013 budget outline contains several revisions which overall would raise $16.8 billion in FY2014. Note that some of these are complex to explain, and are described in more detail in a Treasury Department document.[105]

- Disallowing interest deductions of parent companies to the extent that income is deferred. This provision is similar to the allocation proposal in Grubert and Mutti but confined to interest and affecting deferred income. An earlier tax reform proposal by Chairman Rangel (H.R. 3970 in the 110th Congress, 2007) would have allocated a broader range of deductions, not just interest. This provision would reduce, although not eliminate, the disincentive to repatriate. ($5.9 billion).
- Limiting foreign tax credits available to the same share of total credits as the overall share of income that is repatriated. This approach would limit tax minimization by repatriating income to absorb foreign tax credits. ($5.5 billion).
- Treating excess intangibles profits as U.S. income, the same provision as Option A is the Ways and Means Discussion Draft, although the budget proposal does not specify the magnitude of the cost mark-up. ($2.5 billion). The proposal would also clarify some rules relating to the valuation of intangibles ($0.1 billion).

- U.S. insurance companies can reduce taxes by purchasing reinsurance from foreign affiliates, with a deduction of the premiums by the U.S. firm but no tax on the income of the foreign affiliate. This provision would disallow these deductions under certain circumstances ($0.2 billion).
- Stricter limits on interest deductions would apply to U.S. subsidiaries of firms that inverted (moved their headquarters abroad) prior to the anti-inversion rules adopted in 2004 ($0.4 billion).
- Foreign taxes paid in part to receive a benefit (i.e., the firm is paying a tax in a dual capacity) would not be credited unless the income tax is generally imposed on the country's own residents as well as foreign persons. The current rule does not require the tax to be imposed on the country's residents. This provision typically relates to taxes being substituted for royalties in oil producing countries ($1.0 billion).
- A codification of regulations that impose on a foreign corporation or nonresident alien tax on gain from a partnership interest to the extent the gain reflects property effectively connected with U.S. business ($0.2 billion).
- A provision to prevent a foreign affiliate from avoiding characterization as a dividend by making the distribution through a related affiliate with limited earnings and profits, causing the distribution to adjust the cost basis of stock rather than create dividend income ($0.3 billion).
- Preventing foreign tax credits from offsetting tax on the gain from certain types of asset acquisitions (0.1 billion).
- A provision that prevents the reduction of earnings and profits without the reduction in foreign tax credits that can currently occur in some transactions ($20 million).

The Administration also presented a framework for tax reform that mentioned five elements: the allocation of interest for deferred income (first bullet point above), a tax on excess intangibles (third bullet point), a minimum tax on foreign source income in low tax countries, disallowing a deduction for the cost of moving abroad and providing a 20% credit for costs of moving an operation from abroad to the United States.[106]

The minimum tax on foreign source income, which would be a potentially important provision, is not discussed in detail. A minimum tax that could be imposed in the framework of an effective territorial system is discussed below.

Partial or Targeted End to Deferral

A variety of more limited ways of reducing or partially eliminating deferral include eliminating deferral for specified tax havens, eliminating deferral in countries with tax rates that are below the U.S. rate by a specified proportion, eliminating deferral for income from the production of goods that are in turn imported into the United States, eliminating deferral for income from the production of goods that are exported to any other country from the foreign location, and requiring a minimum payout share. These provisions would partially achieve the goals of a general elimination of deferral.[107]

Formula Apportionment

Another approach to addressing income shifting, whether in the current system or a revised territorial system, is through formula apportionment. With formula apportionment, income would be allocated to different jurisdictions based on their shares of some combination of sales, assets, and employment. This approach is used by many states in the United States and by the Canadian provinces to allocate corporate income. In the past, a three factor apportionment was used, but some states have moved to a sales based system. Studies have estimated a significant increase in taxes from adopting formula apportionment.[108] The ability of a formula apportionment system to address some of the problems of shifting income becomes problematic with intangible assets which, unlike production income, cannot be allocated based on tangible assets.[109] There is also a problem of coordinating with other countries so that income would not be double-taxed or never taxed.[110]

Hybrid Approaches: Minimum Tax, Partial Territorial Tax

Using the basic territorial approach embodied in the Ways and Means Draft Discussion, it would be possible to generate a relatively straightforward hybrid approach, by a modification of Base Erosion Option B to impose a simpler general minimum tax with no exceptions for active trade or business. Such a revision would technically begin with an elimination of deferral and per country foreign tax credit limit. Income, however, would be taxed at a lower tax rate. This approach would avoid the incentives to shift to a slightly higher tax jurisdiction. Moreover, it would be simpler, because it would not require any measure of a specific type of income, would not require a measure of effective tax rate, and would not require a determination of the type of activity to allow an exception. It would use U.S. rules for measurement of income, but would apply a lower statutory rate to taxable income. Foreign tax credits would need to be allowed on a country by country basis. For example, suppose the statutory rate to be applied were half the U.S. rate, or given current rates, 17.5%. In that case any income from a country with an effective tax rate on taxable income at that level (and probably a lower effective rate overall) would not be subject to U.S. tax. Such a tax regime would only affect tax havens and low tax jurisdictions.[111]

An alternative would be to require income to be repatriated (or deemed repatriated) but subject some share of it to U.S. tax and exempt the rest. An appropriate share of foreign tax credits would be disallowed. For example, if half of income is taxed, the system would be 50% a territorial tax and 50% a world wide tax without deferral. Foreign tax credit limits could be allowed on an overall basis or country by country. This approach bears some resemblance to the foreign tax credit pooling proposal in the President's budget except there is no discretion about repatriation. Comments made on the combining of a minimum tax with a territorial system suggested that the tax rate would be important, with two observers suggesting a rate of 20%, similar to the rate used by Japan, and indicating that a 10% tax rate is too low.[112]

Both of these proposals would have the effect of eliminating the repatriation disincentive as well as reducing the incentive to shift profits (or at least the cost). Unlike proposals to tax this income at full U.S. rates, such a minimum tax is less likely to shift income to other jurisdictions that have higher rates than the United States.

In any proposal aimed at tax havens, there is a possibility that the haven or low tax country would raise its taxes and capture some of the profits. This problem is more significant with a minimum tax that it would be with full elimination of deferral, which would remove the incentive to profit shift altogether. Tax havens attracting other country's firms might be reluctant to raise taxes and it might be possible to deny credits for taxes that are increased for that purpose.

APPENDIX. HISTORY OF INTERNATIONAL TAX RULES

As this history indicates, most of the proposals made over the years, whether adopted or not, moved not toward a territorial tax and a reduction in taxation of foreign source income, but toward a worldwide tax and increased taxation.

Deferral of tax on income from foreign incorporated subsidiaries dates from the earliest years of the income tax based reflecting legal principles of the time. The earliest income tax allowed a deduction for foreign taxes, which was replaced by an unlimited credit in 1918. In 1921 an overall limit on the foreign tax credit. similar to current law, was adopted. Beginning in 1932, a per country limit was allowed or required, although regulations that sourced income to holding companies allowed firms to achieve overall limits on their own. The per country limit was eliminated in 1976, although income was sorted into passive and active baskets to prevent this type of cross-crediting.

A number of proposals for changing the system were made but were not (or have not yet been) adopted. Eliminating deferral was proposed by President Kennedy and President Carter. The Kennedy proposals led to the anti-abuse rules (Subpart F) that tax passive and easily shifted income currently.

The Burke Hartke proposal in the 1970s would have repealed deferral and allowed a deduction rather than a credit for foreign taxes. A per country limit was proposed by the Reagan Administration as part of the Tax Reform Act of 1986, but the legislation expanded the number of baskets from two to several instead. The baskets were reduced to two again in legislation in 2004. The main consequence according to tax data, was to include income from financial services in the general basket.

Legislative proposals which would have increased taxation of international income by allocating parent company expenses, such as interest, to deferred income and not allowing it as well as allowing overall foreign taxes to be considered Proposals similar to those of President Obama were included in tax reform legislation proposed by then Ways and Means Committee Chairman Rangel in 2007. A predecessor to the Wyden Coats bill was the Wyden Gregg bill in the 111th Congress. International tax provisions are discussed in detail, through 1989, in William P. McClure and Herman B. Bouma, "The Taxation of Foreign Income from 1909 to 1989: How a Tilted Playing Field Developed," *Tax Notes*, June 19, 1989, pp. 1379.

End Notes

[1] The President's Advisory Panel on Federal Tax Reform, Final Report, November 1, 2005, at http://govinfo.library.unt.edu/taxreformpanel/final-report/index.html. The Grubert-Mutti

proposal was the territorial proposal under discussion for a number of years. It is outlined in Harry Grubert and John Mutti, Taxing International Business Income: Dividend Exemption Versus the Current System (Washington, DC, AEI Press, 2001). It is discussed in further detail in Rosanne Altshuler and Harry Grubert, "Where Will They Go if We Go Territorial? Dividend Exemption and the Location Decisions of U.S. Multinational Corporations," National Tax Journal (December 2001), pp. 787-809. Because the current U.S. tax system collects little revenue, and because of features of the Grubert-Mutti proposal to allocate parent company deductions, this proposal would raise revenue.

[2] See various discussions and drafts at the Ways and Means Committee website, at http://waysandmeans.house.gov/ taxreform/.

[3] The National Commission on Fiscal Responsibility and Reform, The Moment of Truth, at http://www.fiscalcommission.gov/sites/fiscalcommission.gov/files/documents/TheMomentofTruth12_1_2010.pdf.

[4] The President's Framework for Business Tax Reform: A Joint Report by the White House and the Department of the Treasury, February 2012, at http://www.treasury.gov/resource-center/tax-policy/Documents/The-PresidentsFramework-for-Business-Tax-Reform-02-22-2012.pdf.

[5] Melissa Costa and Jennifer Gravelle, "Taxing Multinational Corporations: Average Tax Rates," presented at a Conference of the American Tax Policy Center, October 2011, and forthcoming in Tax Law Review at http://www.americantaxpolicyinstitute.org/pdf/Costa-Gravelle%20paper.pdf.

[6] Fundamental economic issues are discussed in CRS Report RL34115, Reform of U.S. International Taxation: Alternatives, by Jane G. Gravelle.

[7] This discussion generally refers to foreign subsidiaries that are sometimes wholly owned and sometimes partially owned by a U.S. parent. The tax law defines a controlled foreign subsidiary or a controlled foreign corporation (CFC) as one in which the U.S. firm has a 10% share and 50% of the shares are owned by five or fewer 10% U.S. shareholders. A corporation in which a U.S. firm owns a 10% share but 50% is not owned by five or fewer 10% shareholders is called a non controlled Section 902 corporation or a 10/50 corporation. Smaller share ownership is portfolio investment. New data from the Internal Revenue Service reports dividends from firms that are less that 20% owned, more than 20% owned and wholly owned at 7%, 65%, and 27%, although any of these firms could potentially be CFC's and the payout ratios may differ. Filled in 1120 form at http://www.irs.gov/pub/irs-soi/08colinecount.pdf.

[8] Check-the-box allows a firm, including a subsidiary of a U.S. firm, to choose to disregard (not recognize) its own subsidiary as a separate entity and consolidate that income with the parent (higher tier subsidiary) firm. For example, if a U.S. parent's subsidiary in a low-tax country lends money to its own subsidiary in a high-tax county (with deductions for interest paid), the interest income received by the low-tax subsidiary would normally be taxed as Subpart F income even if this income is not repatriated to the U.S. parent. Check-the-box allows the high-tax subsidiary to be disregarded for tax purposes so that no interest income appears.

[9] See David R. Sicular, "The New Look-Through Rule: W(h)ither Subpart F?" Tax Notes, April 23, 2007, pp. 349-378 for a discussion of this provision.

[10] Fewer excess credit firms in recent years also led to transactions designed to generate foreign tax credits, but these have now been limited by regulation. See Steven Schneider, Regulations Address Foreign Tax Credit Generator Structures, at http://www. taxlawroundup.com/2011/07/regulations-address-foreign-tax-credit-generator-transactions/.

[11] A per country limit was used in the past at various times, but because it did not have look-through rules, holding companies could be used to accomplish the effects of an overall limit. While an overall credit limit has been used for some time, between 1986 and 2004, the credit was applied within nine different baskets.

[12] Scott Luttrel, "Corporate Foreign Tax Credit, 2007," Internal Revenue Service, Statistics of Income Bulletin, 2011, at http://www.irs.gov/pub/irs-soi/11cosumbulcorpforeign.pdf. There are two very small baskets for income from countries sanctioned by the United States and income resourced by treaty, which accounted for less than two-tenths of a percent. Prior to 2007 when there were nine baskets, but the only important difference was a separation of the financial services basket, with 19.7% of income, from the general basket.

[13] These treatments were referred to as reverse hybrids, and they occurred when, from the U.S. perspective, the subsidiary has its own subsidiary where profits can be deferred, but from the foreign perspective the subsidiary and its own subsidiary are the same firm. The top tier subsidiary thus confronts a foreign tax it is liable for and which could be claimed as a credit even though the income is not reported because it is eligible for deferral. It is the reverse of the check the box arrangement.

[14] This provision was adopted in the P.L. 111-226. See Joint Committee on Taxation, General Explanation Of Tax Legislation Enacted In The 111th Congress, JCS-2-11, March 24, 2011, for the revenue estimate for this provision and for several other revisions of the foreign tax credit to address abuses. See also CRS Report R40623, Tax Havens: International Tax Avoidance and Evasion, by Jane G. Gravelle.

[15] See Internal Revenue Service http://www.irs.gov/pub/irs-soi/08colinecount.pdf.

[16] Internal Revenue Service, Statistics of Income, Controlled Foreign Corporations, at http://www.irs.gov/taxstats/ bustaxstats/article/0,,id=96282,00.html. Firms represented in these statistics have a 50% ownership or more.

[17] Department of Commerce, Bureau of Economic Analysis, Table 6.16D, at http://www.bea.gov/international/ di1usdop.ht.m.

[18] For 2006 total payments were 25% with 12% as discretionary dividends. The data for Canada were similar, but in Switzerland 16% was paid out in total but only 3% as dividends.

[19] Residual U.S. tax in Table 3 divided by net income from statistics reported in Table 1.

[20] Harry Grubert and Rosanne Altshuler, "Corporate Taxes in the World Economy: Reforming the Taxation of Cross-border Income," in John W. Diamond and George R. Zodrow, eds., Fundamental Tax Reform: Issues, Choices, and Implications (Cambridge: MIT Press, 2008).

[21] Data on distribution by basket from Scott Luttrell, Corporate Foreign Tax Credit, 2000, Internal Revenue Service, Statistics of Income, at http://www.irs.gov/pub/irs-soi/00cftcar.pdf.

[22] Pre-tax income would range from $112 billion for 2007 to $142 billion for 2008 (with deemed tax apportioned 73% on active dividends. 12.6% of the total tax in Table 3 would result in $3.7 billion in 2007 and $2.8 billion in 2008, for an effective tax rate of 3.3% and 1.6% on dividends received. However, estimates above indicate that only about 23% of dividends are paid out, so that these tax rates need to be multiplied by 0.23, yielding rates of 0.36% to 0.76%.

[23] Camp Releases International Tax Reform Discussion Draft, October 26, 2011, at http://waysandmeans.house.gov/ News/DocumentSingle.aspx?DocumentID=266168.

[24] If the rate of return were 10%, the steady state nominal growth rate were 6% (a typical value reflecting a real growth rate of 3% and an inflation rate of 3%), then the remainder would be paid out as a 4% dividend yield. These are typical historical values in the United States.

Thus, in a steady state growth model with these values, 60% of nominal earnings would be retained in any case (and would be retained if taxes did matter), and 40% paid out.

[25] See CRS Report R40178, Tax Cuts on Repatriation Earnings as Economic Stimulus: An Economic Analysis, by Donald J. Marples and Jane G. Gravelle. Another repatriation holiday was voted on in the Senate in 2009, but not adopted.

[26] Data from 1992 to 2008 were from Internal Revenue Service Statistics of Income, Data on Controlled Foreign Corporations, http://www.irs.gov/taxstats/bustaxstats/article/ 0,,id= 97151,00.html. Data from 1968-1992 reported in James R. Hines, Jr., The Case Against Deferral: A Deferential Consideration, National Tax Journal,Vol. 52, September 1999, pp. 385-404.

[27] The evidence does not support the idea that the fall in repatriations was due to check-the-box, which was first announced at the beginning of 1997. Subpart F income did not begin to decline as a share of income until 2004.

[28] Mehir A. Desai, C. Fritz Foley, and James R. Hines, Jr., Dividend Policy Inside the Multinational Firm, Financial Management, March 22, 2007, at http://www.thefreelibrary. com/Dividend+policy+inside+the+multinational+firm.- a0167305683.

[29] Testimony of Mr. Gary M. Thomas Before the Committee on Ways & Means, U.S. House of Representatives, Hearing on How Other Countries Have Used Tax Reform To Help Their Companies Compete in the Global Market and Create Jobs, May 24, 2011, at http://www.whitecase.com/files/Uploads/Documents/GThomas-HWM-Testimony24May2 011.pdf.

[30] Peter Egger, Valeria Merlo, Martin Ruf, and Georg Wamser, The Consequences of the new UK Tax Exemption System: Evidence from Micro-level Data, Working Paper, January 26, 2012.

[31] Mehir A. Desai, C. Fritz Foley, and James R. Hines, Jr., "Repatriation Taxes and Dividend Distortions," National Tax Journal, Vol. 54, December 2001, pp. 829-851.

[32] See Rosanne Altshuler, T. Scott Newlon, and William C. Randolph, "Do Repatriations Matter? Evidence from Tax Returns of Multinationals," in The Effects of Taxation on Multinational Corporations, Ed. by Martin Feldstein, James r. HInes, Jr. and R. Glenn Hubbard, Chicago: University of Chicago Press, 1995, pp. 253-277.

[33] Mehir A. Desai, C. Fritz Foley, and James R. Hines, Jr., "Repatriation Taxes and Dividend Distortions," National Tax Journal, Vol. 54, December 2001, pp. 829-851.

[34] Rosanne Altshuler and Harry Grubert, "Repatriation Taxes, Repatriation Strategies and Multinational Financial Policy, Journal of Public Economics, Vol 87, 2002, pp. 73-107.

[35] Some methods of returning cash to the United States involve corporate reorganizations. See Jesse Drucker, "Dodging Repatriation Tax Lets Companies Bring Home Cash," Bloomberg, December 29, 2010, http://www.bloomberg.com/ news/2010-12-29/dodging-repatriation-tax-lets-u-s-companies-bring-home-cash.html. For an in depth discussion of methods, see Hal Hicks and David J. Sotos, "The Empire Strikes Back (Again) – The Killer Bs, Deadly Ds and Sec. 367 As The Death Star Against Repatriation Rebels,". International Tax Journal, May-June 2008, pp. 37-58. The Internal Revenue Service has periodically attempted to address various methods of repatriating cash without paying tax, most recently in July 2012. See Richard Rubin, "IRS Ends Deals That Let Companies Avoid Repatriation Tax," Bloomberg, July 13, 2011, at http://www.bloomberg.com/news/2012-07-13/irs-ends-deals-that-let-companies-avoidrepatriation-tax.html.

[36] Mehir A. Desai, C. Fritz Foley, and James R. Hines, Jr., Dividend Policy Inside the Multinational Firm, Financial Management, March 22, 2007, at http://www. thefreelibrary.com/Dividend+policy+inside+the+multinational+firm.- a0167305683.

[37] CRS Report R40178, Tax Cuts on Repatriation Earnings as Economic Stimulus: An Economic Analysis, by Donald J. Marples and Jane G. Gravelle.

[38] The repatriations under the repatriation holiday, enacted on the basis of increasing investment, were largely used to repurchase shares, the equivalent of paying dividends. See CRS Report R40178, Tax Cuts on Repatriation Earnings as Economic Stimulus: An Economic Analysis, by Donald J. Marples and Jane G. Gravelle, for a review of the evidence.

[39] Using repatriations to increase employment in an underemployed economy in the short run are unlikely to be effective because transferring foreign earnings into U.S. dollars is contractionary and likely overwhelms any direct spending effects. See CRS Report R40178, Tax Cuts on Repatriation Earnings as Economic Stimulus: An Economic Analysis, by Donald J. Marples and Jane G. Gravelle.

[40] Note that economic analysis has focused on efficient allocation of investment, rather than the effects on jobs because in the long run (the focus of a permanent tax law), an economy will tend to naturally create jobs.

[41] The issues discussed in this section are discussed in more detail in CRS Report RL34115, Reform of U.S. International Taxation: Alternatives, by Jane G. Gravelle.

[42] Harry Grubert and John Mutti, Taxing International Business Income: Dividend Exemption Versus the Current System," Washington, DC, The AEI Press, 2001.

[43] The President's Advisory Panel on Federal Tax Reform, Simple, Fair and Pro-Growth: Proposals to Fix America's Tax System, November, 2005, at http://govinfo.library.unt.edu/taxreformpanel/.

[44] The proposal is estimated to raise revenues by $6.9 billion in FY2014. See Congressional Budget Office, Reducing the Deficit: Spending and Revenue Options, March, 2011, p. 187, http://www.cbo.gov/sites/default/files/cbofiles/ ftpdocs/120xx/doc12085/03-10-reducing thedeficit.pdf.

[45] Countries can adopt anti-abuse provisions that are more limited. See Marco Rossi, "European Commission Blesses Italy's Anti-Inversion Rules," at http://www.euitalianinternationaltax.com/2011/05/articles/european-commissionblesses-italys-antiinversion-rules/.

[46] See Jane G. Gravelle, Does the Concept of Competitiveness Have Meaning in Formulating Corporate Tax Policy? November 2011, forthcoming, Tax Law Review, at http://www.americantaxpolicyinstitute.org/pdf/ Jane%20Gravelle%20paper.pdf. Critiques of competitiveness arguments were also made, primarily with respect to trade policy, by Paul Krugman, See "Competitiveness: A Dangerous Obsession," Foreign Affairs, Vol. 73, No. 2 (March-April, 1994), pp. 28-44. Links to the journal can be found at http://www.foreignaffairs.com/issues/1994/73/4.

[47] Mergers that involve shifting the location of incorporation do occur occasionally. The announced merger of Eaton Corporation and Cooper Industries is an example of how mergers can be used to shift headquarters although even in this case the stated primary reason was non-tax issues. Cooper was already incorporated in Ireland, but is effectively a U.S. company with management in Houston. See Robert Schoenberger, "Eaton Corporation Plans to Buy Cooper Industries, Move Incorporation to Ireland," The Plain Dealer, May 12, 2012. http://www.cleveland.com/business/ index.ssf/2012/05/eaton_corp_plans_ to_merge_with.html. Aon's shift of incorporation to the U.K. will trigger a shareholder level capital gains tax. See "Aon Shareholders May Pay Hefty Taxes With Headquarters Shifting to London," Ameet Sachdev's Chicago Law, at http://articles.chicagotribune.com/2012-01-20/business/ct-biz-0120- chicago-law-20120120_1_aon-global-aon-corp-tax. Among solutions to limit tax motivated international mergers is imposing a tax on shareholder gain at ordinary rates.

[48] Susan Morse and Eric Allen, "Firm Incorporation Outside the U.S.: No Exodus Yet," December 2011, at http://papers.ssrn.com/sol3/papers.cfm?abstract_id=1950760.

[49] This idea is most recently addressed in Mihir Desai and James Hines, "Evaluating International Tax Reform," National Tax Journal, Vol. 56, September 2003, pp. 487-502.

[50] See CRS Report RL34115, Reform of U.S. International Taxation: Alternatives, by Jane G. Gravelle, for a more detailed discussion of this issue.

[51] See CRS Report R41743, International Corporate Tax Rate Comparisons and Policy Implications, by Jane G. Gravelle.

[52] Melissa Costa and Jennifer Gravelle, Taxing Multinational Corporations: Average Tax Rates, Presented at a Conference of the American Tax Policy Center, October 2011, and forthcoming in Tax Law Review, at http://www.americantaxpolicyinstitute.org/pdf/Costa-Gravelle%20paper.pdf.

[53] Charles Duhigg and David Kocieniewski, "How Apples Sidesteps Billions in Taxes," New York Times, April 29, 2012, p.1, 20-21. at http://www.nytimes.com/ 2012/04/29/business /apples-tax-strategy-aims-at-low-tax-states-andnations.html?pagewanted=all.

[54] See CRS Report R41743, International Corporate Tax Rate Comparisons and Policy Implications, by Jane G. Gravelle.

[55] The overall evidence suggests an elasticity of around three which is used in the calculations above; see Jennifer C. Gravelle, Corporate Tax Incidence: Review of General Equilibrium Estimates and Analysis, Working Paper 2010-03, May 2010, at http://www.cbo.gov/sites/ default/files/cbofiles/ftpdocs/115xx/doc11519/05-2010-working_papercorp_tax_incidence-review_of_gen_eq_estimates.pdf. See Harry Grubert and Rosanne Altshuler, "Corporate Taxes in the World Economy: Reforming the Taxation of Cross-border Income," in Fundamental Tax Reform: Issues, Choices, and Implications, Ed. John W. Diamond and George R. Zodrow, Cambridge, MIT Press, 2008 who reference a number of studies showing that investment by multinationals is sensitive to tax rates. A review is also contained in Michael Smart, Repatriation Taxes and Foreign Direct Investment: Evidence From Tax Treaties, Working Paper, June 20, 2010, at http://www.sbs.ox.ac.uk/ centres/tax/symposia/Documents/2010/05%20Smart.pdf; and in Lars Feld and Jost Heckemeyer, "FDI and Taxation: A Meta Study," Journal of Economic Surveys, Vol 25, April, 2011, pp.233-272. The working paper version is at http://www.cesifo-group.de/ portal/pls/portal/docs/1/1186528.PDF.

[56] Estimates from CRS Report R41743, International Corporate Tax Rate Comparisons and Policy Implications, by Jane G. Gravelle, based on perfect mobility of capital and perfect product substitution.

[57] CRS Report R40623, Tax Havens: International Tax Avoidance and Evasion and CRS Report R41743, International Corporate Tax Rate Comparisons and Policy Implications, both by Jane G. Gravelle. Data on earnings and profits of controlled foreign corporations were taken from Lee Mahoney and Randy Miller, Controlled Foreign Corporations 2004, Internal Revenue Service Statistics of Income Bulletin, Summer 2008,http://www.irs.ustreas. gov/pub/irs-soi/ 04coconfor.pdf. Data on GDP from Central Intelligence Agency, The World Factbook, https://www.cia.gov/library/ publications/the-world-factbook. Most GDP data are for 2008 and based on the exchange rate but for some countries earlier years and data based on purchasing power parity were the only data available.

[58] See CRS Report R40623, Tax Havens: International Tax Avoidance and Evasion and CRS Report R41743, International Corporate Tax Rate Comparisons and Policy Implications, both by Jane G. Gravelle. For the most recent estimates see Kimberly A. Clausing "The Revenue Effects of Multinational Firm Income Shifting Tax Notes, March 28, 2011, pp.

1580-1586, who finds estimates for 2008 from $57 billion to $90 billion and Martin Sullivan, "Transfer Pricing Costs U.S. at Least $28 Billion," Tax Notes, March 22, 2010, pp. 1439-1443.

[59] Martin Sullivan, "Transfer Pricing Abuse Is Job-Killing Corporate Welfare," Tax Notes August 2, 2010, pp. 461-468.

[60] The lobbying group has apparently ended at least part of their campaign. See "WIN America, Tax Repatriation Holiday Lobby Group, Ends Advocacy Work" Reuters, http://www.huffingtonpost.com/2012/04/23/win-america-taxrepatriation-holiday_n_1447581.html?ref=business. For a report on the repatriation holiday and its issues see CRS Report R40178, Tax Cuts on Repatriation Earnings as Economic Stimulus: An Economic Analysis, by Donald J. Marples and Jane G. Gravelle.

[61] Harry Huizinga and Luc Laeven, "International Profit Shifting Within Multinationals: A Multi-Country Perspective," Journal of Public Economics, vol. 92. 2008, pp.1164-1182.

[62] Jesse Drucker, "Google 2.4% Rate Shows How $60 Billion Lost to Tax Loopholes," Bloomberg, October 21, 2010, at http://www.bloomberg.com/news/2010-10-21/google-2-4-rate-shows-how-60-billion-u-s-revenue-lost-to-taxloopholes.html.

[63] Department of the Treasury, General Explanations of the Administration's Fiscal Year 2013 Revenue Proposals, February 2012, http://www.treasury.gov/resource-center/tax-policy/Documents/General-Explanations-FY2013.pdf.

[64] Harry Grubert and John Mutti, Taxing International Business Income: Dividend Exemption Versus the Current System (Washington, DC, AEI Press, 2001).

[65] The President's Advisory Panel on Federal Tax Reform, Simple, Fair and Pro-Growth: Proposals to Fix America's Tax System, November, 2005, at http://govinfo. library.unt.edu/taxreformpanel/.

[66] Author's conversation with Harry Grubert, July 2, 2012.

[67] Congressional Budget Office, Reducing the Deficit: Spending and Revenue Options, March 20, 2011, p. 187. http://www.cbo.gov/sites/default/files/ cbofiles/ftpdocs/120xx/doc12085/ 03-10-reducingthedeficit.pdf

[68] Documents, including bill language, technical discussions and shorter summaries can be found at the Ways and Means Committee website at http://waysandmeans.house.gov /taxreform/.

[69] Ernst & Young has provided a summary of this bill, "Senator Enzi Introduces and International Tax Reform Bill," http://www.ey.com/Publication/vwLUAssets/ Senator_ Enzi_introduces_ an_international_tax_reform_bill/ $FILE/Senator%20Enzi%20introduces%20reform%20bill.pdf, March 1, 2012.

[70] Jeffery M. Kadet, "Territorial W&M Discussion Draft: Change Required," Tax Notes, January 23, 2012, pp. 463-464.

[71] See Senator Enzi's press release, at http://www.enzi.senate.gov/uploads/3.pdf.

[72] Comments of Stephen Shay, KPMG, Will the U.S. Shift to a Territorial System: A Discussion of Chairman Camp's Territorial Tax Draft, http://www.us.kpmg.com/microsite /taxnewsflash/Corporate/2011/tgi-exec-sum-territorialtax.pdf.

[73] Rosanne Altshuler and Harry Grubert, "Where Will They Go if We Go Territorial? Dividend Exemption and the Location Decisions of U.S. Multinational Corporations," National Tax Journal, December 2001, pp. 787-809.

[74] The proposal refers to allocating the parents interest to firms and not worldwide interest, although a worldwide allocation would be an option.

[75] See data from Economic Report of the President at http://www.gpo.gov/fdsys/pkg/ERP-2012/pdf/ERP-2012- table15.pdf.

[76] Internal Revenue Service, http://www.irs.gov/taxstats/article/0,,id=170692,00.html. In 2006, the manufacturing sector has 247 billion of interest payments, $183 billion of interest income and $481 billion in net income. In 2007, these numbers were $304 billion, $203 billion and $468 billion respectively.

[77] Rosanne Altshuler and Harry Grubert, "Where Will They Go if We Go Territorial? Dividend Exemption and the Location Decisions of U.S. Multinational Corporations," National Tax Journal, December 2001, pp. 787-809.

[78] Ibid.

[79] International Revenue Service statistics, at http://www.irs.gov/taxstats/article/ 0,,id= 164402, 00.html.

[80] When the Grubert Mutti proposal was developed, worldwide allocation was not in the law. Harry Grubert, in a conversation on July 5, 2012, indicated that worldwide allocation would be appropriate.

[81] This measurement problem is pointed out by Harrington, Subcommittee on Select Revenue Measures, Ways and Means Committee, November 27, 2011, testimony of John L. Harrington, at http://waysandmeans.house.gov/ UploadedFiles/Harringtonsrm1117.pdf.

[82] This complication of Options A and C is pointed out by Stephen Shay and Paul Oosterhuis, KPMG, Will the U.S. Shift to a Territorial System: A Discussion of Chairman Camp's Territorial Tax Draft, at http://www.us.kpmg.com/ microsite/taxnewsflash/Corporate/ 2011/tgi-exec-sum-territorial-tax.pdf and by Michael Reilly, discussion reported in Shamik Trivedi, "Agreement on Territorial Plans Unlikely Despite Commonalities," Tax Notes, February 20, 2012, pp. 949-950.

[83] Subcommittee on Select Revenue Measures, Ways and Means Committee, November 27, 2011, Testimony of T. Timothy Tuerff, at http://waysandmeans.house.gov/Uploaded Files/Tuerffsrm1117.pdf.

[84] Kristen A. Parillo, "Camp Plan Would Likely Violate WTO Rules, Buckley Says," Tax Notes, December 12, 2011, pp. 1327-1328.

[85] Subcommittee on Select Revenue Measures, Ways and Means Committee, November 27, 2011, testimony of David G. Noren, at http://waysandmeans.house.gov/ UploadedFiles/ Norensrm1117.pdf.

[86] Conversation with Harry Grubert, July 2, 2012.

[87] Subcommittee on Select Revenue Measures, Ways and Means Committee, November 27, 2011, testimony of John L. Harrington, at http://waysandmeans.house.gov/ UploadedFiles/ Harringtonsrm1117.pdf. He notes that the purpose may be able to deal with individuals transferring their earnings to corporate form, but suggests that should be dealt with in a more targeted fashion.

[88] Subcommittee on Select Revenue Measures, Ways and Means Committee, November 27, 2011, testimony of Paul W. Oosterhuis, at http://waysandmeans.house.gov/UploadedFiles/ Oosterhuissrm1117.pdf.

[89] See comment of Ray Beeman, KPMG, Will the U.S. Shift to a Territorial System: A Discussion of Chairman Camp's Territorial Tax Draft, at http://www.us.kpmg.com /microsite/taxnewsflash/Corporate/2011/tgi-exec-sumterritorial-tax.pdf.

[90] Subcommittee on Select Revenue Measures, Ways and Means Committee, November 27, 2011, testimony of John L. Harrington, at http://waysandmeans.house.gov/ UploadedFiles/ Harringtonsrm1117.pdf.

[91] Subcommittee on Select Revenue Measures, Ways and Means Committee, November 27, 2011, testimony of T. Timothy Tuerff, at http://waysandmeans.house.gov/Uploaded Files/Tuerffsrm1117.pdf.

[92] Subcommittee on Select Revenue Measures, Ways and Means Committee, November 27, 2011, testimony of John L. Harrington, at http://waysandmeans.house.gov/UploadedFiles/Harringtonsrm1117.pdf.

[93] Subcommittee on Select Revenue Measures, Ways and Means Committee, November 27, 2011, testimony of Paul W. Oosterhuis, at http://waysandmeans.house.gov/UploadedFiles/Oosterhuissrm1117.pdf.

[94] Report on comment of Jose Murillo at an Ernst and Young Conference, Kristen A. Parillo and Marie Sapirie, "Territorial Plan Drafters Aware of Transition Concerns," Tax Notes, November 14, 2011, pp. 810-812.

[95] Subcommittee on Select Revenue Measures, Ways and Means Committee, November 27, 2011, testimony of John L. Harrington, at http://waysandmeans.house.gov/Uploaded Files/Harringtonsrm1117.pdf.

[96] Kristen A. Parillo, "Camp Plan Would Dramatically Affect Withholding, Buckley Says" Tax Notes, November 21, 2011, pp. 948-949, reporting comments by John Buckley.

[97] Subcommittee on Select Revenue Measures, Ways and Means Committee, November 27, 2011, testimony of John L. Harrington, at http://waysandmeans.house.gov/Uploaded Files/Harringtonsrm1117.pdf.

[98] Subcommittee on Select Revenue Measures, Ways and Means Committee, November 27, 2011, Testimony of T. Timothy Tuerff, at http://waysandmeans.house.gov/UploadedFiles/Tuerffsrm1117.pdf. See also Paul Oosterhuis, KPGM, Will the U.S. Shift to a Territorial System: A Discussion of Chairman Camp's Territorial Tax Draft, at http://www.us.kpmg.com/microsite/taxnewsflash/Corporate/2011/tgi-exec-sum-territorial-tax.pdf.

[99] Subcommittee on Select Revenue Measures, Ways and Means Committee, November 27, 2011, testimony of John L. Harrington, at http://waysandmeans.house.gov/ UploadedFiles/Harringtonsrm1117.pdf.

[100] Kristen A. Parillo, "Camp Plan Would Dramatically Affect Withholding, Buckley Says" Tax Notes, November 21, 2011, pp. 948-949, reporting comments by Jeff Vandervolk.

[101] Subcommittee on Select Revenue Measures, Ways and Means Committee, November 27, 2011, testimony of Paul W. Oosterhuis, at http://waysandmeans.house.gov/UploadedFiles/Oosterhuissrm1117.pdf.

[102] Subcommittee on Select Revenue Measures, Ways and Means Committee, November 27, 2011, Testimony of T. Timothy Tuerff, at http://waysandmeans.house.gov/UploadedFiles/Tuerffsrm1117.pdf.

[103] CRS Report RL34115, Reform of U.S. International Taxation: Alternatives, by Jane G. Gravelle; CRS Report R40623, Tax Havens: International Tax Avoidance and Evasion, by Jane G. Gravelle.

[104] Congressional Budget Office, Reducing the Deficit: Spending and Revenue Options, March, 2011, p. 186, at http://www.cbo.gov/sites/default/files/cbofiles/ftpdocs/120xx/doc12085/03-10-reducingthedeficit.pdf.

[105] See U.S. Department of Treasury, General Explanations of the Administration's FY2013 Revenue Proposals, February 2012, http://www.treasury.gov/resource-center/tax-policy/Documents/General-Explanations-FY2013.pdf.

[106] The President's Framework for Business Tax Reform: A Joint Report by the White House and the Department of the Treasury, February 2012, http://www.treasury.gov/resource-center/tax-policy/Documents/The-Presidents-Frameworkfor-Business-Tax-Reform-02-22-2012.pdf.

[107] CRS Report R40623, Tax Havens: International Tax Avoidance and Evasion, by Jane G. Gravelle This reports also discusses a variety of minor changes in rules including foreign tax credit provisions.

[108] Slemrod and Shackleford estimate a 38% revenue increase from an equally weighted three-factor system Douglas Shackelford and Joel Slemrod, "The Revenue Consequences of Using Formula apportionment to Calculate U.S. and Foreign Source Income: A Firm Level Analysis," International Tax and Public Finance, vol. 5, no. 1, 1998, pp. 41-57. Clausing and Avi-Yonah estimate a 35% increase in taxes using sales. Kimberly A. Clausing and Reuven A. AviYonah, Reforming Corporate Taxation in a Global Economy : A Proposal to Adopt Formulary Apportionment, Brookings Institution: The Hamilton Project, Discussion paper 2007-08, June 2007.

[109] These and other issues are discussed by Rosanne Altshuler and Harry Grubert, "Formula Apportionment: Is it Better than the Current System and Are There Better Alternatives?" Oxford University Centre for Business Taxation, Working paper 09/01.

[110] CRS Report R40623, Tax Havens: International Tax Avoidance and Evasion, by Jane G. Gravelle, for further discussion.

[111] A 2000 Treasury Study proposed a similar treatment and also discussed a tax at a low rate without foreign tax credits. See U.S. Department of Treasury, The Deferral of Income Earned Through U.S. Controlled Foreign Corporations, p. 91, at http://www.treasury.gov/resource-center/tax-policy/Documents/subpartf.pdf.

[112] These observations were made by Reuven Avi-Yonah and Edward Kleinbard, reported in Julie Martin, "Minimum Tax on Multinationals," Tax Notes, March 19, 2012, pp. 1498-2000.

INDEX

A

abuse, 8, 10, 12, 22, 23, 40, 113, 114, 117, 118, 119, 121, 127, 131, 133, 140, 144
access, 7, 98
accommodation, 10
accounting, 54, 60, 76, 78, 99
acquisitions, 137
adjustment, 65
age, 21
allocative efficiency, 39
American Jobs Creation Act, vii, 1, 3, 6, 7, 38
annuals, 59
apples, 145
assets, 7, 14, 20, 29, 30, 31, 36, 45, 50, 54, 60, 84, 95, 108, 111, 118, 122, 124, 127, 138
Austria, 45
authorities, 43, 129
avoidance, 23, 30, 37, 43, 44, 47, 122
awareness, 7

B

base, x, 11, 21, 35, 37, 38, 45, 49, 51, 53, 54, 60, 70, 73, 75, 80, 83, 87, 89, 111, 114, 120, 121, 123, 124, 125, 128, 133, 135
behavioral change, 70, 129
Belgium, 46
benefits, viii, 1, 3, 6, 7, 13, 15, 29, 38, 53, 54, 62, 68, 71, 72, 79, 113, 116, 135
Bermuda, vii, 1, 6, 8, 9, 30, 42, 71, 84, 113, 115
bias, 30
blueprint, 94
bonds, 20, 79
Brazil, 57
budget deficit, 11
business activity test, viii, 2, 8, 10
businesses, 71, 76, 77, 79, 81

C

capital flows, x, 52, 64, 66, 68, 73, 80, 84, 86, 112
capital gains, 9, 10, 44, 45, 49, 50, 80, 81, 89, 144
capital goods, 55, 60, 64
capital inflow, 66, 67, 69, 70, 85, 86
capital markets, 7
cash, 7, 108, 132, 143
category a, 78
Cayman Islands, vii, 1, 6, 8, 9, 15, 30, 42, 113
challenges, 11
Chicago, 14, 16, 143, 144
Chile, 63
China, 57

citizens, 110
Clinton Administration, 44
closed economy, 64, 79, 86
combined effect, 75
comparative advantage, 24, 46
compensation, 85
competitiveness, 16, 24, 144
competitors, 5
complex interactions, 94
complexity, 36, 116, 129, 130, 135
compliance, vii, 2, 71, 76, 94, 105, 116
complications, vii, 3, 127, 131
composition, 86
computer, 111
conference, 47
conflict, 130
Congress, ix, xi, 1, 2, 3, 12, 13, 16, 38, 45, 49, 51, 77, 79, 83, 86, 88, 89, 91, 93, 105, 136, 140, 142
Congressional Budget Office, 47, 49, 64, 75, 84, 85, 86, 88, 144, 146, 148
conservation, 79
construction, 60, 76
consumers, 66
consumption, 86
coordination, 43
corporate sector, 66, 70, 80, 81
correlation, 85
cost, x, xi, 6, 7, 22, 24, 31, 35, 41, 44, 50, 52, 57, 65, 70, 71, 74, 76, 77, 78, 87, 88, 105, 110, 112, 116, 125, 128, 136, 137, 139
cost benefits, 77
cost saving, 6
criticism, 106
crowding out, 65
crowds, 70
Czech Republic, 46

D

data set, 98
debt service, 65, 70, 86
deduction, ix, 20, 25, 41, 47, 49, 54, 55, 56, 57, 60, 63, 64, 71, 72, 75, 76, 77, 79, 83, 97, 109, 119, 120, 123, 128, 137, 140
deficiencies, 86
deficit, x, 47, 51, 53, 83
denial, 35
Denmark, 46
Department of Commerce, 142
Department of the Treasury, 3, 17, 48, 87, 89, 141, 146, 148
depreciation, xi, 49, 52, 54, 57, 59, 62, 67, 75, 76, 79, 81, 87, 89, 121, 127
depth, 143
developed countries, 48
direct investment, 25
direct payment, 95
directors, 5
distortions, 31, 83
distribution, 94, 98, 103, 113, 130, 137, 142
domestic capital, 83
domestic economy, 35, 112
domestic investment, ix, 12, 16, 20, 29, 32, 33, 37, 38, 93, 110
draft, xi, 13, 39, 40, 76, 78, 91, 93, 117, 119, 121, 124, 125, 128
drugs, 113

E

economic activity, vii, 1, 2, 6, 7, 8, 42
economic efficiency, 12, 21, 36, 42, 43, 45, 93, 110
economic growth, 89
economic theory, 24, 35, 65, 66
economic welfare, ix, 20, 25
economics, 28, 85
efficient resource allocation, 135
election, 121, 132
electricity, 76, 77
empirical studies, 110
employees, 85, 121
employment, 6, 31, 109, 138, 144
energy, 79
enforcement, xi, 52
environment, 42

equilibrium, 66, 68, 85
equipment, 31, 38, 54, 55, 56, 57, 59, 60, 75
equities, 46
equity, 28, 46, 67, 80, 83, 86, 108, 120, 124
erosion, viii, 2, 3, 7, 11, 37, 111, 114, 120, 121, 123, 124, 125, 128, 135
Europe, 14, 16, 83
European Commission, 144
European Court of Justice, 8
European Union, 9, 10, 63, 84, 110
evidence, xii, 11, 16, 30, 49, 62, 67, 70, 75, 84, 85, 87, 92, 102, 103, 106, 107, 108, 114, 130, 143, 144, 145
exchange rate, 145
exclusion, 9, 30, 102, 115, 119, 120, 121, 123, 130, 131, 133
expatriation, vii, 3, 42
expenditures, xi, 40, 52, 60, 73, 75, 76, 78, 81, 123, 124
exploitation, 36, 127
export subsidies, 126, 129
exports, 20, 49, 113, 118, 125
extraction, 76, 96, 99, 100, 101

F

factories, 31
fairness, 7, 41, 43, 88
fear, 32
Federal Reserve, 46, 59
Federal Reserve Board, 59
financial, 15, 20, 30, 42, 44, 54, 95, 101, 103, 107, 140, 142
financial data, 107
financial firms, 95
financial institutions, 101
Finland, 46
flexibility, 7, 93
fluid, 13
force, 9
foreign companies, 111
foreign corporation, vii, 1, 4, 5, 6, 13, 15, 16, 23, 42, 101, 102, 119, 137, 141, 145
foreign direct investment (FDI), 20, 28, 44, 145
foreign firms, 4, 22, 26, 28, 30
foreign investment, ix, xii, 16, 19, 20, 25, 28, 32, 33, 37, 38, 92, 110
foreign person, 137
formation, 131
formula, 88, 138
France, 46, 58, 72
franchise, 55, 60, 64
freedom, 9, 110
frictional unemployment, 66
fringe benefits, 69
funds, 9, 49, 50, 89, 116, 123, 130

G

GAO, 68, 86, 87
Germany, 46, 54, 55, 58, 72, 114
global economy, 24, 64, 78, 80, 86
globalization, 44
google, 84, 87, 146
governments, 38, 68, 69
graph, 72
Greece, 46
gross domestic product (GDP), 20, 42, 45, 56, 57, 58, 59, 60, 61, 63, 66, 70, 72, 73, 82, 83, 86, 87, 112, 113, 145
growth, 12, 25, 28, 36, 65, 80, 83, 86, 106, 107, 142
growth rate, 106, 142
guidelines, 124

H

Harvard Law School, 46
health, 110
health insurance, 110
history, 139
holding company, 9
host, 21, 22, 32, 37
House, 13, 16, 45, 53, 78, 143
House of Representatives, 143
housing, 76, 79
human, 59, 60
human capital, 59, 60

Hungary, 46
hybrid, ix, x, xii, 19, 20, 21, 32, 33, 34, 35, 92, 94, 105, 106, 134, 138

I

Iceland, 46, 55, 63
identification, 128
imports, 20
incentive effect, 21, 32, 33
incidence, 66, 85, 145
income effects, 86
income tax, vii, xi, 1, 2, 3, 6, 10, 33, 42, 49, 54, 69, 83, 91, 93, 129, 137, 140
India, 58
individuals, 9, 31, 43, 49, 50, 66, 68, 130, 132, 147
industries, 49, 76, 107, 113
industry, 9, 77, 111
inefficiency, 35, 47
inflation, 54, 61, 67, 76, 79, 142
infrastructure, 42
institutional change, 30
integration, ix, 19
intellectual property, 12
Internal Revenue Service, 48, 64, 84, 99, 100, 141, 142, 143, 145, 147
international competitiveness, 45
international investment, 21, 28
inversion(s), viii, viii, 1, 3, 4, 5, 6, 7, 8, 9, 10, 11, 13, 14, 15, 30, 42, 88, 110, 111, 137
investments, 25, 30, 32, 42, 66, 76, 108, 109, 111, 112, 120, 121, 130, 133
investors, 3, 21, 28, 31, 32, 38, 68, 112
Ireland, viii, 2, 6, 8, 9, 71, 84, 113, 126, 127, 128, 129, 144
isolation, 64
issues, vii, xi, xii, 7, 12, 21, 24, 45, 46, 52, 53, 64, 67, 76, 83, 92, 94, 98, 105, 110, 116, 117, 119, 122, 130, 131, 132, 133, 134, 135, 136, 141, 144, 146, 149
Italy, 46, 144

J

Japan, 30, 46, 54, 55, 56, 58, 72, 139
job creation, 65
jurisdiction, ix, 5, 10, 19, 25, 27, 33, 97, 138
justification, 28, 35, 78, 79, 106, 109, 114

K

Korea, 46, 63

L

labor force, 27, 84, 108
Laffer Curve, 83, 87
laws, xi, 9, 42, 52, 110
lead, x, xii, 28, 30, 52, 69, 71, 76, 92, 131
leakage, 134
legislation, ix, 2, 3, 8, 111, 133, 140
legislative proposals, 13, 44
lending, 42
liberalization, 48
light, vii, 3, 21, 31, 119, 122
limited liability, 71, 80
loans, 40, 133, 134
lobbying, 114, 146
local government, 79
low tax foreign countries, viii, 2
Luxemburg, 113

M

machinery, 31
magnitude, 66, 67, 68, 69, 94, 98, 112, 113, 114, 136
majority, 5, 6
management, ix, 2, 7, 13, 31, 111, 144
manipulation, 42
manufacturing, 31, 47, 49, 76, 77, 97, 111, 113, 124, 147
marginal product, 86
marketing, 127, 128
matter, 29, 107, 117, 122, 143

measurement, 129, 135, 139, 147
media, 49, 58, 59, 75, 87, 88, 105
mergers, vii, viii, 2, 3, 9, 10, 12, 111, 144
methodology, 67
Mexico, 46, 63
models, 67, 85
multinational companies, 25
multinational corporations, xi, 56, 91
multinational firms, viii, 2, 16, 43, 54, 123

N

national income, x, 52, 64, 67
national income accounts, 67
national policy, 24
nationality, 28, 31, 94, 111
natural gas, 76
Netherlands, 8, 9, 46
neutral, vii, ix, xi, 20, 24, 25, 28, 29, 30, 37, 38, 39, 52, 53, 64, 76, 77, 78, 79, 80, 89, 110, 123, 134
New Zealand, 46, 63
Norway, 46

O

Obama, x, 51, 53, 83, 87, 88
oil, 8, 96, 99, 100, 101, 137
openness, ix, 19
operations, viii, ix, 1, 3, 5, 8, 19, 20, 21, 22, 26, 28, 29, 33, 36, 80, 95, 96, 113, 117, 121, 131, 133, 135
opt out, 131
optimization, 25, 109
Organization for Economic Cooperation and Development (OECD), x, 11, 30, 43, 49, 52, 54, 55, 56, 57, 58, 59, 60, 61, 62, 63, 71, 72, 73, 81, 82, 83, 87
organize, vii, 3
overhead costs, 97, 100, 109, 123, 124, 126, 127
overseas investment, 21, 35, 39
ownership, viii, 2, 7, 25, 28, 29, 30, 31, 35, 46, 141, 142
ox, 145

P

parents, 34, 86, 101, 111, 116, 133, 146
passive type, 4
patents, 31
payroll, 69
permit, ix, 20, 34, 40, 45, 50, 73, 76, 77, 79, 89, 135
pharmaceutical, 9
physical activity, 62
Poland, 46
policy, vii, viii, xi, 2, 3, 10, 17, 24, 25, 26, 28, 43, 47, 48, 52, 53, 71, 75, 88, 113, 116, 141, 143, 146, 148, 149
policy options, viii, 2, 3
policymakers, 6, 21, 47
pools, 76
portfolio, 20, 25, 28, 30, 31, 34, 37, 44, 45, 47, 66, 67, 84, 85, 141
portfolio investment, 20, 25, 28, 30, 34, 37, 141
Portugal, 46, 54
present value, 76, 86, 107
President, viii, x, xi, xii, 2, 12, 34, 39, 40, 41, 44, 45, 47, 48, 49, 51, 53, 74, 75, 77, 79, 85, 86, 91, 92, 93, 109, 114, 117, 118, 120, 136, 139, 140, 141, 144, 146, 148
President Obama, xi, 40, 44, 74, 75, 77, 91, 93, 114, 117, 120, 140
price manipulation, 42
principles, 21, 140
production function, 85, 86
productive efficiency, 29
profit, viii, x, xii, 2, 11, 12, 13, 16, 33, 37, 40, 51, 52, 54, 62, 64, 70, 71, 73, 77, 79, 87, 92, 94, 105, 111, 112, 113, 114, 115, 116, 118, 124, 125, 126, 128, 133, 134, 135, 139
project, 43, 54
property taxes, 55, 60, 62
proposition, 45
protection, 114

purchasing power, 145
purchasing power parity, 145

R

rate of return, 66, 68, 142
reactions, 53
reasoning, 35, 110
recall, 87
recession, 59, 85, 104
recognition, 131
recovery, 76, 104
reform(s), i, iii, v, viii, ix, x, xi, 10, 12, 13, 16, 17, 19, 20, 21, 24, 34, 38, 45, 46, 47, 48, 51, 52, 53, 63, 71, 73, 75, 79, 81, 83, 85, 86, 87, 88, 89, 91, 93, 98, 104, 111, 112, 114, 130, 140, 141, 142, 143, 144, 145, 146, 148
regulations, viii, 2, 3, 9, 40, 137, 140, 141
reinsurance, 137
relative prices, 84
relative size, 112
relief, 34, 37, 44, 50, 130
rent, 29
repatriate, xii, 40, 92, 94, 102, 107, 115, 123, 130, 135, 136
requirements, 29, 44
researchers, 62, 98
resources, 24, 31, 63, 83, 110
response, viii, 2, 8, 49, 72, 134
restrictions, 30, 36, 40, 47, 77, 81, 96, 126, 127
retail, 55, 60, 64
retained earnings, 115
retaliation, 25
retirement, 45, 50
risk, 30, 86
royalty, 96, 105, 109, 115, 120, 125, 126

S

savings, vii, 1, 3, 7, 8, 42, 43, 45, 83, 110
scope, 20, 21, 33, 44, 96, 116, 122, 131, 135
Secretary of the Treasury, 49
securities, 30
Senate, xi, 12, 13, 39, 48, 49, 76, 78, 87, 88, 91, 143
services, 83, 103, 128, 133, 140, 142
shape, 37
shareholders, viii, 2, 4, 5, 6, 9, 10, 13, 71, 80, 89, 101, 107, 108, 118, 119, 132, 135, 141
shelter, 21, 50, 83
showing, 105, 145
simulations, 84
Social Security, 69
SOI, 46
solidarity, 43
solution, 30, 85
South Korea, 54
Spain, 46
specific tax, 129, 132
spending, 68, 144
state(s), 30, 46, 55, 60, 61, 63, 71, 74, 75, 77, 79, 83, 86, 89, 106, 107, 108, 123, 124, 130, 138, 142, 145
statistics, 101, 124, 142, 147
stimulus, 65, 84
stock, xii, 4, 9, 14, 23, 25, 28, 30, 46, 50, 60, 66, 67, 69, 83, 85, 86, 92, 106, 112, 115, 119, 121, 137
stock appreciation, 9
stock exchange, 4
stockholders, viii, 1, 2, 7, 9, 13, 14, 23
structure, vii, ix, 1, 6, 19, 22, 42, 45
structuring, 42
Subsidies, 74
subsidy, 50, 97, 113
substitutes, 66, 109
substitution, 26, 28, 29, 30, 31, 44, 45, 66, 67, 77, 83, 84, 85, 145
substitution effect, 83
surplus, 31
Sweden, 46
Switzerland, viii, 2, 8, 9, 46, 54, 102, 142

T

target, viii, 2, 8

tax administration, vii, 2, 36, 131
tax base, viii, 2, 3, 7, 22, 23, 32, 35, 105
tax benefit, viii, 1, 2, 3, 6, 7, 13, 38, 53, 54, 62, 119
tax collection, 134
tax credits, ix, x, xi, 7, 19, 20, 22, 23, 34, 35, 40, 41, 44, 46, 52, 65, 77, 86, 87, 88, 92, 96, 97, 98, 109, 116, 120, 121, 125, 130, 132, 135, 136, 137, 139
tax cuts, 50, 72, 80, 81
tax data, 107, 140
tax deduction, 38
tax evasion, 42, 43, 48
tax havens, viii, x, xii, 1, 8, 20, 30, 41, 42, 43, 44, 48, 92, 126, 128, 138, 139
tax incentive, ix, 19
tax increase, 12, 49, 68, 107, 116, 125, 129
tax policy, ix, x, 19, 24, 41, 44, 45, 51
tax rate comparisons, vii, xi, 52, 53, 57
tax rate differentials, vii, xi, 52, 53, 54
tax rates, ix, x, 4, 19, 30, 31, 39, 42, 45, 47, 50, 51, 53, 54, 55, 56, 57, 58, 59, 60, 61, 62, 63, 68, 71, 72, 76, 80, 82, 86, 96, 98, 104, 110, 111, 112, 113, 117, 121, 126, 127, 128, 129, 138, 142, 145
tax reform(s), vii, viii, xi, 2, 12, 13, 21, 23, 25, 31, 34, 38, 40, 41, 45, 47, 52, 53, 64, 79, 91, 93, 109, 119, 121, 133, 136, 137, 140
tax return data, 98
tax system, viii, ix, 2, 7, 8, 10, 11, 12, 19, 20, 21, 23, 24, 25, 26, 28, 29, 32, 33, 34, 36, 37, 45, 53, 83, 93, 94, 105, 109, 111, 115, 141
taxpayers, 11, 23, 41, 44, 47, 48, 49, 99, 130
techniques, 13, 14, 31, 42, 71, 86
technologies, 29
technology, 35, 125
tenants, 79
territory, 21
Title I, 16
Title IV, 16
trade, 20, 45, 120, 122, 123, 127, 128, 138, 144
trade policy, 144
trading partners, 95
transactions, xi, 7, 11, 13, 23, 42, 44, 49, 52, 122, 137, 141
transfer pricing, 11, 36
transparency, 44, 49
Treasury, viii, 2, 3, 7, 8, 9, 10, 14, 15, 30, 44, 47, 48, 70, 75, 80, 87, 89, 136, 148, 149
treaties, 5, 44, 95, 130, 132
treatment, xi, xii, 22, 57, 71, 76, 78, 80, 91, 92, 96, 110, 113, 116, 117, 118, 119, 123, 125, 130, 131, 132, 133, 135, 149
triggers, 107, 127, 128
Turkey, 46

U

U.S. corporate income tax, vii, 1, 2, 3
U.S. Department of Commerce, 45
U.S. Department of the Treasury, 15, 48, 75, 88
U.S. economy, ix, xii, 19, 44, 64, 65, 66, 69, 85, 92, 112, 125
U.S. policy, 24
U.S. Treasury, 7, 38, 41
unemployment rate, 65, 108
unions, 79
United Kingdom (UK), viii, 2, 5, 8, 9, 10, 15, 46, 48, 56, 58, 72, 107, 110, 143

V

valuation, 136
value added tax, 110

W

wage increases, 84
wage level, 66
wage rate, 66, 85
wages, x, 26, 52, 66, 67, 84, 85, 109
Washington, 15, 45, 46, 47, 48, 49, 83, 141, 144, 146
weakness, 39

wealth, 55, 60, 62, 83
welfare, vii, ix, xi, 20, 25, 27, 28, 43, 52, 53, 64, 68, 69, 72, 77, 78, 86, 109, 112
White House, 47, 48, 141, 148
workers, 26, 66
World Bank, 57
worldwide, vii, ix, x, xi, xii, 2, 4, 7, 11, 15, 19, 20, 21, 22, 23, 25, 26, 28, 30, 31, 32, 33, 38, 39, 55, 57, 68, 77, 91, 92, 93, 94, 95, 97, 104, 105, 109, 115, 120, 122, 124, 126, 127, 134, 140, 146, 147
worldwide tax liabilities, vii, 3
WTO, 126, 127, 129, 147

Y

yield, 10, 11, 29, 49, 142